Bookmarks
London, Chicago and Melbourne

Lenin's Moscow

Alfred Rosmer

translated by Ian Birchall

Lenin's Moscow
by Alfred Rosmer
translated into English by Ian Birchall

Moscou sous Lenine
First published by Editions Pierre Horay, Paris 1953
Copyright © Pierre Godeau

This translation first published 1971
Copyright © Bookmarks and Ian Birchall
Published by agreement with Editions la Découverte, Paris
This edition published with a new introduction, July 1987
Bookmarks, 265 Seven Sisters Road, London N4 2DE, England
Bookmarks, PO Box 16085, Chicago, Illinois 60616, USA.
Bookmarks, GPO Box 1473N, Melbourne 3001, Australia.

ISBN 0 906224 37 3

Printed by Cox and Wyman Limited, Reading, England.
Typeset by Kate Macpherson, Bristol.
Cover design by Roger Huddle.

Bookmarks is linked with an international grouping of socialist orgnisations:

AUSTRALIA: *International Socialists*, GPO Box 1473N, Melbourne 3001.
BELGIUM: *Socialisme International*, 9 rue Marexhe, 4400 Herstal, Liege.
BRITAIN: *Socialist Workers Party*, PO Box 82, London E3.
CANADA: *International Socialists*, PO Box 339, Station E, Toronto, Ontario.
DENMARK: *Internationale Sosialister*, Morten Borupsgade 18, kld, 8000
    Arhus C.
FRANCE: *Socialisme International* (correspondence to Yves Coleman, BP
    407, Paris Cedex 05).
IRELAND: *Socialist Workers Movement*, PO Box 1648, Dublin 8.
NORWAY: *Internasjonale Sosialister*, Postboks 5370 Majorstua, 0304 Oslo 3.
UNITED STATES: *International Socialist Organization*, PO Box 16085,
    Chicago, Illinois 60616.
WEST GERMANY: *Sozialistische Arbeiter Gruppe*, Wolfgangstrasse 81,
    D–6000 Frankfurt 1.

Contents

Alfred Rosmer was born to French parents in New York in 1877. He became a committed revolutionary syndicalist in the early years of this century, and was one of only a handful of French socialists who opposed the First World War. The victory of the Bolshevik revolution in Russia led him to become a communist. He attended the Second, Third and Fourth Congresses of the Communist International, and was a member of its executive committee; he played a leading role in the founding of the Red International of Labour Unions and was a member of the political bureau of the French Communist Party. A close friend of Trotsky, he was expelled from the French Communist Party in 1924, but remained a convinced revolutionary until his death in 1964.

Ian Birchall is a long-standing member of the Socialist Workers Party. His previous publications include **France: the struggle goes on** (with Tony Cliff, London 1968), **Workers against the monolith** (London 1974), **The smallest mass party in the world** (London 1981) and **Bailing out the System: Reformist Socialism in Western Europe 1944-1985** (Bookmarks, London 1986). He is senior lecturer in French at Middlesex Polytechnic in London.

This book is published with the aid of the **Bookmarks Publishing Co-operative**. Many socialists have a few savings put aside, probably in a bank or building society. While it's there, this money is being lent out again to some business or other to further the aims of capitalism. We believe it is better lent to a socialist venture to further the struggle for socialism. That's how the co-operative works: in return for a loan, repayable at a month's notice, members receive free copies of books published by Bookmarks, plus further advantages. The co-operative has about 150 members at the time this book is published, from as far apart as London and Australia, Canada and Norway.

Like to know more? Write to the **Bookmarks Publishing Co-operative**, 265 Seven Sisters Road, Finsbury Park, London N4 2DE, England.

Introduction
by Ian Birchall

REVOLUTIONARIES have to know both how to swim against the stream and how to swim with it. When the workers' movement is in retreat, when the traditional organisations of the left are crumbling around them, they have to hold firm to a clear and principled analysis without bending to the pressures of the times. But such tenacity is useless unless, when a new phase of mass struggle begins, they can respond quickly and imaginatively to it, and give the leadership that is required.

Alfred Rosmer, the author of **Lenin's Moscow**, faced both these tasks. In his long life as a revolutionary he went on fighting for his vision of internationalist socialism when the European labour movement collapsed in 1914, during the high tide of the years following 1917, and then through the bleak, bitter isolation that came when the Russian Revolution was betrayed and lost.

Rosmer — his family name was Griot — was born in New York in 1877 to French parents.[1] They had not been directly involved in the Paris Commune of 1871, but probably left France because of the period of repression that followed it. The family returned to France in 1884. Rosmer became an office-worker, then an employee of the *Préfecture de la Seine* and a proof-reader. The name Rosmer, which he used throughout his life, was taken from the hero of Ibsen's **Rosmerholm**, an incurable idealist.

Rosmer began his political life as an anarchist around 1896 at

1. For a biography of Rosmer see C Gras, **Alfred Rosmer (1877-1964) et le mouvement révolutionnaire international** (Paris 1971).

the time of the Dreyfus case; he evolved towards revolutionary syndicalism and in the years before 1914 worked with Pierre Monatte on the journal **La Vie Ouvrière**. As an intransigent syndicalist he refused all contact with organisations of the Second International. Rosmer was also a resolute advocate of the right of women to take employment, something rejected by many French trade unionists at this time. In 1913 he was involved in supporting Mme Couriau, a Lyons woman who had taken a job as a printing worker. Not only did the union refuse to accept her into membership, but it instructed her husband to tell her to give up her job, and, when he refused, expelled him from the union.[2]

Rosmer's first experience of a sudden massive shift in the level of class struggle came in 1914. In the last week of July 1914 there was a huge anti-war demonstration in Paris, so large that the police could not control it.[3] But within days the opposition had crumbled; as Rosmer noted: 'When war starts, it means the working class has already been defeated.'[4] Syndicalists and socialists alike betrayed; only a tiny handful kept internationalism alive. From October 1914 Rosmer and a minute group of anti-war militants met weekly at the **Vie Ouvrière** office. They were joined by a Russian exile who had fled from Vienna at the outbreak of war, one Leon Trotsky. Rosmer worked to prepare for the Zimmerwald Conference, but did not himself attend as he was conscripted in May 1915. The limited anti-war propaganda that was possible was forced into clandestine channels; Rosmer's pamphlet on Zimmerwald was published in a small format so that it could be distributed unobtrusively in ordinary letter-sized envelopes.

With the new wave of struggle that followed the Russian Revolution, Rosmer had to reconsider his previous political allegiances. He now devoted himself entirely to the building of the Communist International; between 1920 and 1924 he held numerous posts of responsibility in both the International and the French Communist

2. Gras, page 40.
3. A Rosmer, **Le mouvement ouvrier pendant la guerre: De l'Union Sacrée à Zimmerwald** (Paris 1936) page 102.
4. Rosmer, **Le mouvement ouvrier**, page 9.

Party. The contribution of Rosmer and others like him was highly valued by Lenin and Trotsky. Trotsky recalls that on one occasion Lenin said to him: 'Couldn't we advise the French Communists to throw out those corrupt parliamentarians like Cachin and Frossard, and replace them with the **Vie Ouvrière** group?'[5]

But Rosmer's dedication to the revolution did not blind him to its weaknesses, and he was one of the first to recognise the degeneration of the International. Together with Monatte and Souvarine he sided with Trotsky from the beginning of his struggle against Stalin; they published Trotsky's articles on the New Course in French. Yet the opposition of Rosmer and his friends was so firmly based in Leninism that it was necessary for Treint and his associates in the party leadership to distort the issues totally and present them as a Right Opposition. (The charge was largely based on Rosmer's opposition to Lozovsky's claim in **L'Humanité** of 2 February 1924 that the British Labour government represented 'a victory of the bourgeoisie over socialism'.)

Rosmer, Monatte and Delagarde were expelled by an extraordinary conference of the French Communist Party in December 1924. The conference was called at four days' notice and most of the delegates had not read the open letter to party members which was the main ground for expulsion. Rosmer declared: 'We will work from outside to hasten the day when the party becomes a real communist party.' And in 1925 he joined with Monatte in founding **La Révolution Prolétarienne**.

For the rest of his life Rosmer remained an uncompromising revolutionary. He strove to build a left opposition tendency in France, and in the 1929-30 period he worked closely with Trotsky in the attempt to regroup the international left opposition. But in 1930 he broke with Trotsky over what he considered the excessive trust the latter was putting in Molinier. Rosmer was later personally reconciled with Trotsky, and visited him in Mexico in 1939. He participated in the 'Committee for Inquiry into the Moscow Trials and the Defence of Free Opinion in the Revolution' and in the Dewey Commission. He never again, however, formally involved

5. **Les Humbles** (special issue on Marcel Martinet), January-March 1936.

himself in the Trotskyist movement.[6] (His disagreement with Trotsky on the class nature of Russia may have been one of the reasons for this.) After Trotsky's death Rosmer was asked by Natalia Sedova to find European publishers for Trotsky's works.

Rosmer remained a Leninist and an anti-Stalinist until the day of his death in 1964. It is possible to criticise some of his detailed positions, such as his willingness to accept the Congress for Cultural Freedom as authentic anti-Stalinists,[7] while making a peremptory dismissal of Sartre as worthless,[8] but on essentials he never wavered. He continued to write for **La Révolution Prolétarienne**. When Isaac Deutscher published the third volume of his **Trotsky** Rosmer wrote to him congratulating him on distinguishing himself from 'those anti-Stalinists who are simply reactionaries.'[9] In 1960, when over eighty years of age, he signed — alongside Sartre and others — the Manifesto of the 121, supporting those who refused to take arms against the Algerian people. The American historian Robert Wohl, who interviewed him in 1960 and 1961, records: 'To the end he never gave up his belief in the Leninism of 1917-22, which in his view was corrupted but not called into question as a doctrine.'[10]

Above all, Rosmer wrote. His most substantial work was his study of working-class opposition to the First World War, **Le mouvement ouvrier pendant la guerre**.[11] This combines scrupulous documentation with a record of personal involvement.

6. It has long been believed that the Founding Conference of the Fourth International, in September 1938, was held at Rosmer's home (see I Deutscher, **The Prophet Outcast** (London 1970) page 419). However Charles Van Gelderen, who attended part of the Conference, claims this was not the case (see S Bornstein and A Richardson, **The War and the International** (London 1986) page 24).

7. He was a personal friend of Nicola Chiaromonte, editor of **Tempo Presente**, and attended meetings organised by **Preuves**. (Gras, pages 414 and 423.)

8. Letters of 1950, in Gras, page 424.

9. Gras, page 416.

10. R Wohl, **French Communism in the Making 1914-1924** (Stanford 1966) page 427.

11. Volume 1: **De l'Union Sacrée à Zimmerwald** (Paris 1936); Volume 2: **De Zimmerwald à la Révolution Russe** (Paris and The Hague 1959).

But it is **Lenin's Moscow (Moscou sous Lénine)** that remains Rosmer's most relevant and readable work. It was originally published in the bleak year of 1953. After launching a last wave of purges, Stalin departed this life; his heirs fought for his succession with squalid ruthlessness, but friend and foe alike accepted the orthodoxy that Stalin was Lenin's true heir. In the United States McCarthy was at the peak of his witch-hunting power, tracking down ex-Communists, while in France a series of right-wing governments were attacking the living standards and organisation of the working class.

The Cold War seemed to have led the working class — and with it the whole of humanity — into a dead-end. The working class was not, however, so easily silenced. This was also the year of the East Berlin rising. In France a strike — originally called by anarcho-syndicalists in the Bordeaux post office — spread to four million workers.

There are, of course, numerous other histories of the early years of the Communist International — many bad, a few good.[12] But Rosmer's text is especially valuable, if not unique, in that it combines careful historical analysis with a record of personal experience. The truth is always concrete, and Rosmer shows us how the principles and policies of the Comintern were put into practice by real human beings, with their individual strengths, eccentricities and failings.

Not that Rosmer believed that individual character was the major determining factor in history. On the contrary, he shows how a period of massive social struggle transformed the characters of those called on to play leading roles. The success of the revolution brought out the best in many revolutionaries; but as the tide turned and Russia found itself isolated, the crisis of the movement manifested itself through individual weaknesses.

All this Rosmer grasps vividly yet simply. Thus he shows us the complexity of a figure such as Zinoviev, revealing both his strengths and weaknesses. In retrospect it is easy to agree with Victor Serge

---

12. Among the good ones are D Hallas, **The Comintern** (London 1985) and T Cliff, **Lenin: The Bolsheviks and World Communism** (London 1979), republished as part of **Lenin: Revolution Besieged** (London 1987).

that Zinoviev was 'Lenin's biggest mistake'[13] (and Rosmer himself had been a victim of Zinoviev's regime in the International in 1924), but Rosmer's honesty enables him to demonstrate how the contradictions of an epoch are revealed in the contradictions of an individual.

Rosmer also reminds us of the ravages of defeat by recalling the subsequent fates of many who appear in his pages. All too often the best and most dedicated militants fell victim to Hitler or Stalin, while the more dubious characters ended up as apologists for one or other of those butchers.

But Rosmer's interest is not in the past for its own sake, but rather for what it teaches the present. His account is honest, but it makes no claim to be dispassionate. Rosmer was deeply engaged in the debates of the period, and presents them to us because he believes that they deal with issues that are still alive. The age of the first four congresses of the Comintern represents the highest level of working-class struggle and organisation we have yet seen, and as such it is an unparalleled school of tactics.

Thus the united front is one of the most vital yet difficult tactics that revolutionaries have to apply, for it must always be formulated concretely, in terms of the specific demands and organisational forms required in a particular historical situation. Rosmer takes us beyond the conference resolutions and shows us the problems of fighting for the united front line within the International and of implementing it on the ground.

In the early 1920s the united front tactic raised particular problems. In order to establish the International in the first place it had been necessary to carry through a sharp fight to split existing working-class parties, and a major effort had to be made (not always successfully) to exclude from the International centrists and indeed open reformists who wanted to jump on the bandwagon of a victorious and popular revolution. Hence the notorious 'twenty-one conditions'. But having established itself on a clear political basis, the Comintern had to fight for united action with those it had just split from. Many in the ranks of the new International could not — or would not — understand the logic of this strategy. Rosmer's study illustrates the

13. V Serge, **Memoirs of a Revolutionary 1901-1941** (London 1963) page 177.

problems of the period — problems which have their parallels in our own times.

The work of revolutionaries in the trade unions is another area on which Rosmer assists our understanding. As a syndicalist, Rosmer had a key role to play in the founding and early development of the Red International of Labour Unions. Tony Cliff and Donny Gluckstein have recently argued that the RILU was 'fundamentally wrong' as a concept and 'bound to fail'.[14] It is interesting to compare this retrospective judgment with Rosmer's account of the aims and perspectives of the RILU. For if it is true that the Russian initiators of the RILU 'did not understand Western trade unions'[15] this charge can scarcely be levelled at Rosmer. Despite its weaknesses — and Rosmer does not conceal the problems — the RILU was not a piece of ultra-left madness but a serious attempt to grapple with a set of complex and demanding questions. Whatever the mistakes it is an experience we can learn from.

Rosmer also has much to tell us about 'centrism' and 'ultra-leftism'. Often these words seem to be no more than terms of abuse hurled by one leftist group at another. But when the level of struggle rises, those who vacillate between reform and revolution can become a real danger. It is then that such centrists look most left-wing and yet are most likely to mislead the struggle. Again, Rosmer makes the argument concrete for us by pointing to the varieties of centrist and opportunist who crept into the leadership of the French Communist Party. His portraits of Cachin and Frossard help us to understand why the apparently draconian 'twenty-one conditions' were not only necessary but indeed inadequate.

In the same way, when the general movement is to the right ultra-leftism tends to be confined to the verbal excesses of marginal groupings. But when the struggle rises ultra-leftism returns with a rush. Long-standing revolutionaries find themselves overtaken by newly radicalised militants who are inspired by success. In such a situation revolutionaries have to shake off the conservative pessimism

14. T Cliff and D Gluckstein, **Marxism and Trade Union Struggle: The General Strike of 1926** (London 1986) pages 49-50.
15. Cliff and Gluckstein, page 9.

bred of an age of defeat while at the same time firmly resisting adventures that can lead to disaster (like the notorious March Action in Germany).

Again Rosmer gives us a concrete and sensitive account. With his own roots in anarchism, he was able to respond sympathetically to those of a similar background who were being won over to the International; but at the same time he deals severely with the various forms of ultra-leftism that flourished in the heady atmosphere of the early 1920s. Supporters of the 'revolutionary offensive', opponents of participation in parliament, 'pure syndicalists' hostile to the notion of a revolutionary party — all had their say in the early congresses of the Comintern.

For the Comintern of Lenin's time did not resemble the monolith of the Stalinist epoch. The International Rosmer paints for us was sometimes fraternal, sometimes impassioned; but serious differences were always debated seriously.

Today more than ever capitalism is an internationally integrated system, and more than ever an internationally co-ordinated struggle against it is needed. An International based on an assembly of small groups is not a viable prospect (as the experience of the various 'Fourth Internationals' shows only too clearly) but the aspiration to build a new International remains. Rosmer's picture of the Third International in its early years gives us a model of what such an organisation could look like. Rosmer has no illusions about the Comintern's weaknesses, but he shows us what 'democratic centralism' on the international scale implies. The economic and political chaos of the world after the first world war meant that every country was intimately affected by events in every other, and that each party had to be held responsible to its fellows for its actions.

Rosmer shows us, too, how the Comintern brought together revolutionaries from very different traditions. The upheaval of the war had broken down the old dividing lines between syndicalists and social democrats and replaced them by new demarcations. For such diverse traditions to come together in a centralised body was possible only if centralism was balanced by democracy; and as Rosmer shows us, the debates of the early congresses allowed open and honest exchanges on the most fundamental questions of revolutionary strategy.

Of course as a participant Rosmer can give us only a partial view of the work of the Comintern, and there are regrettable omissions from his account. For example he tells us nothing of the extensive debates on the position of women in the Comintern.[16]

Again, Rosmer's deep respect for the Russian leaders makes him underestimate the dangers of Russian domination over the International that existed from the very beginning. This theme would have emerged more clearly if Rosmer had extended his account to include the 'Bolshevisation' of 1924-25. Likewise, the chapter on the trade-union debate of 1921 is a disappointment. In his concern to show that both Lenin and Trotsky had valuable points to make, Rosmer tends to blur the issues on a question he was especially qualified to deal with.

A fuller account of the events at Kronstadt in 1921 would also have been welcome, though Rosmer does draw out the essential points clearly, and while he is under no illusions that Kronstadt was one of Bolshevism's finer moments, he presents the situation in terms of the practical needs of the time and does not lapse into moralising or retrospective self-justification. In this respect Rosmer's account is to be preferred to that given by Victor Serge in his **Memoirs of a Revolutionary**.[17]

For some, Rosmer's book, and indeed its title (the French original means 'Moscow under Lenin'), may seem to focus too much on the revolutionary leader and not enough on the creativity of the masses. But for Rosmer it was not just the individual Lenin, but 'Leninism' which was at stake, Lenin remains the incomparably great revolutionary figure of the twentieth century, and he must be saved from both his foes and those who claim to be his friends. The obscene personality cult of the dead leader built up by Stalin (preserved by post-Stalinist Russia and parodied by diverse Trotskyist and Maoist sects) serves only to repel any right-thinking revolutionary from looking seriously at Lenin's ideas. On the other hand many on

16. For a brief summary see Hallas, pages 51-3. It is also noteworthy that at no point in the book does Rosmer mention his own wife, Marguerite, although she was actively involved in the manoeuvring in the French Communist Party (Wohl, page 304).

17. Serge, pages 124-133.

the left dig up the bogeyman of 'Leninism' as an excuse to justify their refusal to join an organisation which might discipline their activity and make them accountable for their actions (and make them sell papers in the rain).

To rescue Lenin from his admirers and his enemies, and subject him to a critical assessment of both strengths and weaknesses is thus a crucial task for revolutionaries who believe they can learn from history without expecting history to repeat itself.[18] Rosmer, an eye-witness who knew Lenin personally, offers an account from which we can learn a great deal.

In 1929 Rosmer wrote to Trotsky about the weakness and demoralisation of the left opposition in France: 'the great misfortune of all these groups is that they find themselves outside all action; and this fatally accentuates their sectarian character.'[19] Five years on from his expulsion from a mass International Rosmer had adjusted to a very different level of struggle and organisation. Yet he knew too that political clarity could not be preserved without involvement in practical struggle. This remains as true as it ever was, although the isolation of revolutionaries since 1968 has been incomparably less bleak than that of the pioneer Trotskyists. Even when the possibilities of intervention are limited, however, we can expand our understanding by looking at a period when struggle was at far higher level. **Lenin's Moscow**, studied alongside Tony Cliff's **Lenin** and Duncan Hallas's **The Comintern**, can provide both an inspiration and a practical text-book for a new generation of revolutionaries.

Ian Birchall
March 1987

18. T Cliff, **Lenin** (four volumes, London 1975-79) is exemplary in this respect.
19. 16 April 1929: cited Deutscher, page 45.

Lenin's Moscow

A note on the translation

Rosmer's book contains extensive documentation. As well as giving commentaries on the texts of Lenin and Trotsky, he quotes from many works otherwise inaccessible. Readers concerned with textual accuracy should note that in the case of several of Lenin's and Trotsky's speeches he does not give the text as printed in their works, but a summary of it, although it is printed as quotation. The summary may be either Rosmer's own or that of some contemporary publication. In no case that I have examined does he distort the sense of the argument. In the case of Lenin's and Trotsky's works I have normally used the standard English translations with minor changes for the sake of clarity or consistency.

I have replaced the brief biographical notes that Rosmer added to the original edition with a fuller appendix, intended for English readers. This is not because the text requires any supplement; far from it. But if today's militants are freer from Stalinism than Rosmer's original readers, they are also more remote from the traditions and the people of the Third International. For example, in 1953 the shifty Cachin was still being paraded as the grand old man of French communism. I hope these notes will assist the reader, and, in the accounts of the subsequent fates of some of the participants, underline the price of defeat.

Ian Birchall

Author's Foreword

'Marx's doctrines are now undergoing the same fate, which, more than once in the course of history, has befallen the doctrines of other revolutionary thinkers and leaders of oppressed classes struggling for emancipation . . . After their death . . . attempts are . . . made to turn them into harmless saints, canonising them, as it were, and investing their name with a certain halo by way of "consolation" to the oppressed classes, and with the object of duping them; while at the same time emasculating and vulgarising the real essence of their revolutionary theories and blunting their revolutionary edge.'
Lenin: **State and Revolution**, August 1917.

IT IS only thirty years since the period which stretched from October 1917 to the death of Lenin in January 1924, a period which saw the origins of Soviet Russia and the first congresses of the Communist International; but already, in the socialist movement, this period has become a sort of prehistory. The ravages of the Second World War have destroyed a considerable part of the works and periodicals dealing with the period, and only fragments and partial collections, hard to get hold of, remain. But that is not the worst of it. The worst is that the very people who claim to be the heirs and continuers of the tasks undertaken in 1917 have been the most ruthless agents of this destruction. They invoke their heritage only to distort it; they have imposed a string of falsifications on it, and finally reduced it to a text-book containing the maximum possible number of lies, omissions, gaps and additions, the distinctive feature of which is that it contradicts all the works previously written by the official historians of the régime. In commercial language they say: 'This catalogue replaces all previous editions.'

My memories of this period are many and accurate; I can add my evidence on all the important events, the first-hand evidence of a participant. I have often spoken about the period to my friends and at meetings, and those who heard me always commented that I should write down what I had told them.

I have decided to do so today for several reasons. From time to time books are published on the 'Birth of the USSR', or on the Communist International, or on Lenin, and sometimes the authors present themselves, or are presented, as Lenin's 'confidants', 'friends' or even 'advisers'. I know that their claims are laughable. But the tactic of the big lie is effective; it cannot simply be ignored. The most recent of these works, published in New York in 1947, **Pattern for World Revolution**, and in Paris in French in 1949, under the title **Du Comintern au Stalintern**, is anonymous. The author, or authors, used the pseudonym of Ypsilon. As well as some astounding errors, it contains a good proportion of correct information, and on the whole is an important document. But obviously, if such a book is to acquire its real value and be used, it is essential that we know who is the author. But he (or they) is so keen to conceal his identity, that he even invents characters or disguises some of those that he presents, to cover up his sources or for some such reason. It is therefore time for me to speak on my own behalf, to present a true account in opposition to distortions and the work of hacks.

I spent several periods in Soviet Russia between 1920 and 1924, the longest spell being seventeen months from June 1920 to October 1921. I went back to Moscow again in February 1922, and again every year, sometimes several times in the same year. I participated in the Second Congress of the Communist International as a member of the bureau, then in the Third and Fourth Congresses. I was a member of the Executive Committee of the Communist International from June 1920 to June 1921, and of the 'small bureau' from the Congress of Tours (December 1920), when the French Socialist Party voted for affiliation to the Communist International. I worked with Lozovsky on the founding of the Red International of Labour Unions. I was a member of the delegation of the Communist International to the Conference of the three Internationals at Berlin, and to the Conference held at Hamburg at the time of the fusion between the Second International and the International Union of Socialist Parties. In the French Communist Party I was on the central committee, the Political Bureau and on the editorial board of **L'Humanité** from 1923 to March 1924. I have given this list, without omissions, although I never took personal pride in these positions. Most of them were imposed on me; I accepted them reluctantly, and I was never happier than when I could get rid of them and return to the ranks. I am recalling them merely in order to give my credentials; the reader will recognise that at all events I was in a position to be acquainted with the men and the facts during Lenin's lifetime.

I have found enough documents to support my account, to check facts and dates when I had any doubts. My memories were so clear and so certain that the mistakes I might have made could only be tiny errors of detail. For the revolutionaries of my generation who answered the call of the October Revolution, these years left a deep mark. We then reached our highest aspirations; the internationalist faith that we had kept intact during the mutual slaughter of workers found its reward when the new International was born. The shameful abdications of 1914 were avenged; the Soviet Republic proclaimed socialist society and the liberation of mankind. Such ages are inscribed on one's memory in such a way that they cannot be erased.

The fate of the Russian Revolution, the daily acrobatics of recent years which pass for 'Marxism-Leninism', pose important questions: is Stalin the continuer of Lenin? Is the totalitarian régime another form of what used to be called the dictatorship of the proletariat? Was the worm already in the fruit? Is Stalinism 'a logical and almost inevitable development of Leninism', as Norman Thomas affirms? . . . To answer these questions it is first of all necessary to know the facts, the ideas, the men, as they really were in the heroic years of the Revolution. A preliminary excavation job is necessary, for they have been systematically buried under successive layers of ever-changing lies. My work must help to recreate them in an authentic form. I shall simply say: I was there; this is how it happened. My intention is to make easier the task of those who are interested in the history of this period by putting every fact in its true light, by giving every text its full meaning.

Before writing my account, I decided to reread the work by the

English writer Arthur Ransome, **Six Weeks in Russia**, published in 1919. Ransome had the priceless privilege of being able to go to Russia at the beginning of 1919, when Clemenceau's blockade had not yet been broken. His knowledge of the language and the country, the sympathy he felt for the new régime even though he was not a communist, allowed him to give a lifelike and faithful picture of the régime and the men. With him we go right into Lenin's office, we follow the conversation, we see Lenin laugh and wink . . . Behind the 'awesome' theoretician, we see the real Bukharin, youthful and warm-hearted, skipping out of the hall of Hotel Metropole, after having explained the development of world revolution to his un-believing but fascinated listener. The book was written in the most simple style, without rhetoric; it was a unique asset.

I have tried to take it as a model. When the difference between yesterday and today was obvious, blatantly so, I was often tempted to stop a moment to ask the question: 'Are these two the same thing?'; but I deliberately did not do so. I want to confine myself to giving a long report on life in the Soviet Republic, on the Communist International and the Red International of Labour Unions, on men and events. I am writing it today as I could have written it in 1924; my sources are all in the official publications of the Communist International; it is easy to check.

As far as congresses and conferences are concerned, there is no question of giving complete accounts; the history of the Communist International and the Russian Revolution in these decisive years would require several volumes. The agendas were always full; there were numerous meetings of commissions and plenary sessions, countless theses, innumerable resolutions . . . But since I participated in it all, I can draw out what is essential, bring out the points that were stressed, show the continuity of the successive debates and emphasise their conclusions. I have therefore given only a minimum of quota-tions. But I have brought together the main texts of Lenin in this period; they go from **State and Revolution** to the speech to the Fourth Congress (November 1922) — his last intervention in the affairs of the Communist International. They will be found in the Appendix.

Alfred Rosmer
November 1949

1920

1: Europe in 1920

EARLY IN 1920, I was staying with my friend Marcel Martinet at Toulon when I got a letter from Paris informing me I had been appointed by the Committee for the Third International to go to Soviet Russia. Time was short; I had to be ready to set out in a week. But that was more than I needed to make preparations. For me, as for all those with whom I had spent the long years of what was then called the Great War, the October Revolution had been the revolution we expected — the revolution which was to follow the war. It was the dawn of a new era, the beginning of a new life. Everything that came before it had lost its charm; I had lost interest in my books, pamphlets and collections and the works I had prepared. I was more than ready, I was impatient to go.

This journey to Moscow had been continually in our thoughts, especially in mine, since I had been selected in advance to make the journey. But it was, at that time, a difficult undertaking, especially for Frenchmen. Of all countries, the France of Clemenceau and Poincaré had shown itself the most viciously hostile to the Soviet Republic. Clemenceau had boasted of isolating it from the world, of treating it as a plague victim that had to be put in 'quarantine', both to stifle it and to protect the peoples of the world from infection. We could only envy those, for the most part English and Americans, who were able to overcome the obstacles of various sorts which constituted the 'quarantine'.

We were, however, able to distinguish the true from the false in the mass of information published in the newspapers. The October Revolution had taken the bourgeoisie by surprise; its representatives, even those who were not stupid, could not understand it at all. How could this little bunch of exiles whom the Provisional Government had allowed to return to Russia manage to stay in power? It was indeed a nightmare, but one that could last only a few days.

The newspaper correspondents hitherto stationed in Petrograd had moved out to the capitals of neighbouring countries, to Riga, Stockholm or Warsaw, from where they dispatched daily gloomy tales. Lenin had had Trotsky executed; and then again, it was the other way round, another palace revoution, in which Lenin was executed and Trotsky the executioner. For everything hinged on those two names, which had immediately stood out from all the rest. Their ignorance made them accept the most fantastic rumours, and if by any chance they had been able to hear or discover the truth, they knew quite well that their bosses would never let them tell it.

One had to read the dispatches sent at the time and the commentaries that accompanied them to get a clear idea of the furious hatred that the October Revolution inspired in the bourgeoisie; they considered that any means of crushing the revolutionaries was legitimate. Moreover, they believed famine would inevitably spread through the country, and they got some sort of consolation from the thought of such a disaster. In the train bringing me back from Marseilles to Paris at the end of a spell of leave, I found myself in the company of three adjutants on the day when the newspapers had finally to admit that the Bolsheviks had taken power. Seized with the most violent indignation, my neighbours took it in turns to heap crude insults on the heads of the leaders of the insurrection, whose names they did not even know — and that was, for them, a further cause for complaint. Then, in conclusion as it were, one of them shouted out: 'But they'll all starve to death! They haven't got supplies for three days!'

We were safeguarded against the various lies of the correspondents in Riga and elsewhere, because for our part, we knew these 'unknown' men well; their names and their ideas were familiar to us. Some had lived in France during the war, notably Trotsky, from November 1914 until his expulsion (in September 1916) by the

Minister of the Interior, Malvy, colleague of the Socialist Ministers Guesde and Sembat. Then there was Antonov-Ovseënko, manager of the daily paper produced in Paris throughout the war by the Russian socialists of different tendencies who united on the platform of opposition to the imperialist war and the defence of proletarian internationalism; plus Dridzo-Lozovsky, Manuilsky and others. We had first met in the autumn of 1914, when a chance circumstance had enabled us to discover that our basic position on the great problems posed by the war was identical. Chicherin and Litvinov were in London, Lenin and Zinoviev in Switzerland. Contact had been established between the socialists of all countries who were faithful to internationalism at the conferences of Zimmerwald (September 1915) and Kienthal (April 1916). We were amused by the errors committed by journalists of the 'respectable press' who, in their ignorance, got lost in biographical details, and produced some extraordinary hybrids. Even the photographers were mistaken in identifying the people in their pictures.[1]

But despite everything, it happened that from time to time our faith in the stability of the new régime was shaken by detailed dispatches announcing the fall of Petrograd, or the collapse of the Red Army in the face of the victorious thrust of one of the counter-revolutionary generals. The attempted assassination of Lenin, on 30 August 1918, once it was no longer open to doubt, plunged us into worry and anguish; was counter-revolution finally going to triumph?

★   By the time of my journey to the Soviet Republic in the spring of 1920, the situation had become so favourable, the régime had stood up to all attacks so well, that the most bitter enemies of Bolshevism had to admit that they had been wildly wrong in their judgment on it. They had seen merely a rising prepared by a handful of demagogues who were able to win an easy victory because of exceptional circumstances, but whom it would be just as easy to overthrow. They had the unpleasant shock of coming up against a

1. In the learned **Revue des Deux Mondes**, Charles Benoist, seeking to appear well-informed, had written 'Lenin or Zederblum?' Then he corrected himself, rather resentfully, saying, 'It appears that he is definitely called Ulianov.'

movement capable of creating a new order, already firmly rooted in the soil of what, yesterday, had been the empire of the Tsars. For the first time since October 1917, the soviet of workers, peasants and soldiers breathed freely. With an immense, stupendous effort, the Republic had freed itself from the triple threat against it. Yudenich, Kolchak, Denikin and, behind them, the Allied bourgeoisies, had been successively repulsed. The blockade had been broken at one point; the treaty made with Estonia gave the Soviet Republic a window on to Europe, and, thereby, on to the world. England, following the United States, had renounced all open intervention. Working-class protests had even become so strong that Lloyd George was preparing British opinion for the conclusion of a commercial agreement with the Soviet government. France alone remained obstinate, maintaining a warlike and chauvinistic mood in Poland. For Poland, which had scarcely been reconstituted, already wanted to annex the Ukraine. But it was only later that we could accurately assess the price that had been paid to liberate the land of revolution.

★   In France, the revolutionary upsurge which developed as soon as the war ended involved — alongside the workers — peasants, intellectuals, sections of the petty-bourgeoisie, and those ex-servicemen, many in number, who had come home, crippled or unhurt, with the clear intention of settling accounts with the government and the régime which, for four years, had reduced them to the bestial life of the trenches, where they were ordered to attack so that the generals could have good reports to send! The bourgeoisie was bewildered: it was nonplussed at consequences of the war that it had had no inkling of; it had lost faith in its own destiny.

This revolutionary upsurge, despite its breadth and clear intentions, was held in check by the men who led the trade unions and the socialist parties throughout the world at that time. Taking advantage of the inexperience of the newcomers to the movement, they succeeded, by disguising their manoeuvres with dogmatic utterances, in diverting them from any revolutionary action. Membership had risen considerably: in France, the Socialist Party had grown from 90,000 members in July 1914 to 200,000. At the start of the war, the CGT had been cut down until it contained the mere skeletons of unions. Now, for the first time in its history, it could claim to be a mass organisation with its two million regular union members. The reformist leaders argued that it was enough to remain united in order to be strong, to be capable of imposing the will of the working class on the ruling class on every important issue. They affirmed in words their solidarity with the Russian Revolution, but added that in the democratic nations of the West there would be no need to have recourse to violence, for here a new order could be established merely by putting into effect an economic programme drawn up by the working-class organisations which governments and employers would have to accept. In this way the hard struggles, the suffering and wretchedness which had afflicted the countries ravaged by revolution, could be avoided.

I was later able to observe during my travels through Europe that it was relatively easy to deceive men who had been made into revolutionaries by the war by means of such an illusion: for what was the good of further fighting if the objective could be achieved without conflict? Thus in France, Jouhaux and his friends in the union leadership who had thoroughly compromised themselves in the 'sacred union' of national unity, in the war to the last drop of blood — we could now see what huge and unnecessary sacrifices it had demanded — managed to remain at the head of the CGT. In the Socialist Party, meanwhile, the wartime chiefs who had been removed were merely replaced by unreliable elements, whose main concern was to swim with the stream.

Early in 1920, the first big post-war strike, by railway workers, showed that the revolutionary wave was still very strong. This was often embodied in its finest form in the new leaderships thrown up by the local organisations in opposition to the disguised reformism of the national leaders of the Confederation. They often showed remarkable maturity. While I had been at Toulon I had had the opportunity to follow closely the activity of the railway union in the *département*. When the railway strike broke out, I was struck by the intelligence shown by the secretary of this union in the preparation and organisation of support for the strikers. He explained clearly the meaning of the strike, showed the course it might follow in a general situation which was objectively revolutionary, and foresaw the repressive measures which the government would not fail to take. To ensure the continuity of the workers' action, he immediately created teams of substitutes in the strike committee. All this was said and done in a very simple manner, with none of the bombast common in inhabitants of the region. Surprised by the suddenness and extent of the movement, by the firmness and disciplined quality of its development, the railway companies rapidly gave way. They were to take their revenge three months later, with the assistance of the government and of the leaders of the CGT, who sabotaged a solidarity strike which had been forced on them.

2: The Journey to Moscow

Travel across Europe in the post-war period was very complicated. The new nations established with the help of Wilsonian ideology were barricading themselves behind their frontiers. They were defending themselves against Bolshevik penetration, and also against illicit traders of the special type thrown up in periods of upheaval. To get into them, you needed entry visas; and then exit permits to leave again. You had to put up with meticulous customs inspections, with endless and intolerable formalities, and you were glad enough if you got away unscathed. Finally — the last and most serious obstacle — the bordering states, which had seceded after being part of Tsarist Russia, did not allow travel through their territory.

As a result, my journey from Paris to Moscow lasted six weeks. I found it long indeed, yet it taught me a great deal, for it involved long detours which took me through the new nations of central Europe and the new Germany. I was able to make on-the-spot observations, and, moreover, enter into contact with the various parties and groupings which had already joined the Third International or proposed to do so, and to get to know men whom I would meet later in Moscow.

First of all, I devoted a few days of my week's wait to a journey to Catalonia. I had friends and relations there, and I wanted to see them before setting out. I don't want now, any more than I did then, to exaggerate the dangers of the long journey I was about to undertake, or the consequences that it might have. In any case the thought that I was finally going to be present at the very heart of the Soviet Revolution prevented me from dwelling on such thoughts. But there were dangers and they were by no means imaginary ones. Moreover, this rapid visit would allow me to see for myself the present state of the syndicalist movement which was so powerful in this region. By chance during my journey, on the station bookstall at Gerona, I picked up a book which had just appeared on revolutionary syndicalism and the CNT (National Confederation of Labour). It gave some interesting details on the recent congress of this organisation, anarcho-syndicalist in orientation, held at Madrid, in December 1919, where there had been a unanimous vote for joining the Third International. Moreover, the congress had declared in favour of the dictatorship of the proletariat. It was an event of extreme importance, which allowed us to measure the impact that the October Revolution had had throughout the world. The leaders of the victorious insurrection were Marxists, social democrats, albeit of a type different from those encountered hitherto in the international socialist movement. And yet these Spanish revolutionary syndicalists, declared enemies of 'politicians' and political parties, had not hesitated to reply to their appeal. Joaquín Maurin, commenting later on these decisions, wrote: 'The syndicalist movement underwent a veritable transformation.' It was the same with the revolutionary syndicalists in Italy, and with ourselves.

But this was Spain, and while the syndicalists had been able to hold a great public congress at Madrid, at the same time the same organisation was illegal in Barcelona. Here its members were hounded by the ordinary police as well as by a special police created by the employers' groups, the *somatenes*, and a special law gave the police the right to execute summarily men they wanted to get rid of, under the pretext that they were trying to abscond. The anarcho-syndicalists replied by individual assaults against those responsible for such crimes and against informers. It was a bitter and unending struggle. I had a great deal of difficulty in finding some of the friends I had known on previous visits. They confirmed and completed the information I had been able to get from newspapers and correspondence about the working-class movement during the war.

Catalonia had had a period of exceptional prosperity. Its factories were working flat out for the countries at war, for Germany as well as for France. This prosperity, far from lulling the revolutionary spirit of the workers, aroused it, and the Russian Revolution brought it to its peak. In 1917 a general strike had grown so large that it threatened the régime. Moreover, the industrialised and proletarian Catalonia had not been the only region affected by profound agitation. In the agricultural provinces of the South too, although on a lesser scale, there had been attempts at insurrection against the owners of the latifundia, especially in Andalusia. For the revolutionaries, the urgent task was now simply to co-ordinate the two movements. But at present all their energies in Catalonia were absorbed in clandestine activity. As I was taking my final cup of white coffee at the stall on the Rambla, the evening news-vendors suddenly appeared, shouting out the day's news: an employer assassinated at San Gervasio.

★ In Paris I met the Russian comrade who, I was told, had made arrangements for my journey. I shall quite often have occasion to speak of him in the following pages, and as he disappeared from the political scene quite early on, and never played a rôle of any importance, I shall call him Ivan for the convenience of the narrative. He explained to me the plan that he had thought up: the Italian Socialist Party had just decided to send a large delegation to Russia, which would include the Party leaders and the principal trade union leaders. It would therefore be a substantial party, it would travel without difficulty, with regular passports and all the necessary visas. The Socialists were the largest party in parliament, their influence in the towns and countryside was enormous, and the government had shown that it was quite willing to look favourably on their expedition. It would be possible to take advantage of these favourable circumstances to include me in the delegation. It was in fact very simple; it looked almost too good to me. We arranged to meet in Milan.

I got there just in time. In Modano I caught the last train allowed to set out before work stopped — the railwaymen's union had just called a strike. During these days the National Council of the Socialist Party was meeting in Milan. I asked for Bordiga whom I imagined to have a position quite close to ours. He was the leader of the abstentionist faction and defended his position brilliantly in his tendency's weekly **Il Soviet**. Contrary to my expectations he was concerned to differentiate himself immediately and clearly from us. With his extraordinary volubility, which in congresses brought shorthand writers to despair, he explained to me that he was not at all in agreement with us, that he considered revolutionary syndicalism to be an erroneous, anti-Marxist and hence dangerous theory. I was surprised at this unexpected outburst; at least I now had no further doubts on the position of this group of anti-parliamentarists.

We were then taken to the private home of G-M Serrati, at the time editor of **Avanti!** — the daily paper of the Party — where a more intimate meeting of a quite different type was taking place. Serrati had been a very active supporter of Zimmerwald; he was producing an excellent paper, which was the best informed on the international movement. He had come to Paris during the war and I had met him at Merrheim's office, at the time when this office was a home and meeting-place for internationalists from all countries. Besides Serrati and two Italian deputies, there were also Hungarians, Austrians, a Russian, and people from the Balkans — a Rumanian and a Bulgarian — and Fernand Loriot, the Socialist leader of the French Zimmerwaldians, who had already arrived the day before. As can be seen, there were the ingredients of a real international conference.

This little conference, and the others of the same sort that I was to participate in on my way to Moscow, were above all meetings for a mutual exchange of information. Each of the participants knew in general terms what had happened in Europe and in the world, but was impatient to know more, especially about the Balkan nations and the nations of Central Europe, which had been thrown into upheaval by the war and the revolutionary movements of the post-war period. They wanted to know what had been the developments of Wilsonian Europe, this Utopia of an American liberal intellectual, of a Presbyterian professor. For their part, our Balkan comrades were eager for news about the labour movement in the great nations of the West.

However, since we were in Milan, and since the situation in Italy could rightly be considered to be a pre-revolutionary one, it was on this country that our attention was concentrated. Asked to give an account of the situation, Serrati refused, asking the deputy Sacerdoce to do it instead. He gave us a sort of administrative report, listing the number of Socialist deputies, the local authorities controlled, the whole regions in town and countryside that had been won for socialism, the continual growth of the unions, the general strikes by which the working class was intervening in political life every time an important problem arose. It was interesting, impressive and encouraging; but we expected something different. Serrati realised that he would have to give his comments; in a few words he drew the conclusion for the statistical data we had noted. 'Town and countryside are with us,' he said; 'the workers follow our calls. The peasants are no less keen; in many rural communes, the mayors have replaced the portraits of the King in the town-halls with pictures of Lenin. We have the strength; we have it so absolutely that no one, friend or foe, would think of disputing it. The only problem for us is how to use that strength.' This was indeed the great problem for workers of all countries. Here it was more urgent than anywhere else.[2]

I had just made some new acquaintances, but I had some older ones in Milan itself. These were the anarchist Errico Malatesta, and the secretary of the *Unione Sindacale Italiana*, Armando Borghi. Malatesta was one of the most attractive figures of anarchism. More than once he was obliged to flee from Italy to escape repression, but he reappeared as soon as a favourable opportunity allowed him to, and resumed his activity as though he had left the day before. This

---

2. A non-socialist writer described the situation at this time as follows: 'Until September 1920, Italy really gave the impression of having fallen prey to the most excessive disorder and the most exaggerated revolutionary madness — mainly in verbal form. The strike-mania among all categories of workers, even in the public services, verged on tragi-comedy. The slightest cause was a pretext for stopping production. Everything that had a "bourgeois" appearance was subject to attack; cars could not travel through the countryside or the surbubs of certain "red" towns without running the risk of being the target for stones thrown by workers and peasants . . . The Russian myth was more widespread than ever. Communist Russia became the ideal of the great majority of the working class.' G. Prezzolini, **Le Fascisme**, pp 65-67.

time his return had been forced on the government, which was equivocating, by the threat of a strike by those enrolled for naval conscription. I knew him well. I had already been long familiar with his writings when I met him for the first time in London, where he found asylum when life in Italy became impossible for him. The insurrectionary wave which shook Italy on the eve of the world war, the 'red week', had reached its full pitch in Ancona where Malatesta at the time was publishing a weekly paper **Volontà**. For a week he and his friends had controlled the town and the surrounding area. Obstructed by the socialist leaders, the insurrection was crushed by government forces, and once more Malatesta took refuge in London.[3] Returning to Italy at the beginning of 1920, he established himself in Milan, and immediately prepared to publish a daily paper, **Umanità Nuova**. It was at the paper's offices that I went to see him. These consisted of a square room, not very big, with scarcely room enough for the four tables, one in each corner, for the editors. Malatesta was working at his table; they were in the middle of preparing the issue, so we fixed up a meeting for the evening. I brought along Armando Borghi, whom I had fetched from the *Unione Sindacale*.

That very day Malatesta had devoted his article to the Third International. He asked the question: What is it? He asked in a friendly and sympathetic manner, but for the moment there was no point in asking more of him. He wanted to have precise information before making up his mind. The Socialist Party had already affiliated, without reservations, and among those who were answering Moscow's appeal, a certain sympathy was spontaneously growing up, so that the old enmities were beginning to be forgotten. None the less Malatesta, who knew the leaders of the Italian Socialist Party well, might well wonder how certain elements in the Party, especially the

3. The following is an appraisal of the man and his ideas by a socialist: 'The anarchist Malatesta, who is about 67 years old, and who returned from exile a few days ago, was the only true revolutionary to be found in Italy in the period 1919-1920. For him, the word "revolution" has a precise meaning . . . Malatesta thinks we should make the revolution as soon as possible. "For," he says, "if we let the favourable moment go by, then afterwards we shall have to pay with tears of blood for the fear we are now causing the bourgeoisie.' A. Rossi, **La naissance du fascisme**, p 45.

reformist leaders of the **Confederazione Generale del Lavoro**, could have approved this decision. This was doubtless one of the reasons for his desire to wait and see. One of the qualities he rated highest in relations between men was frankness; he was himself incapable of disguising or toning down his opinions. He had proved this during the war when he had stood out firmly against Kropotkin and those anarchists who had supported the war, in a harsh article entitled 'Governmental Anarchists'. Although he had great sympathy for revolutionary syndicalism, he always stressed that syndicalism and anarchism remained two quite distinct concepts. Borghi and his revolutionary syndicalist organisation, on the other hand, had not hesitated to commit themselves straight away. They had voted for affiliation, like their Spanish comrades and the minority of the French CGT.

The next day we had a long conversation with Ivan and the Russian Communist whom I had met at the international meeting at Serrati's home. He was very different from Ivan. Though I had no information about his origins and political biography, I imagined he might belong to the category of intellectuals and technicians that the October Revolution had brought into revolutionary activity — a category exemplified by the engineer Krasin. It was this comrade who, together with Serrati, published the monthly magazine **Comunismo**. 'The magazine gives me a great deal of work,' he said in the course of the conversation. 'I have to do almost everything. I haven't even been able to go to a concert since I've been here!'

It very quickly emerged in the course of our conversation that the magnificent device dreamt up to make my journey easier had collapsed as soon as it was discussed in any detail. For all sorts of reasons the Italian socialists were quite unwilling to put up with me. They intended to travel as respectable citizens, with genuine passports, and to go to Moscow as customers of Thomas Cook. So I had to find an alternative. The improvisation we arrived at involved a long detour through Vienna, with a first stop at Venice where Ivan was to join us.

We did indeed meet there, but in circumstances that led me to cast serious doubts on Ivan's capacities as far as organising clandestine travel was concerned. He did not arrive by the train he had agreed to take, nor by the following one. It was only in the middle of the next day that we caught sight of him, by chance as we were walking through the town; he was up at the top of the Rialto, observing the progress of a gondola on the Grand Canal.

3: May Day in Vienna

The Austrian frontier clearly marked the boundary with the other half of Europe; it took a whole morning to get through the interminable controls, checks and inspections. The train had only two carriages in which we were all piled up. Finally it started. Its speed would have given me time to admire the magnificent region we were travelling through at my leisure — the line ran along the high wooded mountains of Carinthia — had it not been for the talkativeness of my companion. He went on telling me all kinds of stories, some of which had a certain interest: for example when he told me of his veneration for Krupskaya. He had worked for several years in Switzerland, and, at one time, he had been on the verge of sinking into an aimless life of dissipation; it was Krupskaya, Lenin's companion, who had saved him by her wise advice, by the discreet influence that she exercised on all those who came close to her, above all because of her simple way of life.

But such interesting items were exceptional; more usually, he would tell stupid lies. 'In Soviet Russia there is still famine, but everything you get there is of the highest quality,' he said, among other things. Yet he knew that when I got there I would find foul black bread, and that a bowl of millet *cacha* would be a feast. It was rather disconcerting; for if I could appreciate that for its couriers Moscow had to put up with men who were no more than reliable, the discovery that I was making of this second- or even third-rate Bolshevik left a bad impression. On questions where he was better informed than I was, and where he could have told me something useful, he showed himself very reticent. At the congress held the previous October at Heidelberg, the young German Communist Party had split into two sections over the questions of parliamentarism and trade-union organisation. A considerable part of the delegates had declared vigorously against any participation in parliamentary action, and in favour of breaking with the reformist unions which they proposed to replace with new mass workers' organisations. They had come up against an intransigent leadership; expelled from the Party they had immediately created another one, the KAPD (Communist Workers Party of Germany). I had only general and sketchy information about this, and I would have liked to know more. But when I interrogated Ivan he was evasive. He knew that I was a syndicalist and therefore hostile to parliament; childishly, he was afraid that I might be influenced by this disagreement.

★   The situation in Vienna, in the spring of 1920, was terrible. There was deep poverty everywhere, poverty which it was painful to look at. From the moment we got to the hotel, the ragged linen, the state of physical exhaustion that the staff were in, revealed it. In the shop windows there were nothing but empty boxes lying here and there. Hostilities had scarcely ended when traders flocked in from all over to plunder the capital of the great empire that had collapsed; first of all the Italians, for they, being the nearest, had arrived first, and they had felt an extra thrill of joy at plundering their 'hereditary enemy'. Everything one saw and heard was distressing.

The three days we spent there followed the same pattern as our stay in Milan: a small international meeting and a visit to a well-known anarchist. Here the meeting was dominated by the Hungarians — those who had managed to flee when the young Republic had fallen before the attack of the Rumanian mercenaries sent in by the Allies; Bela Kun had been captured and was in prison. Among them was the economist Eugene Varga. He had some knowledge of French affairs; and he questioned me, among other things, about Francis Delaisi and his book **Democracy and the Financiers**. Delaisi argued that the true masters of France were not the 'democratic' rulers; they were the 'financiers', a small number of men to be found on the boards of directors of all the big firms — an anticipation of the theme of the '200 families' which was to be taken up later at the time of the Popular Front. Lively and superficial, the book had made a certain impression in France, and, as I could now observe, it had travelled beyond our frontiers. This Viennese communist group also published a review, **Kommunismus**, but in comparison with **Comunismo** of Milan, it was of a 'leftist' tendency. Its editorial board was certainly more original, more individual, less dependent on the positions then considered to be official.

The anarchist that I visited next, Nettlau, was quite different from Malatesta: he was a man devoted to study rather than a man of action. Among other things he had written an important work on Bakunin. Not having found a publisher, or not having looked for one because he was proud and sensitive and felt horror at soliciting, he had had a limited number of copies printed, to be placed in the great libraries where researchers, historians and students would always be able to consult them. The war years, bringing privations of every sort and making it impossible to leave Austria, had weighed heavily on him. He was not rich, but had sufficient means to live as he pleased. He liked to travel for pleasure and for the research that his work required. He had collected such a large number of works on the working-class movement in general, and on anarchism in particular, that he had them stored in several towns. Would he find them all again? That was his great worry.

When I arrived at his home, he was busy making his evening meal: a bowl of beans that he had covered with a layer of coffee-grounds. Noticing my surprise at this unusual mixture, he said to me: 'There are nutritious elements in coffee-grounds; we can't afford to waste them.' As we went out together, I pointed out that he had a coupon sticking in his hat. 'That's deliberate,' he said, 'so that I don't risk forgetting the cigarette distribution; as I don't smoke, I can exchange them for some food.' Such was life in Vienna, in the month of April 1920. Such was the state to which the long war and its privations had reduced a free man.

One afternoon, as we were walking in the suburbs of Vienna, Nettlau stopped and said in a bitter tone: 'Even from here you can see what they call Czechoslovakia.' He held the same position on the war as Kropotkin, but from the other side; he was for the defence of Germanic culture against Asiatic barbary. We stopped in one of those pleasant inns, normally crowded on a Sunday, but where there were few customers. A glass of white wine and a pastry were enough to change my friend's expression; his cheeks took on a new colour and the expression of sadness and despondency which had been permanently with him finally gave way to a sort of exuberance.

★ We had arrived on the first of May; the traditional demonstration was very impressive. It had an international character with its contingents of Italians, Hungarians and Balkan peoples. The Hungarians were there in great number, and despite their defeat gave an impression of strength. They sang the *Internationale* very rhythmically, as a marching song, quite different from the usual drawling chant.

4: Masaryk's Czechoslovakia

After Vienna, Prague provided a complete contrast. Poverty gave way to abundance, sadness and resignation to gaiety. The shops were overflowing with food. If one could judge from the impressions of a single day, the new state was being born in the most favourable conditions. The friendliness shown towards the French was so great as to be embarrassing; you couldn't stop a young Czech from taking hold of your case and putting himself at your disposal to show you round the town. Although demands for national independence had never meant much to me, the joyful vitality manifested by this young and favoured nation had a likeable side to it. Czechs and Austrians had clashed in everything. Even in the international socialist and trade-union conferences, their powerful antagonism had always created sharp conflicts, the Czechs claiming independent national representation. Now they could live as good neighbours.

None the less one did not have to stay long in Prague to feel serious doubts about the matter. The money-changer to whom I gave Austrian crowns gave them back to me, saying contemptuously that he didn't take that sort of money. At Vienna we had visited the secretary of the Austrian section of the Women's International League for Peace and Freedom; she had fought for her ideas during the war, putting herself at some risk, and despite the distress of Austria and the absurd divisions which made Austria into an unviable nation, she remained faithful to her pacifist internationalism. The Czech representative that she sent to us was quite different. Her husband held an important position in the new state — there had been plenty of places going at the liberation. She herself was managing a recently created institution and there was no question of her compromising herself by getting involved in internationalist activity. The Czechs were very proud of the great men of the Republic, Masaryk and Beneš, and of the consideration shown them by Wilson. They spoke of the Russian Revolution unsympathetically, in an aloof manner; Czechoslovakia was going to show the world what a real democracy was. From these examples one can imagine what the chauvinism of the average Czech was like. The new state had no fewer national minorities than the old Hapsburg Austria and it was already to be feared that it would treat them no better.

Prague was decidedly something different; unlike Milan and Vienna, we had no international meeting: communists had no reason to come there, and good reason to stay away. Masaryk — the great man — was clearly and openly hostile to Bolshevism and the October Revolution. The convoy of Czech prisoners that the Soviet government had premitted to return through Siberia and Vladivostok had suddenly turned against it, and gone to join Kolchak as reinforcements. All I was able to arrange was a meeting with some socialist journalists. They belonged to the left, and there was a sharp struggle within the Party. The leadership wanted to maintain the coalition established during the war between the national bourgeoisie of Masaryk and Beneš and the Social Democratic Party, despite the criticisms of a strong opposition which demanded a break and a return to socialist politics based on the class struggle. (The split took place some months later, in September 1920 — the left wing of the Socialist Party formed the Communist Party which affiliated to the Third International in May 1921.) I was struck by the way the people we were talking to spoke of Bohumir Šmeral — the man who was to become the leader of the Communist Party. He was an avowed opportunist, who had been a deputy in the Imperial Council under the Hapsburgs and had, as it were, proved what kind of man he was. They were embarrassed by him, but none the less did not conceal a certain admiration for his skill as a wily politician. They repeated several times 'we can do nothing without Šmeral', as if replying to an ever-present objection.[4]

5: Clara Zetkin. Shlyapnikov. Great demonstration at Berlin

In Berlin we met Ivan again; we had not seen him since Vienna. He had had unexpected difficulties at the Czech frontier, which was better controlled than he had thought. Our first visit was to Clara Zetkin. Normally she lived in Stuttgart, but she kept a small flat in Berlin, near the Potsdamerplatz. A girl who was her secretary was anxious that she should get enough rest. 'Don't make her talk too much,' she advised us; 'she's very tired at present.' But it wasn't us she should have given this advice to, for, whether she was replying in the course of conversation, or crying out *'Genossinnen und Genossen'* (comrades) to the audience at a meeting, Clara Zetkin always launched into things with great energy and it was not so easy to stop her. She gave us a very interesting picture of the general situation in the country and of the internal life of the various socialist parties, rather in the style of a speech at a public meeting — that is, without going into the disagreements in depth, but sticking to generalities. Then, when we tried to leave, she cried: 'Oh! you know my organism has extraordinary resilience; doubtless it's because I have French blood in my veins.'

She had advised us to see Paul Levi, who was now leading the Party together with her, and who was more intimately involved in its internal life. I didn't know him, but a Dutch communist I had just met, and who was closely in touch with the German socialist movement, had sketched a portrait of him for me. A barrister, son of a banker, quite rich, living in a comfortable flat, he had lived in Switzerland during the war. Then he had moved closer to Lenin and

---

4. Speaking of Šmeral in his **Souvenirs**, Beneš mentions his 'opportunist pro-Austrian politics' during the war, which he justified in Marxist terms: 'Say I am a cynic, a materialist, or whatever else you like; but politics is not a question of morality.' Beneš adds: 'He was then considered a politician of the first rank, whom the whole world had to reckon with.' (Beneš, **Souvenirs de guerre et de révolution**, French translation, pp. 26-30.)

the Bolsheviks, and had participated in the Kienthal Conference. On his return to Germany he had fought alongside Karl Liebknecht and Rosa Luxemburg, and had also been their lawyer. He was an educated, well-informed man, capable of making brilliant analyses, but not of coming to conclusions, nor even of formulating the logical conclusions of his analyses. His origins and way of life seemed incompatible with being the leader of a revolutionary workers' party. Clara Zetkin had been optimistic and full of drive, but he was gloomy and fretful. His main aversion was the communists who had opposed him at Heidelberg. He was obsessed with them, and the conflict took on the appearance of a personal quarrel. In his eyes the syndicalists were not politically reliable comrades and there was the danger they would be attracted by the anti-parliamentarism of the KAPD. We tried to get him to talk of other things, for the conversation was becoming wearisome. But it was impossible, he always came back to the terrible opposition; it was almost like a persecution mania.

The Italian delegation, which had left Milan well after me, was now making a brief stop in Berlin. The Russian communist whom I had met at Serrati's home was now here and he had sent a message to ask me to go and see him. As I was approaching the address he had given me, I bumped into Serrati. He was furious. 'They asked me to wait in the street. I'm not risking anything; I've got a passport; but as for him . . . Very odd conspiratorial methods!' He was still declaiming when they came for us. The strangest thing was that they had nothing to tell us, nothing but platitudinous advice for the rest of the journey.

In Berlin we met other travellers going to Moscow who, like us, were waiting for a possible route to be found. First of all Angel Pestaña, secretary of the CNT, the Spanish anarcho-syndicalist trade union; then the men from the Balkans I had seen in Vienna; another day it was three Bulgarians, among them Kolarov. These represented a new type of communist, for, in their manner and dress, they looked like notaries or wealthy businessmen. There was no danger of the police questioning them during a raid. They none the less claimed to be authentic Bolsheviks, for they belonged to the *tesnyaki* (Narrow Socialists), who defended socialism based on the class struggle as opposed to the 'broad-minded ones'. In fact it was no more than a version of the Guesde-Jaurès dispute, as a decisive experience was soon to show. We made contact with several Young Communist militants; they were all very likeable, full of go. They too had grievances against the Party leadership — and even against the Communist International — but not the same as those of the KAPD. Above all they complained, though in a rather vague manner, that it was not revolutionary enough.

Once again at this time the Poles, under Pilsudski, had invaded the Ukraine and were declaring their intention of annexing it. The aggression was so blatant that the British government under Lloyd George refused them any assistance, and the leaders of the Second International called on their sections to call meetings denouncing it, and on the unions to refuse to transport any munitions to Warsaw. The German Socialist and Communist Parties organised a joint demonstration through Berlin. The assembly point for the processions was in the great square in the heart of the city, between the former Imperial Palace, the cathedral and the museum. An enormous crowd of people had responded to their appeal and had gathered, according to their political sympathies, in front of any of about ten rostrums. In any case, all the speeches developed the same theme and had the same tone, for Pilsudski had awakened the hostility latent in all Germans, even sometimes in socialists, towards Poland; and now the Germans had the additional grievance against the Poles of the 'corridor' which the Treaty of Versailles had attributed to Poland, and which had the ridiculous effect of cutting Germany into two separate parts. At the time fixed for the end of the meeting, a bugle call rang out. A resolution was read out and all the groups voted on it at the same time amid cheering. The speeches from all the rostrums had ended at the same moment, except for the one occupied by the Youth Section, where the speaker continued even after the warning from the bugle. Finally their march formed up and set off briskly into Unter den Linden, to the rousing strains of the *Internationale*. When they reached the Friedrichstrasse, the whole march turned and headed towards the working-class Wedding quarter.

★   At this time, Shlyapnikov[5] was in Berlin; he had come as a delegate from the Russian trade unions to the German metalworkers' union congress. He was extending his stay, taking advantage of the rare opportunity to get as much information as possible on this Western world from which Moscow was still cut off, and also to question travellers who were anxious to continue their journey but who had got stuck in Berlin. He had arranged to meet me at the union headquarters, and, when he arrived, I felt he had kept me waiting a long time. But he was overjoyed, and said to me with a laugh: 'Do you know who I had in my office? Cachin and Frossard.' For me this neither made up for being kept waiting nor was it any source of joy. Cachin was editor of **L'Humanité**, Frossard was secretary of the Socialist Party. The congress of this Party, held at Strassburg, had decided to send them to Moscow 'on a fact-finding mission' before making a decision on affiliation to the Third International. In the meantime they had taken the provisional measure of withdrawing from the Second International.

I had no liking for either of them. Cachin was a man devoid of character, who had been an ultra-chauvinist at the beginning of the war, running errands to Mussolini on behalf of the French government. Then he had swum with the stream, and now professed to be a sympathiser with Bolshevism, although, in his articles, he had condemned the October rising and basically loathed the Bolsheviks. Of Frossard it is enough to say that he was a second-rate imitation of Briand. Starting out with sympathies for Zimmerwald, he was to end up as a minister under Laval and even Pétain. We will meet him again in the course of this narrative.

Our stay in Berlin was certainly not without interest, but it went on too long. To calm our impatience we had nothing but conversations among the delegates. New ones kept arriving. At the café Bauer the coffee was wretched, but you could see newspapers from all the different countries. Our little group used to get excited at picking up rumours which suggested we might be off again soon. It was said that the Youth Sections had arranged the journey, or that

5. Trade-union militant and leader of the 'Workers' Opposition'; he had been Commissar for Labour at the beginning of the Revolution.

we would make a detour through Scandinavia and arrive at Murmansk . . . But our hopes were vain, and our wait continued. We had to resign ourselves to taking an interest in the city, or in the curious theatrical experiments that Max Reinhardt was presenting in the vast amphitheatre where he was staging a repertory that was quite disconcerting by its sheer variety, ranging from *The Weavers* to *Orpheus in the Underworld*. When the play fitted the setting it was very fine, for example *Julius Ceasar*. But I wasn't very impressed by *The Weavers*, which I had been looking forward to and which I considered inferior to the version that Antoine had produced, in Paris, on his tiny stage. At the Lessing Theatre, the production and interpretation of *Peer Gynt* were second-rate. At the Opera we had some fine evenings of Wagner. We also made trips out of the city to lakes situated amid the woods, and we made a boat journey as far as Potsdam.

6: From Stettin to Reval (Tallinn)

At last Pestaña and I were suddenly informed that we should set out without delay. It was already late in the evening and the next morning we were to take the first train for Stettin. Then everything developed in the simplest manner imaginable — except towards the end, when a final unforeseen obstacle turned up. We embarked on a fine boat which was to take us as far as Reval (which had now become Tallinn). We strolled on the deck, and ate meals that were very pleasant in comparison with the diet we had put up with in Vienna and Berlin. The only embarrassing moment was when we caught sight of two other passengers, travelling clandestinely, the Englishman Murphy and the American Fraina, who, in the evening, were taking the risk of emerging from the coal-bunker where they had had to be accommodated. Although it was in no way my fault, Murphy always bore me a grudge for it.

We had had a pleasant crossing, with three days of calm sea, but at Reval we had an unpleasant awakening. The validity of our passports was accepted, but we had not asked for Estonian visas at Berlin, so we were separated from the other passengers and taken to the government headquarters. The ideology of Wilsonism and the desire to carve up Soviet Russia had together led to the re-establishment of the Baltic states, Estonia, Latvia and Lithuania, as independent nations. As we had already observed in Czechoslovakia, this national resurrection was accompanied by a chauvinism, the intensity of which seemed to develop in inverse proportion to the size of the country. Here, at any rate, it was in a robust state, for it was the Foreign Minister in person who came to give us a sermon and to threaten us. 'They want to ignore us,' he shouted, 'but we shan't allow it!' And as we tried to explain to him, with all due humility, that nothing could be further from our minds, he only got more excited, and shouted louder than ever: 'We are determined to be respected!' He was a little man, and he was pacing up and down his office, gesticulating and raising his voice as he came closer to us. The scene must have been pretty ridiculous, comical even, but we weren't in a position to appreciate it. We were wondering if we were going to end up with a stupid failure after having got so near our destination. Finally we were asked to leave; our case would be studied and we would be informed of the decision.

We went to our place of refuge, the Soviet mission, to tell them our story. The minister was dining with his family and his secretaries. We were invited to sit down and take some refreshments; our mishaps would be discussed later, after the meal was finished. A secretary took us into her office where we were to await the government's decision. Hours went by; Pestaña had found a topic of conversation that he was always glad to expand on — namely, the fact that the present situation in Spain was more favourable to the overthrow of the régime of Alfonso than it had ever been.

For the first time, in fact, revolutionary agitation was not limited to the workers in Catalonia. It was developing at the same time in the agricultural regions of the South, where a feudal régime still existed. The peasants were in revolt and their movement had become so large that it was not only possible, but an urgent necessity, to link up the two movements. The secretary seemed to be taking a great interest in this account, which was brusquely interrupted by the arrival of a messenger bringing an encouraging piece of news. There was no firm decision yet, but the authorities' intransigence seemed to be weakening. The secretary then disappeared rapidly, making us think that perhaps she was not so interested in Spanish affairs as she had led us to suppose.

★   The journey across Estonia, from Reval to the frontier, took a whole morning. This was not because the distance was so great, but because in places the railway was in a terrible condition. A large bridge, which had not been fully repaired, could be crossed only if one took serious precautions. It was not so long since Yudenich had passed that way . . . We were kept waiting again at Narva for exit formalities; finally we arrived in Soviet Russia at Yamburg. We all leapt out of the train and ran across to the station building. Now there was a whole group of us, for delegates whom we hadn't yet seen suddenly emerged. The joy we all felt excited even the most placid; it was expressed by embraces all round.

The ceremony that took place in the station was very simple; on the walls the only decoration was four large photographs — Lenin, Trotsky, Zinoviev and Lunacharsky. The Russian communists who had come to welcome us returned with us, so that our railway carriage was rapidly transformed into a discussion group. Fraina was very proud to be able to show us a thick volume of selected articles by Lenin and Trotsky which he had edited and had just published. He had managed to bring a copy all the way with him, certainly a meritorious achievement.

One Russian communist was determined to get me to discuss the question of parliamentarism; his pretext was to get me to translate theses of which he had only the English text. The author had obviously made great efforts to lay down a set of rules that was so precise that in future there would be no danger of party members, once elected, escaping party discipline, carrying on political activity on their own account and using their mandate to make a career for themselves — a kind of behaviour of which there had been many examples in the past. When I had finished reading the translation, my neighbours expressed their approval, and they were surprised to see me remain unmoved. 'Don't you think it's an excellent text?' they asked me. 'Yes, it's very good, but in France it would have been easier to make the revolution than to enforce it. Men like Millerand

and Briand don't give a damn for the strictest mandates, and their successors can learn from their example.' Whereupon the discussion picked up again; other comrades intervened, and our Russian friends came to the rescue. 'If you think this text is inadequate, propose that it should be strengthened; your amendments will certainly be accepted.'

With these impromptu discussions, jumping from one subject to another, the journey was now going very quickly. None the less we had time to look at the countryside, at this new Russia which had, in a single act, passed from the hated Tsarist rule to the liberating revolution on which revolutionaries of all lands now had their eyes fixed. In one of the rare moments when I had been able to get away from the debates, I was approached in the corridor by an English-woman, a journalist, the correspondent, she told me, of the **Daily News**, a liberal paper from which I had often got interesting information about Soviet Russia. She quite rapidly came to the question of the Third International and of the Congress which was soon to meet. Discreetly a Russian comrade led me aside, and after having enquired about the questions she had been asking, he said to me: 'Keep away from her; she looks suspicious to us. She's come here after a stay in Poland and the interest she's showing in the Third International only strengthens our suspicions.' 'But why are you letting her in?' 'Because we are very concerned to unmask spies. The bourgeois governments are trying to infiltrate agents into the very centre of the Third International, and above all, most of the delegates to the Congress will have come here illegally. We must ensure their safety.'

7: Petrograd. Zinoviev

We arrived in Petrograd early in the evening, an evening which was to have no end, for this was the season in which it never went dark. We had already had the experience on the boat. The Gulf of Finland was not yet entirely clear of mines, and the boat had to hug the coast cautiously. Everything was odd: the passage through the Åland Isles at reduced speed because a special pilot was steering us; the night which never fell . . . you couldn't make up your mind to go to your cabin to sleep. And even less so in Petrograd.

We had scarcely arrived when Ivan turned up with a text that I had to check straightaway. In his view it was an admirable piece, and he was sure I would be pleased with it. In the course of our discussions, I had told him over and over again that it seemed to be impossible to construct a communist party with the leaders of the Socialist Party, especially those like Cachin who had abandoned socialism and betrayed the workers in the critical hours of the war, and had become raving chauvinists. If, under the impact of the Russian Revolution, they had more or less sincerely revised their positions, it had been above all in order to stay at the head of the Party. The text in question was the draft of an open letter to the members of the French Socialist Party, recalling and condemning the betrayal of their leaders, with no punches pulled and no details omitted. Thereby the Congress would appeal to the working class over the heads of the Party leaders. Obviously it was intended to 'prepare the way' for the return to France of the two emissaries, Cachin and Frossard. I couldn't get excited about it, and above all I wanted to get down to other things. Victor Serge arrived just in time to save me. 'Leave that,' he said; 'that's our job.'

Serge was one of the anarchists who had responded to the appeal of the October Revolution and the Third International. He had come a long way, for in his youth he had belonged to the individualist anarchist tendency; but he had come through some tough experiences. When the Russian Revolution broke out, he was in Spain. He set out immediately, hoping to be able to get to Petrograd through France. But he had been arrested, and interned in a concentration camp. By joining a convoy of prisoners being repatriated he had finally managed to get to Petrograd. He had been appointed to the editorial board of the review of the Communist International, where his knowledge of languages, his talents as a writer and his experience of participation in the labour movement in various countries were put to good use. For us he was the best possible guide. There was a flood of questions on both sides. We had plenty to ask him, and for his part he was anxious to know exactly what was happening in the Western democracies, for communications were still difficult, newspapers came only at irregular intervals, and correspondence was possible only by taking advantage of exceptional circumstances.

One example will be enough to show how inadequate communication was, and how difficult it was to get exact information. At the time when **La Vie Ouvrière** — which then represented the new International — was able to resume publication, a new weekly appeared with the strange name of **Le Titre Censuré** (The Censured Title), the text of which led readers to understand that the title forbidden by the censorship was **The Bolshevik**. This paper was a creation of Clemenceau's head of police, Mandel, whose clear aim was to obstruct **La Vie Ouvrière** by deceiving the workers. It was quite cleverly done, so that even in France some people in the provinces were taken in by it. Victor Serge could therefore be forgiven for including it in one of his reports as being among the journals which supported Soviet Russia and the Third International.

Our long walk through town took us to places I was already familiar with through my reading. There were still many traces of war; in some places the wood-paved streets had been torn up. Because of its geographical situation the town was the most exposed, the most difficult to provide with supplies and to defend, and the suffering there had been terrible. We were on the famous Nevsky Prospect at the end of which we could see the golden spire of the Admiralty Building. We saw the Kazan Cathedral and its porticoes, and the Winter Palace which immediately made us think of the tragic events of 22 January 1905: the peaceful crowd led by the priest, Father Gapon, bringing a petition to Nicholas II and getting rifle-fire as their sole reply.

Over the Troitsky Bridge, along the side of the sinister Peter-Paul fortress, we crossed the Neva and returned through the revolutionary suburb of Vassili Ostrov. Our tour ended up in St Isaac's Square, at the Astoria hotel, where the leaders of the Petrograd Soviet were living. Victor Serge had a room there. At the back of the vestibule we saw a machine-gun trained on the entrance, for it was not long since the town had lived through anxious days, under the dangerous threat of an offensive by Yudenich's army. The civil-war atmosphere could still be felt, and Pilsudski's soldiers had just invaded the Ukraine.

Zinoviev set off for Moscow the next day, for the Executive Committee of the Communist International had been convened to meet there. He took with him the delegates who had already arrived in Petrograd and he wanted to take advantage of the journey to make contact with them and ask them questions. He was exactly like the picture that we had formed of him: his large head and broad, solid frame gave him the appearance of a classical tribune. The conversations were wholly cordial, and he was obviously pleased when he got the opportunity for a harmless joke. To one delegate who refused a bowl of soup, he said with a laugh: 'You've got to eat it; it's part of the discipline.'

8: Moscow: at the Executive Committee of the Communist International. Sadoul/Radek/Bukharin

In Moscow, we were picked up by cars which took us straight to the office of the Communist International. Several of the members of the Executive Committee were already there, among them Jacques Sadoul. He had gone to Russia with the French military mission, and Albert Thomas had made him his personal informant. Before the war Sadoul had belonged to the most moderate wing of the Socialist Party, but, caught up in the October Revolution, he had gone over to the Bolshevik side. The letters that he wrote at that time to his friend Thomas showed that he had fulfilled his task intelligently. [6] He had been one of the few among the Frenchmen who were in Russia at that time who understood the meaning of the events they were witnessing. The Bolsheviks had seized copies of these letters in the course of a search and had published them. They are worth consulting for information on the early days of the Revolution. In 1918, at our meetings in Paris and throughout France, a wave of

6. Published, first in Moscow and then in Berne, under the title of **Notes on the Bolshevik Revolution** (October 1917-July 1918), these letters from Russia were later published in Paris (the Moscow edition being the most complete). Thirty years later Jacques Sadoul wrote a book on **The Birth of the USSR** in which the events described in these letters are adapted to the prevailing Stalinist taste. At the time of the 'Moscow Trials' he distinguished himself by grossly untrue reports; the perspicacious and clear-sighted observer of the early days of the Revolution had given way to a cheap hack.

enthusiasm was unleashed when they were read. They were the best reply to the lies of the journalists at Riga. Sadoul was already aware of this, but he was glad to hear me confirm it. 'How is it,' he asked me, 'that you have become such a friend of Trotsky? He always speaks very warmly of you and your syndicalist comrades. Yet when I was in France there was no love lost between socialists and syndicalists.' And before I had time to reply, he added: 'But you won't be able to see him; he's had to leave Moscow, and he's in a sanatorium.' I had hardly left Sadoul when Radek came up to me and, to open the conversation, said: 'Don't count on seeing Trotsky; he's ill and has had to go out of town for a rest.' These words should have worried me, but amid the bustle of this active morning I had no time to stop and think about them, and in any case, at heart I knew I should see Trotsky.

The session was about to begin when a small man, very slender, entered discreetly. Ivan, sitting near me, said: 'That's Bukharin . . . his brain's as clear as crystal.' My other neighbour, who had heard his remark, turned to me and added: 'It's a pity you weren't here yesterday when your friends Cachin and Frossard appeared before the central committee of the Party. It was Bukharin who reminded them of their chauvinism and their treachery during the war. It was very moving; Cachin was weeping.' 'Oh!' I said, 'tears come easily to him. In 1918 at Strassburg he was weeping when Poincaré was celebrating the return of Alsace to France.'

At this time Radek was the secretary of the Communist International. He read out a statement dealing with the trade-union question; this was the principal topic for the meeting, which explained the presence of Lozovsky, who didn't belong to the Executive Committee of the Communist International, but who was the author of the text under discussion. The problem was to bring together all the syndicalist elements who were favourable to the October Revolution and to the new International. At present they were to be found both in anarcho-syndicalist organisations which had affiliated *en bloc*, and in the reformist unions where they constituted minorities of greater or lesser size. It was proposed to create a 'Provisional International Council of Trade and Industrial Unions' which would have the job of making possible links between them and of co-ordinating their activity.

A phrase in the preamble which spoke of the betrayal of the syndicalist leaders, lumping them all together, drew a comment from Pestaña. One must be more specific, he said. For example, his friends in the CNT could not be included in this accusation of betrayal. I supported him, adding to his example that of the IWW in America, who had suffered persecution and imprisonment just because of their revolutionary activity against the war and in support of the Russian Revolution. As a result Radek changed the text, but with a bad grace. On the way out of the meeting he let me know that he couldn't understand my refusal to criticise Jouhaux for his attitude during the war, whereas they, who were social democrats, did not hesitate to denounce even Kautsky. He was quite well-informed, but not as well as he thought, and he showed from his remark that he had understood nothing from our intervention.

Then we were taken to the hotel where we were to stay during the Congress. Situated at some distance from the Kremlin, beyond the 'Chinese Town', the Dielovoï Dvor Hotel was remarkable for its perfect arrangement. Nowadays it would be called a model of functional architecture. There were two floors of simply furnished bedrooms; each had a bed, a writing-desk and two chairs. Part of the first floor was taken up with a large dining-room, and on the ground-floor there was a meeting-room. The hotel had been quickly rearranged to accommodate the large delegation from the British trade unions which had just left when we arrived. It was a pleasant surprise, and I commented on it to Sadoul. 'It was Trotsky,' he replied, 'who was in charge of the operation.' 'But how did that happen? It's got nothing to do with his commissariat!' 'Of course not, but if you want to get something done, properly and on time, it's always Trotsky you go to.'

The impressive Italian delegation was already settled in; the party and union leaders had arrived in their own train, loaded with food. They had heard so much about the famine that they had taken precautions. They had also taken precautions against typhus, having had overalls made that were closed at the wrists and ankles so as to be immune from the contagion. For this they were the victims of gentle jokes, as they were the only ones to be thus provided for, although, unfortunately, at this time typhus was no invention of the Riga journalists. In their delegation were Serrati, Graziadei and Bombacci, representing the Socialist Party; and among the trade-union leaders, who had come to observe the Congress but not to participate in it, were the secretaries of the CGL and of several of its Federations — D'Aragona, Dugoni, Colombino, and others, who withdrew quite rapidly. Bordiga, the leader of the abstentionist faction, only arrived later, as did Armando Borghi, secretary of the *Unione Sindacale Italiana*.

After these crowded hours, we were trying to collect together the impressions that the rapid succession of events and encounters had made on us. But Ivan came looking for Pestaña and me, to ask us to go and speak about the International to the Red Army soldiers who were quartered in the Moscow suburbs. Our car went out beyond the city boundaries, plunged into the woods, and suddenly emerged in a clearing where the soldiers who were waiting for us were assembled under the trees round the edge. We were put in the middle, and, as best we could, we explained what the Communist International meant to us, what we had done for it in our own countries, and what we expected from it. We were both very moved, even Pestaña, who was more accustomed to public speaking than I was.

9: Trotsky

When we got back to the hotel, the steward informed me that Trotsky had telephoned, asking me to go and see him as soon as I was free. The journey was already fixed up, and I was first to go to the Kremlin. The car soon left the town and set out at a lunatic pace across country. As I was soon to find out this was the normal behaviour of Moscow drivers, but on a roadway in bad condition it led to endless jolting. The road passed through several villages of peasant cabins spaced out along broad avenues. We had been going at this pace for about half an hour when we turned off into the woods, and soon the car slowed down. Trotsky was standing by the roadside, with his elder son, Leon. I had been right not to worry; it was not a sick man who was standing before me.

The house where the family was living had been the princely home of a rich Muscovite. The enormous drawing-room on the ground-floor had been turned into a public museum. In it all the paintings found in the house had been assembled. There were no really valuable pictures here, just the inevitable Canalettos. Trotsky and his family had two large rooms on the first floor. From the windows you could see far into the surrounding country, all the way to the horizon where hills marked the edge of the plain. The grand staircase had been condemned; and the frost had damaged the plumbing throughout so that the comfort of this 'palace' was a very relative affair. It could be lived in only in the summer. To get to the upper floor you had to use a sort of ladder. As Trotsky commented ironically: 'It's very fitting for the new Soviet "masters".'

He had greeted me with a friendly reproach. 'Well, you were in no hurry to come and see us! Revolutionaries and journalists have come from everywhere except France.' When we were all seated round the table for the evening meal, Natalia Ivanovna said: 'Here we are again, just like in Paris.' 'Yes,' I said, 'but one or two things have happened in the meantime.' And we recalled our wartime memories — the boarding-house in the rue de l'Amiral-Mouchez, the little house at Sèvres on the edge of the woods, the modest lodgings in the rue Oudry, and the intolerable police supervision followed by expulsion.

We had two full days to answer the questions we wanted to ask each other. Trotsky asked me about the men he had known in Paris. Two of them, Monatte and Loriot, had been in prison for three months and were due to appear in court. Worried by the progress of communism, Millerand had dreamt up a 'plot against the security of the State' — the normal formula for this sort of police operation. A railway strike had been started in the wrong conditions, and the organisation of working-class solidarity had been entrusted to the leaders of the CGT, who, basically, only wanted to see it fail. This gave the government the pretext it had been waiting for to imprison the socialist and syndicalist militants in France who had taken up the defence of the October Revolution and the Communist International. On the events themselves I did not need to tell him much, for the two years he had spent in Paris had given him an inside knowledge of

French politics and politicians, and, of course, of the development of the various tendencies existing within the CGT and the Socialist Party. He needed only to pick up a packet of newspapers from time to time to put himself fully in touch with the situation.

But for my part I had a lot to learn, for we had had only very vague and general information about the principal stages of the Revolution, the insurrection, the Red Army and the civil war, and the organisation and functioning of the soviets. The Brest-Litovsk Conference had made a considerable stir all over, both in the countries of the Entente and in the Central European empires. Bourgeois spokesmen had done their best to present it as a betrayal and workers had been disturbed by it. A meeting of representatives of Soviet Russia and the men of the Hohenzollern monarchy round the same table, to discuss the conditions for making peace, and finally to sign the peace treaty, had been thoroughly exploited — above all by those socialists who had betrayed the working class in August 1914. Trotsky explained to me what his tactics had been at the time. One thing had been certain, that Russia was no longer in a position to stay in the war. Food supplies were running out, and the army's equipment was increasingly inadequate; the soldiers did not want to go on fighting. The only possibility left open was to take maximum advantage of the appeal for peace.

The response had been considerable, but unfortunately it had been inadequate because the strikes which had then broken out in Germany did not go as far as a general rising against the government. The socialist and trade-union leaders, from Scheidemann to Legien, made every effort to hold the movement in check. The position taken by Lenin became inevitable; they had to accept the conditions laid down by the Germans. But a heated debate followed. Within the Party, on the central committee, there was still an unyielding opposition, which demanded revolutionary war against Germany. The Left Social-Revolutionaries, who had been in the government with the Bolsheviks, broke the agreement violently and abandoned their commissariats. Trotsky painted me a vivid picture of the men he had found himself facing at Brest-Litovsk. There was General Hoffman, stupid, limited, but banging his fist on the table when he saw what the Bolshevik delegation wanted and what it was doing; and von

Kühlmann, intelligent, flexible, with smooth manners ('I'm glad you've come; it's so much more pleasant to deal with the leaders'), but worried about the outcome of the war.

But he was very discreet about the discussions within the Party and the divergences which might be appearing there. He had no liking for gossip or anecdotes, and he observed scrupulously the rules voluntarily accepted by the members of a party. So at that time I knew nothing of the sharp struggle he had had to wage against Stalin and his clique during the civil war; nor did he tell me anything of his disagreement with Lenin about the very important military operations being carried on at this very moment against Poland. It was only much later, when the discussion in the Party obliged him to, that he reminded people of his opposition to the march on Warsaw.

As far as anecdotes were concerned, I had found an excellent informant in Moscow — Henri Guilbeaux. He had gone to Geneva in 1915 as a pacifist and disciple of Romain Rolland, and evolved gradually to a Bolshevik position under the influence of the Russian revolutionaries he had met in Switzerland. He knew a good number of the Soviet leaders personally, and he had energetically collected gossip and anecdotes. He was more interested in individuals than in ideas, and he was moved by equally strong likes and dislikes. Above all he was a writer and as a result his classifications were very summary. In the course of a conversation he had said to me: 'Lenin [the man he admired above all] is the left. Zinoviev and Kamenev are the right, but Lenin wants them in the Political Bureau for that very reason. Trotsky is unclassifiable. The real left is Bukharin.' One day when I reported these remarks to Trotsky, he said: 'It's more or less like this. Bukharin is always in front, but he's always looking over his shoulder to make sure Lenin isn't far behind.' When I got to know the two men well I got a visual image of these judgments — Lenin, solid and stocky, advancing at an even pace, and the slight figure of Bukharin galloping off in front, but always needing to feel Lenin's presence.

10: At the Kremlin: Lenin

The same day that I returned to Moscow, I was called to the Kremlin by Lenin. He was anxious to make direct contact with the delegates, to get to know each of them personally, and to ask them questions. As soon as they arrived he was preparing the interview. One of things that struck me most at this first meeting was the relaxed atmosphere that was established from the first words of the conversation, and which was kept up throughout. And also his simplicity, the way he could say to me, whom he hardly knew: 'I must have written something stupid.'

The Executive Committee of the Communist International had sent out an appeal: 'To all communists, to all revolutionaries!' inviting them to send delegates to the Second Congress, for which the date and place had boldly been fixed — 15 July in Moscow. But for these delegates the blockade still existed and every frontier was a serious obstacle.

There was something intoxicating about the atmosphere of Moscow in that month of June 1920; the quiver of the armed revolution could still be felt. Among the delegates who had come from every country and every political tendency, some already knew each other, but the majority were meeting for the first time. A true spirit of comradeship was born spontaneously among them. The discussions were heated, for there was no shortage of points of disagreement, but what overrode everything was an unshakeable attachment to the Revolution and to the new-born communist movement.

From his vantage-point in the Kremlin, Lenin followed the preliminary work for the Congress attentively. Two of the main theses had been written by him, and he was intending to participate actively in the discussion in the commissions and the plenary sessions. For the first time since the Revolution, he had the opportunity to make contact with communists from Europe, America and Asia. So he hastened to question them; as soon as you arrived you were summoned to his office in the Kremlin.

On the way to his quarters in the Kremlin, you wondered what sort of a man you were going to meet. His works, apart from the most recent ones, we knew only slightly, or not at all, and we had only rather vague ideas about the passionate struggles which in the past had brought him into conflict with the various tendencies of Russian social democracy. His writings showed him to be a revolutionary of a new type: a surprising mixture of 'dogmatism' (it would be better to say unshakeable attachment to certain fundamental principles) and of extreme realism. He gave great importance to tactics, to 'manoeuvring' (a typically Leninist expression) in the battle against the bourgeoisie. You would prepare questions and replies, and then, all at once, you found yourself in the middle of a cordial and familiar conversation with a man you seemed to have known for a long time, though it was the first time you had seen him. This simplicity and easy way of welcoming people could hardly fail to make a deep impression on the delegates, and you could be sure that when they returned they would begin and end the story of their visit by mentioning this impression.

To get to his office, you had to go through the secretaries' office, a large square room, and in passing there was just time to notice that the communists working there were almost exclusively women. One of them got up to accompany me, but Lenin was already there to welcome me. When I entered, he had just broken off a conversation with two attachés from the Commissariat for War, who had brought him the latest dispatches about the military operations. 'I'll have to keep you waiting a minute,' he said, 'excuse me.' Then he quickly turned back to his visitors still standing in front of the great map on which they were following the movement of the armies.

These were the days during which the Red Army was pursuing Pilsudski's soldiers after having dislodged them from positions where they had established themselves once again during a new invasion of the Ukraine. The advance of the Red Army was stunning; it was developing at a pace which nonplussed professional soldiers, as only an army borne on by revolutionary enthusiasm is able to do.

The conversation in front of the map continued for a few more minutes, then Lenin came to sit opposite me. In a few words he told me the gist of the dispatches from the front that had been brought to him. Although this was a campaign whose consequences might be decisive for the Revolution, he was quite calm, fully in control of himself, ready to move straight on to another subject, for he immediately began to question me about the situation in France.

I didn't take notes of this first conversation on the spot, and today, when I try to reconstruct it faithfully I remember that, on Lenin's side, it was limited to short questions, always relevant and showing that he was finding his way perfectly in a complex situation. But one remark he made suddenly revealed to me the secret of the exceptional position he held in his party, and of the predominant influence he had got there. As we were talking about the Zimmerwaldian minority in the French Socialist Party, he said to me: 'It's time for them to leave the Party now to form the French Communist Party; they've waited too long already.' I replied that this was not the view of the leaders of the minority. Previously they had sometimes been impatient to leave the Party *en bloc*, but the recent Strassburg conference had been so favourable that they were now opposed to the idea of leaving. They had hopes of becoming the majority quite soon. 'If that's the case,' he said, 'I must have written something stupid in my theses. Ask for a copy of them at the secretariat of the Communist International and send me the corrections you are proposing.'

Such was the man. He did not claim to know everything, yet he knew a lot, and had a rare grasp of the labour movement in the West. For if, like him, many revolutionaries knew foreign langauges and had spent many years in exile, only a few had participated intimately in the life of the different European countries where they were living as he had always done. This allowed him to follow the events going on there and to assess them at their true value, to give them their precise meaning. But just because he knew a lot he was able to fill out his knowledge when the opportunity arose, and also, an unusual thing in a 'leader', to recognise that he had quite simply been wrong.

Later on, I had many opportunities to observe Lenin, first of all at the Congress, later in the commissions. With him the work in the commissions was particularly pleasant. He followed the discussion from beginning to end, listening carefully to everyone, and interrupting from time to time, always with a lively and mischievous look.

It is well known that, when necessary, he could be hard and pitiless, even with his closest associates, when questions were in his view decisive for the future of the revolution. In such cases he did not hesitate to make the most severe judgments and to defend the most brutal decisions. But first of all he would explain patiently; he wanted to convince. From the moment he arrived in Petrograd right up to the great days of October, he had continually had to fight hard against a faction within the central committee of his party. In 1920, his authority was immense. Events had shown that in the gravest circumstances he had seen aright. He appeared in the eyes of all as the surest guide of the Revolution, but he was still the same man, very simple, cordial, and ready to explain in order to convince you.

★ Some copies of a book by Lenin called **State and Revolution** had arrived in France early in 1919. It was an extraordinary book and it had a strange density. Lenin, a Marxist and a social democrat, was treated as an outcast by the theoreticians of the socialist parties which claimed to be Marxist. 'It isn't Marxism,' they shrieked, 'it's a mixture of anarchism and Blanquism.' One of them even found a witty turn of phrase and called it 'Blanquism with *sauce tartare*.' On the other hand, for revolutionaries situated outside the mainstream of orthodox Marxism, for the syndicalists and anarchists, this Blanquism, sauce and all, was a pleasant revelation. They had never heard such language from the Marxists they knew. They read and re-read this interpretation of Marx, which was quite unfamiliar to them.

In France, the Marxism which had originated with Lafargue and Guesde had become singularly impoverished. Within the united Socialist Party, founded in 1905, there continued to be a clash of tendencies, and polemics were sometimes sharp. But on essential points there was agreement; socialism could be achieved gradually by means of reforms. They still talked of revolution, but it was no more than a cliché, a conventional evocation to wind up an appeal. (The word had not yet been besmirched as it has been since the fascist period; it still meant working-class violence and insurrection.) Things were no different in Germany, considered to be the home territory of Marxism, where Kautsky posed as the defender of the true doctrine.

But it was precisely the revolutionary nature of Marxism which was to be found in **State and Revolution**: texts from Marx and Engels, and commentaries by Lenin. And for him too, in a sense, these texts had been a discovery. He remarked: 'All this was written a little less than half a century ago, and now one has to engage in excavations, as it were, in order to bring undistorted Marxism to the knowledge of the masses.' But why raise the question of the state right in the middle of the war? Because, as Lenin wrote at the very beginning of his study, 'The question of the state is now acquiring particular importance both in theory and in practical politics. The imperialist war has immensely accelerated and intensified the process of transformation of monopoly capitalism into state-monopoly capitalism . . . The international proletarian revolution is clearly maturing. The question of its relation to the state is acquiring practical importance.' Then he quoted this fundamental text of Engels taken from **Anti-Dühring**: 'The first act by virtue of which the state really constitutes itself the representative of the whole of society — the taking possession of the means of production in the name of society — this is, at the same time, its last independent act as a state. State interference in social relations becomes, in one domain after another, superfluous, and then withers away of itself. The government of persons is replaced by the administration of things, and by the conduct of processes of production. The state is not "abolished". *It withers away.*'

Lenin comments on this text sentence by sentence, then writes: 'The proletariat needs the state — this is repeated by all the opportunists, social-chauvinists and Kautskyites, who assure us that this is what Marx taught. But they *"forget"* to add that in the first place, according to Marx, the proletariat needs only a state which is withering away, i.e. a state so constituted that it begins to wither away immediately, and cannot but wither away.' 'This proletarian state will begin to wither away immediately after its victory, because the state is unnecessary and cannot exist in a society in which there are no class antagonisms.' ' "Breaking of the state power", which was a "parasitic excrescence"; its "amputation", its "smashing"; "the now superseded state power" — these are the expressions Marx used in regard to the state when appraising and analysing the experience of the Commune.' And finally 'the proletariat needs the state only temporarily. We do not at all disagree with the anarchists on the question of the abolition of the state as the *aim*.'

So, for Lenin the socialist revolution was no longer a faraway objective, a vague ideal to be achieved piecemeal, within the strictest observance of bourgeois legality. It was a concrete problem, the problem of the present day, which the war had posed and which the working class was going to solve. Besides these texts, in which they could find a language akin to their own, a conception of socialism which resembled their own, what particularly pleased revolutionaries from the anarchist and syndicalist traditions, and attracted them towards Bolshevism, was the merciless condemnation of opportunism. And this was not only of hardened opportunists, the social-chauvinists who had backed up their imperialist governments during the war, but also of those who stopped halfway, who criticised government policies but did not dare draw the logical consequences of their criticism.

For Lenin, the collapse of the Socialist International at the moment when war was declared in August 1914 meant the opening of a new era. While Kautsky wanted to preserve the organisation whose bankruptcy was obvious, saying that the International was valid only in peace time, Lenin exclaimed: 'The Second International is dead! Long live the new International!' The immediate task was to establish it, regrouping the proletarians who had remained faithful amid the torments of war. And since revolution would follow the war, it was necessary to get down immediately to studying the problems of socialist construction.

State and Revolution was actually written only in August and September 1917, when Lenin, hounded by Kerensky and his socialist ministers and accused of treason, had to hide in Finland. But the whole framework, the basic texts which constituted it, had been brought by Lenin from Switzerland. It was in Switzerland, during the war, that he had set out to collect and comment on them. Just before he left Switzerland, on 17 February 1917, he wrote from Zurich to Alexandra Kollontai: 'I am preparing (and have practically finished) a study on the question of the relation of Marxism to the state.' And he saw this work as so important that, during the July

Days, when Bolshevism was going through a difficult phase, he wrote to Kamenev (the same Kamenev that Stalin was to have executed): 'Comrade Kamenev, *in strict confidence*, if I should be killed, I beg you to publish a notebook with the title **Marxism and the State** (it has been left in safekeeping in Stockholm). Bound, with a blue cover. There are collected in it all the quotations from Marx and Engels, as well as those of Kautsky's controversy with Pannekoek. Also a series of remarks and reviews. It has only to be edited. I think this work could be published within a week. I think it is very important, because it isn't only Plekhanov and Kautsky who have gone off the rails. All this on one condition; that it is in strict confidence *between ourselves*.'

Of course there were still disagreements between Lenin and his new supporters. If there was agreement about the withering away of the state, there was still the question of the transitional period during which it would have to be preserved in the form of the dictatorship of the proletariat. But the Russian socialists had not hesitated to make the revisions imposed on them by the collapse of social democracy. For their part, the syndicalists would have to take account of experience — the experience of the war, where syndicalism had partly collapsed, and the experience of the Russian Revolution. Hitherto they had failed to make a serious study of the question of the transitional period. Lenin's book, and, even more, the actions of Bolshevism in power, had created a climate favourable to a reconciliation. As we have already seen, at their congress the anarcho-syndicalists of the Spanish CNT had declared themselves in favour of the dictatorship of the proletariat.[7]

7. The German anarchist Erich Mühsam wrote, in September 1919, in the fortress of Augsburg where he was imprisoned: 'The theoretical and practical theses of Lenin on the accomplishment of the revolution and the communist tasks of the proletariat have provided a new basis for our action . . . There are no more insurmountable obstacles to a unification of the whole revolutionary proletariat. It is true that the communist anarchists have had to yield on the most important point of disagreement between the two great tendencies of socialism. They have had to abandon Bakunin's negative attitude to the dictatorship of the proletariat and accept Marx's opinion on this point . . . The unity of the revolutionary proletariat is necessary and must not be delayed. The only organisation capable of achieving it is the German Com-

★ A few days after we arrived in Moscow, we received two books that had just been published by the Communist International. They were **Left-Wing Communism, An Infantile Disorder** by Lenin, and **Terrorism and Communism**, a reply by Trotsky to a work of Kautsky's which had appeared with the same title. The two books formed a sort of introduction and commentary on the **Theses** prepared for the Congress.

I was already familiar with the contents of **Left-Wing Communism** from conversations and discussions I had listened to during my journey, especially in Germany. The party, the unions, parliamentarism — these were the questions that had produced the split among the German communists. When I read the book, I discovered once again the true Lenin, the author of **State and Revolution**. But here his opponent was no longer the opportunist, the social-chauvinist, the centrist, but rather a communist, of the sort that Lenin described as 'left'. But rather than a sickness which most children go through, Lenin saw this leftism as childishness in the sense of being easy and uncomplicated. And he frequently speaks of 'childish simplicity', 'easiness' and 'the childishness of anti-parliamentarism'.

In his view this tendency often appeared in the new communist groups and parties. People wanted to build something new quickly, to create organisations that were quite distinct from all those that belonged to a period that was now seen as over and done with. They abandoned the unions to create mass assemblies of workers. They wanted nothing more to do with democracy or parliament. They retained the party on condition that it was a 'mass party', which depended on the base for the initiative and development of the revolutionary struggle; not a 'party of leaders', leading the struggle from above, making compromises and sitting in parliaments. We have seen that the KAPD (Communist Workers Party of Germany) had been established on this basis, and everywhere there were groups on the same road to a greater or lesser extent. For example,

munist Party. I hope that anarchist comrades who see communism as the foundation of an equitable social order will follow my example.' (**Bulletin communiste**, 22 July 1920.)

the *Kommunismus* group in Vienna; the Dutch followers of Görter; the Bordigists in Italy. In France we had seen the formation of a Federation of Soviets, a Communist Party where the syndicalist Péricat rubbed shoulders with anarchists.

Lenin stood up against this tendency. He barred its path and fought against it with the same vigour he had shown against opportunists and centrists in **State and Revolution**. Yet here his adversaries were friends, defenders of the October Revolution, supporters of the Third International. And of course Lenin did make a distinction; but that in no way prevented him from criticising harshly conceptions which he knew to be wrong and, moreover, dangerous, because they could lead to a squandering of the energy that the working class needed to be victorious.

Although it was critical and polemical in manner, the book none the less had a rich content. The delegates read it attentively, and it offered them plenty of food for thought and discussion. The argument was solidly supported, but with no concern for form or even construction. Yet it is precisely the absence of the formal construction we are used to that constitutes Lenin's way of presenting his arguments. He comes back tirelessly to the central point of the debate, finds new arguments and new developments, hammers home the same point; and even when his opponent is in a bad way, he does not hesitate to strike the death blow. Furthermore, the book opens with some general considerations on 'the international significance of the Russian Revolution', stresses 'one of the basic prerequisites for the success of the Bolsheviks', sketches out 'the principal stages in the history of Bolshevism'; and only after this substantial preamble does he embark on the critical examination of left communism in Germany, of which the main features have already been described. On the question of anti-parliamentarism, Lenin set out his views as follows:

'To express one's "revolutionism" solely by hurling abuse at parliamentary opportunism, solely by refusing to participate in parliaments, is very easy; but, just because it is too easy, it is not the solution of a difficult, a very difficult problem. It is much more difficult to create a really revolutionary parliamentary fraction in a European parliament than it was in Russia. Of course. But this is only a particular expression of the general truth that it was easy for Russia, in the concrete, historically exceedingly unique, situation of 1917, to *start* a socialist revolution, but that it will be more difficult for Russia to *continue* and bring it to its consummation than for the European countries. Even in the beginning of 1918 I had occasion to point this out, and our experience of the last two years has entirely confirmed the correctness of this argument.' And finally, the empirical argument, the most difficult to refute, was that 'Liebknecht in Germany and Z Höglund in Sweden were able . . . to give examples of a truly revolutionary use of reactionary parliaments.'

Of the Italian abstentionists, he merely remarked in a note: 'I have had very little opportunity to make myself familiar with left communism in Italy. Comrade Bordiga and his groups of "Communist Boycottists" (*Comunista Astensionista*) are certainly wrong in defending non-participation in parliament.' We should note once again in this context Lenin's scrupulous intellectual honesty. Not being sufficiently well-informed, he remains cautious. He has nothing in common with the attitude of the 'leader' who knows everything, decides everything, is never mistaken, is infallible.

Not only should communists stay in the reformist unions and fight for their ideas, but they should dig themselves in there when the reformist leaders try to drive them out, and use trickery to get in when attempts are made to exclude them. 'Millions of workers in England, France and Germany are *for the first time* passing from complete lack of organisation to the lowest, most simple, and (for those still thoroughly imbued with bourgeois-democratic prejudices) most easily accessible form of organisation, namely, the trade unions. And the revolutionary but foolish left communists stand by, shouting, "The masses, the masses!" — and *refuse to work within the trade unions*, refuse on the pretext that they are "reactionary", and invent a brand-new, pure "Workers' Union", guiltless of bourgeois-democratic prejudices, innocent of craft or narrow trade union sins! and which, they claim, will be (will be!) a wide organisation, and the only (only!) condition of membership of which will be "recognition of the Soviet system and the dictatorship of the proletariat!" . . . There can be no doubt that Messieurs the Gomperses, Hendersons, Jouhaux, Legiens, and the like, are very grateful to such "left" revolutionaries who, like the German opposition "on principle" (heaven preserve us from such "principles"!) or like some revolutionaries in the American Industrial Workers of the World, advocate leaving the reactionary trade unions and refusing to work in them. Undoubtedly, Messieurs the "leaders" of opportunism will resort to every trick of bourgeois diplomacy, to the aid of bourgeois governments, the priests, the police and the courts, in order to prevent communists from getting into the trade unions, to force them out by every means, to make their work in the trade unions as unpleasant as possible, to insult, to hound and persecute them.' And it was in this context that Lenin wrote the lines which have been interpreted as a defence of lying as though it were the very basis of Bolshevik propaganda and activity. 'It is necessary to be able to withstand all this, to agree to every sacrifice, and even — if need be — to resort to all sorts of devices, manoeuvres, and illegal methods, to evasion and subterfuge, in order to penetrate into the trade unions, to remain in them, and to carry on communist work in them at all costs.'

It is very significant to observe, in connection with this sentence which has since become notorious, that none of the delegates who read it then for the first time was shocked by it. Why? Were they all inveterate liars, precursors of Hitler's clique who cynically approved the daily use of monstrous lies? Just the opposite. They all spoke and acted frankly, their language was clear and direct, deception was unknown to them. For they were too proud of showing themselves as they really were. But it is necessary to situate oneself in the context of 1920. The reformist leaders denounced by Lenin had abandoned the workers in 1914, they had betrayed socialism, they had collaborated with their imperialist governments, they had endorsed all the lies — and all the crimes — of chauvinist propaganda during the war. They had opposed any possibility of 'premature peace'. After the war they had used every means possible to break the revolutionary upsurge. In particular in the unions they had never hesitated to break the rules of the very democracy they claimed to be defending, every time they felt themselves threatened by an opposition growing openly. Nor did they hesitate to use violence to preserve their leadership against the clearly expressed will of the majority, or to pursue a hypocritical policy of splitting unions. It must be understood that such a state of affairs is, after all, an exceptional situation, it is a state of war, and war requires trickery, above all when one is fighting an enemy who is himself using deception and who has available to him the whole repressive machinery of the state.

Lenin's book was remarkable, but this idea that it is sometimes necessary to conceal the truth does not constitute its originality. What was new was the insistence on tactics. 'The revolutionary parties must complete their education. They have learnt to attack. They must now understand that this knowledge must be complemented by the knowledge of the most appropriate manoeuvres for retreat.' One of the slogans of the German 'Lefts' was 'No compromises' and something similar was to be found among the British.

Lenin began his reply by recalling what Engels wrote in 1874, on the subject of a manifesto by thirty-three Blanquist Communards: 'We are communists,' these had declared, 'because we wish to attain our goal without stopping at intermediary stations, without any compromises, which only postpone the day of victory and prolong the period of slavery.' Engels commented: 'What childish naïvety to put forward one's own impatience as a theoretically convincing argument!' Then Lenin adds on his own account: 'To tie one's hands beforehand, openly to tell the enemy, who is now better armed than we are, whether and when we shall fight him is being stupid, not revolutionary. To accept battle at a time when it is obviously advantageous to the enemy and not to us is a crime; and those politicians of the revolutionary class who are unable "to manoeuvre, to compromise" in order to avoid an obviously disadvantageous battle are good for nothing.'

Thus with Lenin all these questions are posed in a new way. The very words take on a different meaning, or return to their true meaning. 'Compromise', for Lenin, is an intelligent act of self-defence, to preserve one's forces, which may be required by circumstances. It may prevent workers from falling into an ambush, or being caught in a trap set by a better-armed opponent. The book took on the character of a manual of revolutionary strategy and tactics.

Doubtless the various revolutionary movements, syndicalism in particular, had never completely ignored these factors. The experience of struggle itself had taught workers that there are favourable moments for calling a strike, while in some conditions failure is certain; and that sometimes one has to put up with partial satisfaction, or even be willing to give undertakings. But we also knew that they defended themselves badly against the manoeuvres of the bosses, and that more than once a great working-class victory had been followed by a defeat in which the workers lost at one blow more than they had won, because they weren't able to refuse a fight in which they were doomed to defeat. But it was here for the first time that the rules and fundamental principles of tactics were drawn out and formulated so clearly, we might even say brutally. In contrast to the parliamentary socialists, who were more concerned to put off socialist revolution than to help it on, and for whom class struggle was no more than a rhetorical device, Lenin's whole being was located inside the revolution, and for him the class struggle was a daily battle in which the working class paid dearly for the mistakes of those who led it. The conclusion: we must learn to manoeuvre.

Against this replacement of empiricism by technique, there was nothing to be said. This particular point of Lenin's work aroused no criticism. And it was just this point which concealed a danger. That was the very term used at the time by a communist — the Belgian War Van Overstraeten: 'What a dangerous book,' he said to me; 'with Lenin there's no risk, because he will always use a manoeuvre in favour of the working class, and any compromise he makes will be in its interests. But remember the young communists — and even some who aren't all that young any more — who have no practical experience of workers' struggles . . . They will take only the secondary points out of this manual, because that is what is easiest and most convenient for them. They won't bother with the work and study necessary. Since they don't have a solid socialist base to support manoeuvres and compromises, they will tend to see these as the essence of the matter, and find an easy justification for all their actions.'[8] We didn't have long

8. When the book was published in Paris, Jacques Mesnil expressed a similar opinion: 'Lenin never conceals the difficulties of the task to be accomplished.

to wait to see that this danger was by no means imaginary: the 'Zinovievite Bolshevisation' undertaken immediately after Lenin's death saw it raising its head in every section of the International, and with Stalin, 'communism' itself was reduced to the level of a manoeuvre.

The book had an important appendix. After the manuscript had gone to press, Lenin received new information which led him to think that 'leftism' was decidedly stronger and less localised than he had believed, and that the polemics directed against it so far would be inadequate to cure the communist movement of it. This is what he now wrote: 'There is reason to apprehend that the split with the "Lefts", the anti-parliamentarians (in part also anti-politicals, opposed to a political party and to work in the trade unions), will become an international phenomenon, like the split with the "centrists' (i.e. the Kautskyists, Longuetists, "Independents", etc.). Be it so. At all events a split is preferable to confusion which impedes the ideological, theoretical and revolutionary growth and maturing of the party and prevents harmonious, really organised practical work that really paves the way for the dictatorship of the proletariat.

'Let the "Lefts" put themselves to a practical test on a national and international scale; let them try to prepare for (and then to achieve) the dictatorship of the proletariat without a strictly centralised party with an iron discipline, without the ability to master every field, every branch, every variety of political and cultural work. Practical experience will soon make them wiser.

'But every effort must be made to prevent the split with the "Lefts" from impeding (or to see that it impedes as little as possible) the necessary amalgamation into a single party — which is inevitable in the near future — of all those in the working-class movement who stand sincerely and whole-heartedly for the Soviet power and the dictatorship of the proletariat. In Russia the Bolsheviks had the particular good fortune to have fifteen years in which to wage a

This is a book for all conscious and thoughtful militants. But Lenin's methods put into the hands of a newcomer could have disastrous results. It must not be slavishly imitated, but everything in it is worth consideration and is a subject for serious thought.' (**Bulletin communiste**, 10 March 1921.)

systematic and decisive struggle against the Mensheviks (that is to say, the opportunists and "centrists") and also against the "Lefts", long before the direct mass struggle for the dictatorship of the proletariat. In Europe and America the same work has now to be performed by means of "forced marches". Individuals, especially those belonging to the category of unsuccessful pretenders to leadership, may (if lacking in proletarian discipline, and if they are not "honest with themselves") persist for a long time in their mistakes, but the working masses, when the time is ripe, will easily and quickly unite themselves and unite all sincere communists in a single party that will be capable of establishing the Soviet system and the dictatorship of the proletariat.'

Only a few weeks after he had written these lines, Lenin was able to see that his fears had been exaggerated. 'Leftism' survived, especially in Germany, but it never regrouped in a bloc all the elements likely to attach themselves to it, and the most important organisation, the KAPD, was admitted to the Communist International as a sympathetic section.

★   Trotsky's **Terrorism and Communism**, the **Anti-Kautsky**, was a book of a quite different type. Here we found a form, construction and content that were much more familiar to us. While Lenin concentrated his attention on the party and on tactics, and warned against revolutionary childishness and the squandering of effort in the class war, Trotsky dealt with the theoretical and practical problems posed by the revolution, the civil war and the building of the new society.

Until the outbreak of the world war, Kautsky had been generally considered, in the Second International, as the grand master of Marxism. He had considerable prestige even among the Russian socialists, Bolsheviks as well as Mensheviks. Hardly anyone except Rosa Luxemburg had dared cast doubt on his calibre as a revolutionary, and had spoken irreverently of him. She had worked close to him over a long period, and had more than once come up against his lack of boldness in workers' struggles; she knew him better than anyone. When 1914 came, his authority and reputation did not prevent him from capitulating, together with his revisionist opponents, and along with the majority of the German social democratic leaders. During the war, when total alignment with the extreme right became unbearable, he went no further than the centrist position of expressing his reservations on the question of who was responsible for the war, and criticising leaders like Scheidemann who had thrown in their lot with the Imperial government. But in the last resort he was united with them at every important point in the war, he voted with them, and joined with them to fight against Spartacism.

In the wretched Germany of the Weimar republic, stuck midway between the Hohenzollern régime and the socialist revolution, with its governments containing a motley selection of socialists, liberals and Christians, and at the top, the former saddler Ebert, Kautsky tried to regain his elevated position as guardian of Marxist orthodoxy. In the name of Marxism he decreed that Russia was not yet ripe for the socialist revolution, that the 'relation of forces' didn't allow it. He spoke of the 'Red Terror' as bourgeois historians speak of the Terror during the French Revolution. He drew a gloomy picture of the Soviet economy, and made an erudite criticism of the developing revolution just as he had formerly undertaken the refutation of Bernsteinian revisionism — from his armchair.

Trotsky dictated his reply in his military train; one can understand that the style was influenced by this fact. He worked to complete it, interrupting and resuming his work according to how much time he was allowed by the Whites — sometimes led by the Mensheviks and Social-Revolutionaries, and supported by the great democracies which Kautsky now admired. One cannot be surprised at his vehemence, at his burning irony, or at the revolutionary passion with which he defended the revolution.[9]

9. After having presented his work as 'a contribution to the history of revolutions', Kautsky wrote: 'Noske falls resolutely into step with Trotsky, with this distinction, that he doesn't consider his dictatorship as that of the proletariat.' To bring out the meaning of the Commune of 1871, he relied on Louis Dubreuilh, 'the good revolutionary', whose history is the most trite of those written by socialists, and who, in 1914, capitulated to extreme chauvinism. Then as an inveterate pedant, he added: 'Those who have a precise understanding of Marx's theory have always been few in number. This theory requires too great an intellectual labour, too great a subordination of personal

Lenin's Moscow

Socialists hostile to the October Revolution generally accused Bolshevism of being not Marxism, but Blanquism. Kautsky also found elements of Proudhonism in it. As far as the terror was concerned, he did not hesitate to give credence to the crudest and most stupid lies to be found in the bourgeois press, invented by journalists in Riga and Stockholm. Among other things he had picked up a piece of 'information' about the so-called 'socialisation of women'. It was easy to show that this was a falsification. We in France had been able to detect fabrications of this kind.

Trotsky reminded him of the conditions in which the terror had come into being and had developed: 'The first conquest of power by the Soviets at the beginning of October 1917 was actually accomplished with insignificant sacrifices . . . In Petrograd the power of Kerensky was overthrown almost without a fight. In Moscow its resistance was dragged out, mainly owing to the in-decisive character of our own actions. In the majority of provincial towns, power was transferred to the Soviet on the mere receipt of a telegram from Petrograd or Moscow. If the matter had ended there, there would have been no word of Red Terror . . . The degree of ferocity of the struggle depends on a series of internal and international circumstances . . . The more ferocious and dangerous is the resistance of the class enemy who have been overthrown, the more inevitably does the system of repression take the form of a system of terror . . . The campaign of the adventurers Kerensky and Krasnov against Petrograd, organised at the same time by the Entente, naturally introduced into the struggle the first elements of savagery. Nevertheless, General Krasnov was set free on his word of honour . . . If our October Revolution had taken place a few months, or even a few weeks, after the establishment of the rule of the proletariat in Germany, France, and England, there can be no doubt that our revolution would have been the most "peaceful", the most "bloodless" of all possible revolutions on this sinful earth.

desires and needs to the study of objective conditions.' And finally: 'If the present German Assembly is bourgeois in character, Bolshevik propaganda does not bear the smallest share of the responsibility.'

'But this historical sequence — the most "natural" at the first glance, and, in any case, the most beneficial for the Russian working class — found itself infringed: not through our fault, but through the will of events. Instead of being the last, the Russian proletariat proved to be the first. It was just this circumstance, after the first period of confusion, that imparted desperation to the character of the resistance of the classes which had ruled in Russia previously, and forced the Russian proletariat, in a moment of greatest peril, foreign attacks, internal plots and insurrections, to have recourse to severe measures of state terror.'

For us, the most interesting and original part of Trotsky's book was the section in which the author contrasted the true picture of the Soviet economy with the caricature that Kautsky had drawn. He dealt with the organisation of labour, the rôle of the soviets and of the unions, and the use of experts. Here, to reply to Kautsky, Trotsky merely reproduced the report he had given to the Third All-Russian Congress of Councils of National Economy and to the Ninth Congress of the Russian Communist Party.

An interesting chapter dealt with the labour armies; they had only a brief existence since they were to disappear at the end of the civil war. But certainly the most remarkable chapter was the one dealing with the economic plan. It must be remembered that this was written in March 1920. Here Trotsky wrote: 'This plan must be drawn up for a number of years, for the whole epoch that lies before us. It is naturally broken up into separate periods or stages, corresponding to the inevitable stages in the economic rebirth of the country. We shall have to begin with the most simple and at the same time most fundamental problems . . . This plan has great significance, not only as a general guide for the practical work of our economic organs, but also as a line along which propaganda amongst the labouring masses in connection with our economic problems is to proceed.

'Our labour mobilisation will not enter into real life, will not take root, if we do not excite the living interest of all that is honest, class-conscious, and inspired in the working class. We must explain to the masses the whole truth as to our situation and as to our views for the future. We must tell them openly that our economic plan, with the maximum of exertion on the part of the workers, will neither tomorrow nor the day after give us a land flowing with milk and honey: for during the first period our chief work will consist in preparing the conditions for the production of the means of production . . . Needless to say, under no circumstances are we striving for a narrow "national" communism: the raising of the blockade, and the European revolution all the more, would introduce the most radical alterations in our economic plan, cutting down the stages of its development and bringing them together. But we do not know when these events will take place; and we must act in such a way that we can hold out and become stronger under the most unfavourable circumstances — that is to say, in face of the slowest conceivable development of the European and the world revolution.'

Many other passages, outlining the course of the building of the new society as Trotsky foresaw it at this time, caught our attention; but the prediction which seemed to be the boldest was this: 'If Russian capitalism developed not from stage to stage, but leaping over a series of stages, and instituted American factories in the midst of primitive steppes, the more is such a forced march possible for socialist economy. After we have conquered our terrible misery, have accumulated small supplies of raw materials and food, and have improved our transport, we shall be able to leap over a whole series of intermediate stages, benefiting by the fact that we are not bound by the chains of private property, and that therefore we are able to subordinate all undertakings and all the elements of economic life to a single state plan.

'Thus, for example, we shall undoubtedly be able to enter the period of electrification, in all the chief branches of industry and in the sphere of personal consumption, without passing through "the age of steam".'

Though these books were written for a particular situation, they have lost none of their value. They can still profitably be read today and not only for their historical interest; many of the problems they deal with are still with us. In Moscow in 1920 they were, for the delegates, texts of incomparable richness. They were studied and discussed enthusiastically. Their authors had enormous prestige with the delegates. Lenin and Trotsky stood head and shoulders above the other men of the October Revolution. One day when I made this remark to a group of delegates, including John Reed, he, glad to hear expressed an opinion he had long held, exclaimed: 'So you think so too!' We all agreed; the Revolution had made them greater as it had made all the militants greater. It was easy for me to observe this since I found in Moscow men that I had known in Paris. The most typical case in this respect was Dridzo-Lozovsky. I had seen a lot of him in Paris; he had always been a good comrade, devoted and serious. That he was not of the greatest stature or of a steady character was to be shown by events after 1924. But in Moscow in 1920 I observed in him an air of assurance, of self-confidence, decisiveness and certainty which were new features as far as he was concerned.

11: Among the delegates to the Second Congress of the Communist International

In these discussions before the Congress, the dominant feeling among the delegates was a deep desire for agreement, and a firmly based determination to achieve it. They all saw the October Revolution and the Third International as something that belonged to them all. However, few of them had come ready to approve every point of the theses submitted to them. The content of these didn't fit into the usual categories with which they were familiar, and the way in which they approached problems was also different. All the problems had to be looked at afresh and examined in depth.

As far as the anarchists and syndicalists were concerned, **The State and Revolution** had made a reconciliation on essential theoretical notions much easier. But the dictatorship of the proletariat, hitherto a theoretical question, was now posed as a concrete problem — in fact, as the most urgent problem. Yet this transitional period, this passage from capitalism to socialism, had never been studied in depth; in fact, when the issue had come up as an obstacle in discussion, it had been evaded. The transition had been seen as a leap from capitalist society into an ideal society to be constructed at leisure. Even syndicalist militants such as Pataud and Pouget, in a book called **How we shall bring about the Revolution**, had not made any precise contribution to the problem of the transitional period, though they were committed to doing so by the very title of their book. A short general strike, and the régime would collapse . . . after a few days of agitation, and with minimal violence, the syndicalists would peacefully proceed to the building of the new society. But this was the realm of fairy-tales. In Moscow, in 1920, we were facing reality.

The bourgeoisie, even a feeble bourgeoisie like the Russian one, did not let themselves be overthrown so easily. They too were capable of sabotage when they were threatened. They found support from outside, for the bourgeoisie of the whole world rushed to their aid. Far from being able to get down to work in peace, the revolutionaries had to prepare for war, and for a terrible war, since the attack came from all sides. They had wanted peace. They had wanted to be generous and magnanimous to their enemies. They had freed rebel generals on parole. But all in vain. The bourgeoisie forced them to go to war; the rebel generals broke their word. All the moral and material resources of a country already drained and exhausted by war had had to be thrown into war for three years. It was an unforgivable illusion to expect things to happen differently and more easily elsewhere. The struggle would be even more bitter, since everywhere else the bourgeoisie was stronger.

Certain of the delegates who imagined that they were already in full agreement with the theses submitted to the congress were in fact those who were furthest removed from them. MacLaine, delegate of the British Socialist Party, had boasted that he could affiliate unconditionally, being in agreement on the rôle of the party, on participation in elections and on the struggle in the reformist unions. But Lenin had replied to him: 'No, it isn't so easy, and if you think it is, it's because your head is still stuffed with the socialist chatter which was current in the Second International, but which always stopped short of revolutionary action.' On the question of the party, Trotsky said: 'Of course it wouldn't be necessary to persuade a Scheidemann of the necessity and advantages of a party; but in the party we want there would be no place for a Scheidemann.' And to a young Spanish comrade, who, wanting to prove his communist orthodoxy, had proclaimed: 'We are waging a pitiless struggle against the anarchists,' Bukharin replied sharply: 'What do you mean by fighting against the anarchists? Since October, there have been some anarchists who have come over to the dictatorship of the proletariat. Others have come closer to us and are working in the soviets and in the economic institutions. It's not a question of "fighting" them, but of discussing frankly and cordially, seeing if we can work together, and only abandoning the attempt if there is an irremovable obstacle.'

★ In Moscow I had met Jack Tanner again; until 1914 he had sent us 'Letters from London' for **La Vie Ouvrière**. I had seen him in Paris during the war, when he had come to work in a factory in the Paris suburbs.[10] Together with Ramsay, he was representing the 'shop stewards committees' which had developed and acquired great importance during the war in opposition to the attitude of most of the trade-union leaders who had supported the government's war policy. I was in full agreement with them. The struggle inside the reformist unions was nothing new for them; they had always been in favour of it. Like me too they had hitherto always been reluctant to accept parliamentarism and the political party.

There was strong sympathy between us and other delegates even though we still had certain disagreements. John Reed and his American friends agreed with the Bolsheviks on the question of the party, but were not willing at any price to agree to work in the reformist unions. Wijnkoop, delegate of the Dutch 'Tribunists' (left social democrats who took their name from their paper **De Tribune**), differentiated himself clearly from the 'leftists' Pannekoek and Görter. He considered intolerable the very presence in Moscow of 'centrists', opportunist socialists like Cachin and Frossard, who had come for 'Information'. At every opportunity he protested sharply against their presence. 'There is no place for them here,' he cried.

These first contacts between the delegates were very valuable; we learnt a great deal from each other. Our discussions and conversations went on until late at night. They were interrupted by trips to meetings of workers and soldiers. One day Bukharin came for

10. Today (1949) he is president of the Amalgamated Engineering Union.

some of us and took us to a military camp near the town. As we approached a high rostrum, Bukharin called out: 'That's our tank!' — 'What's the connection?' we asked. He explained to us that when Yudenich, coming from Estonia, was directing his attack on Petrograd, he was making rapid progress because of the tanks with which the English had equipped his army. The young recruits of the Red Army had never seen these fearsome machines before, and they seemed to be monsters in face of which they were defenceless. Inevitably disorder and even panic had followed. Faced with this powerful piece of equipment, the Red Army could only turn to its own special weapons, and the most important of these was the rostrum from which the Bolsheviks explained to the workers and peasants the meaning of the war they were confronted with. The soldiers knew why they were fighting!

That day the Italian socialist Bombacci was in our little group. He was a deputy and playing at anti-parliamentarism, though he wasn't a Bordigist. But from an extreme left-wing position which he never defined properly, he played his part in isolating Serrati, who was left without support on his left. He was very handsome. He had golden hair, and his beard and hair gleamed in the sun. On the rostrum he engaged in impressive histrionics with great gestures and movements of the whole body, sometimes throwing himself at the handrail as though he was going to plunge right over it. He always got a good response, and there was no need to translate what he said. We didn't take him too seriously, but we never imagined that he would finish up as a supporter of Mussolini. Our long serious discussions were sometimes interrupted by moments of relaxation, and groups of delegates were then to be seen chasing Bombacci through the corridors of the Dielovoï Dvor shouting 'Abàsso il deputàto!' (Down with the deputy!).

But with another of the Italian delegates we had less cordial relations, which did not extend to joking. This was D'Aragona, secretary of the *Confederazione Generale del Lavoro*. His comrades from the trade-union organisations, Dugoni and Colombino, hardly ever appeared at our meetings, and quite soon they left. It would certainly be fair to say that they had come to find reasons for opposing Bolshevism rather than to confirm their party's affiliation to the Third International. Trying to justify their attitude, they would say in private that Italian workers would never put up with the hardships imposed on Russian workers by the October Revolution. But as D'Aragona had signed the appeal of the Provisional International Council of Trade and Industrial Unions, he could not get away so soon, and had to put up with our questions. We didn't spare him our questioning, as we were convinced of his insincerity; he was just swimming with the stream, like Cachin in France. When he was too hard-pressed by us, he would always go and look for Serrati, who would get him out of the corner we had forced him into.[11]

12: Radek speaks of Bakunin

In this period before the Congress, I had an additional task, on the credentials commission. I had been appointed to it by the Executive Committee, together with the Bulgarian Shablin and Radek, who was at this time secretary of the Communist International.

Radek held a special position in the International. He was a Pole, who had been active mainly in Germany, and now he was more or less russified. He had a reputation as a brilliant and well-informed

---

11. The following lines will show how D'Aragona and his friends behaved on their return to Italy: 'Having announced that the revolutionary climax was coming with the victorious occupation of the factories, they were, suddenly and inevitably, faced with a downturn. It was soon learned that the Russian myth had lost its intoxicating force. The members of the socialist mission who had gone to Moscow the previous July, and who on their return to Italy had taken good care, for fear of the red extremists, not to speak of their deep disillusion, had now recovered their courage, and were proclaiming everywhere that the application of Lenin's ideas in Russia had been an enormous error. Besides interviews in the press by D'Aragona, general secretary of the CGL, presenting this point of view, there was also the appearance of a much more effective indictment — the documented report of the two leaders of the metal-workers' organisation, Colombino and Pozzani, who published a volume describing how the Bolsheviks had accomplished the destruction of the whole vast machinery of production.' (Domenico Russo, **Mussolini et le fascisme**, p. 45.)

journalist, but it was not uncommon to hear uncomplimentary remarks about his behaviour in groupings where he had worked. In the course of the small private meetings of the commissions, and later, on the Executive of the Communist International, I had the chance of getting to know him well. After our first meeting at the Executive Committee, he had asked me to go and see him in his room at the offices of the International, then situated in the building of the former German Embassy, the house where the Ambassador von Mirbach had been assassinated by the Social-Revolutionary Blumkin. He claimed to know French, but he didn't speak it and our conversation took place in English. During his recent imprisonment in Germany, he had, he claimed, perfected his knowledge of English. Perhaps he had learnt to read it, but he spoke it atrociously. However, he was the only person who didn't notice it, for he expressed himself with his usual self-assurance. For this first meeting he was putting himself out to be friendly, and after having asked me for some information on the French movement, he spoke about his recent work, notably a study on Bakunin. 'When I was in prison,' he said, 'I re-read the main writings of Bakunin and I came to the conclusion that the judgments we social democrats made on him were false on many points. It's a job we shall have to take up again.' I had the impression he was making an unexpected concession to the syndicalists and anarchists who counted Bakunin among their great forerunners.

Coming back to French affairs, he asked my opinion of the leaders of the French Socialist Party, and in particular of Cachin and Frossard and their mission to obtain information. He knew of Francis Delaisi through his book on **Democracy and the Financiers**, and he asked me about his present activity and his position during the war, and whether it would be possible to bring him to communism. I had to reply that I didn't know. Delaisi had remained silent throughout the war, though he had predicted its coming and its nature quite accurately in his pamphlet **The Coming War**.

The job of the commission was quite easy. The delegates who submitted their credentials to us were almost all known, and there were hardly any disputes. There was one incident, of no great importance, concerning the French delegation. Jacques Sadoul and

Henri Guilbeaux had participated in the First Congress. Guilbeaux, considered as a representative of the 'French Zimmerwald Left', had speaking and voting rights; Sadoul, mandated by the communist group in Moscow, had been admitted in an advisory capacity. Should they both be included in the delegation? I was at this time the only delegate having a mandate from the Committee for the Third International. I considered that Guilbeaux, by virtue of his activity in Switzerland, was qualified to receive full voting and speaking rights, while Sadoul, attached to the Socialist Party and having come over only under the pressure of circumstances, should participate merely in an advisory capacity. This proposal was not to Radek's liking — he hated Guilbeaux for personal reasons. He told Sadoul of the decision and we received a sharp protest from him. Finally Guilbeaux and Sadoul were put on the same level in an advisory capacity, which satisfied neither of them.

13: Smolny: Solemn opening session of the Second Congress

On 16 July 1920, the whole Congress set out for Petrograd, and a session was held there the next day. It was in Petrograd that the Revolution had started, and it was there that the Second Congress of the Communist International was to open in solemn session. We started from Smolny, formerly a college for young ladies of the nobility, which in October had become the headquarters of the Revolution. When Lenin came to the front of the great hall where we were assembled, the English and American delegates, with some reinforcements because they were few in number, surrounded him, linking hands and singing 'For he's a jolly good fellow', a traditional English way of expressing admiration mixed with affection.

After some short speeches, the delegates, joined by some militants from Petrograd, set out in a procession to the parade-ground, where the victims of the Revolution were buried. Then on to the Tauride Palace, seat first of the Duma, then of the Petrograd Soviet, the debates of which we had followed anxiously from March to November. At first the Bolsheviks had been few in number, but they had advanced rapidly to constitute the majority by September, electing Trotsky as president. It was the second time, at a twelve-year's interval, that Trotsky had presided over the Petrograd Soviet. The first time had been in the previous Petrograd Soviet during the 1905 Revolution.

The debating hall was like that where parliaments meet in every country (except England, which, in accordance with tradition, has the quaint feature of a rectangular hall, which means that grandiloquent rhetoric is necessarily made impossible). There was a high rostrum, an amphitheatre where the delegates were seated, and a gallery for spectators. Here the inaugural session of the Congress took place. The opening speech was given by Lenin. Within the framework of this work there can be no question of giving an account, or even a summary, of the work of this Congress, which in reality was the first Congress of the Communist International. The assembly in March 1919 had had as its main aim the proclamation of the Third International. Anxious to transform his ideas into facts as soon as he deemed it necessary and possible, Lenin had rejected all objections, notably those of Rosa Luxemburg and the German Communist Party. This Party had sent the only real delegate to the Congress, apart from the Russians, and he had a formal mandate to oppose the proclamation of a new International. Rosa Luxemburg said that it was too early, and all that could be done was to prepare the ground.

This Second Congress, on the other hand, was remarkably representative. Delegates had come from all corners of the world, and the agenda contained all the problems of socialism and revolution. For this Congress as for the other two — those that met in Lenin's lifetime — I shall confine myself to selecting the essential points from the debates and theses, and try to recreate the atmosphere in which they took place, and to sum up their achievement.

Lenin's speech was very typical of the man and his method. He seemed oblivious of the ceremonial nature of the meeting in this place. There were no great declamations, though the circumstances would have justified them. There was great surprise when it was seen that his speech was based on the book by the Englishman John Maynard Keynes, **The Economic Consequences of the Peace**. Not that it wasn't an important book. Among all the experts at the

Peace Conference, Keynes had been the only one to speak out with a clear voice and to dare to point out the fatal consequences for the economy of the new Europe of the semi-Wilsonian peace, while there was still time to do something about it. Lenin started from this book, but he soon came to what, I think, was the essential point for him. At this time, the dominant idea in his mind was always — as the book on 'left-wing communism' had shown — the fear that the new communist parties would see revolution as something easy, inevitable even; and he stressed the theme that it was false and dangerous to say that at the end of the world war there was no solution for the bourgeoisie. And following his usual method — which gave his writings and speeches a disjointed appearance — he formulated this warning and then came back to it, took it up again and developed it in other terms. Always variations on the same theme.

The members of the Congress Bureau then gave short speeches. Paul Levi's speech struck an unpleasant note. Twice, speaking of the Polish aggression, he used the word *schlagen* (to beat) in a cutting tone. We were all following with pleasure the response of the Red Army to Pilsudski's aggression, and Tukhachevsky's bold march on Warsaw was filling us all with hope. But what we hoped from it was a popular rising, the revolution in Poland. Levi's tone and the repetition of the word *schlagen* revealed in him something of the chauvinism too often shown by Germans towards Poles, and certainly, on this point, he was not speaking as an internationalist.

In the afternoon there was a meeting in the great square of the Winter Palace, a place rich with memories. Kerensky's ministers had found their last refuge there. A rostrum had been set up in front of the Palace overlooking the crowd which had come to hear the speakers. One couldn't help thinking of another crowd, the one led by Father Gapon to plead with Nicholas II, which the latter had welcomed with a hail of bullets. Gorky came among us for a moment. He was large, square-shouldered and sturdily built. All the same, we knew that he was seriously ill and obliged to take great care of himself, but it was a pleasing sight to see him apparently in such robust health. He had been totally hostile to the Bolsheviks and the October insurrection. Then, without completely abandoning his criticisms and reservations, he had come over to the side of the régime, devoting most of his time to saving men who were being unjustly persecuted, intervening with the Soviet leaders who had long been his friends. He was said to be one of the authors of a new play which we were to have a first view of in the evening.

It would have been impossible to imagine a better situation for this open-air theatre than the one that had been chosen. It was the peristyle and square of the Stock Exchange, and it had been chosen not merely for its symbolic value. The setting was magnificent. The building, Greek in style (apparently a universal custom), was surrounded by a long colonnade. It filled the top angle of the triangle formed here by Vassili Ostrov between the two branches of the Neva. The view stretched from the embankments of the river with their marble palaces as far as the sinister Peter-Paul fortress.

The stage was the peristyle, which was reached by a high staircase. The enormous crowd which had flocked to see the spectacle fitted easily into the great square. In this extraordinary framework we saw a succession of scenes representing 'the march of socialism through struggle and defeat to victory'. The story started with the **Communist Manifesto**. The well-known words of its appeal appeared at the top of the colonnade. 'Working men of all countries, unite! You have nothing to lose but your chains!' The lighting was provided by powerful projectors installed on ships at anchor in the Neva. The three bangs to announce the raising of the curtain were provided by the fortress cannons. Then we had the Paris Commune, with the songs and dances of the Carmagnole; and then the 1914 war, with the leaders of the Second International grovelling before their government and before capitalism, while Liebknecht picked up the red flag they had dropped and cried 'Down with war!'

The overthrow of Tsarism gave the opportunity for an original piece of staging. Cars loaded with armed workers drove up from several parts of the square and knocked down the imperial building of the Tsar and his clique. A short episode showed Kerensky, who was rapidly replaced by Lenin and Trotsky, two great portraits surrounded by a red flag, with maximum illumination from the projectors. The hard years of the civil war had a symbolic conclusion with Budienny's cavalry charge destroying the last remnants of the counter-revolutionary army. This was the end, and the massive strains of the **Internationale** rose into the night air. It was an act of faith that made a worthy conclusion to a day full of emotion.

14: The debates of the Second Congress

On its return to Moscow, the Congress immediately got down to work. The Russian delegation was impressive in both the number and the quality of its members. It included Lenin, Trotsky, Zinoviev, Bukharin, Radek, Ryazanov, Dzerzhinsky, Tomsky, Pokrovsky and Krupskaya. The first point on the agenda was the rôle of the communist parties. But for a certain number of the delegates, it was the very question of the political party which had to be dealt with first of all. Hitherto they had never belonged to a political party, and all their activity had taken place within the organisations of the labour movement.

This was what Jack Tanner came to the rostrum to say. He explained how the 'shop stewards' committees' had developed during the war, and how they had gained new significance by opposing the policies of the trade-union leaders who were committed lock, stock and barrel to the war policies of the British government. The hard and dangerous struggle they had carried on during the war had led them quite naturally to give the factory committees a revolutionary programme, and to support the October Revolution and the Third International from the start. But their action had always developed outside the party, and to a good measure against the party, some of the leaders of which were the same men they came up against in the trade-union struggles. Their own experience of recent years could only strengthen their syndicalist views. The most conscious and able minority of the working class could, on its own, direct and lead the mass of workers in the struggle for everyday demands as well as in revolutionary battles.

It was Lenin who replied to Jack Tanner, saying in effect: 'Your conscious minority of the working class, this active minority which has to guide its action — well, that's the party, that's what we call the party. The working class is not homogeneous. Between the upper layer, the minority which has come to full consciousness, and the lowest category, which has no political notions at all, the sector where the bosses recruit scabs and strike-breakers — between these is the great mass of workers which we must be able to bring along with us and convince if we want to win. But for that the minority must organise, it must create a firm organisation, and impose discipline based on the principles of democratic centralism. Now there you have the party.'

A dialogue on the same basic point took place between Pestaña and Trotsky. Unlike Tanner, who represented groupings still small in size and developing on the fringe of the central trade-union organisation, Pestaña could speak in the name of the *Confederación Nacional del Trabajo* (National Confederation of Labour). It didn't cover all the Spanish trade unionists, for there was another union federation where the socialists were dominant; but the CNT could at this time claim a million members. It was deeply rooted in the industrial regions of the country, especially in Catalonia; it was a true embodiment of the anarcho-syndicalist tradition which was so alive in Spain. So Pestaña spoke more confidently than Tanner, and in a more decisive tone. As far as the party was concerned, he expressed not so much hostility as scorn. 'But,' he conceded, 'it is possible that in some countries workers want to assemble in political parties. In Spain we do not need to. And history shows that revolutions, starting with the great French Revolution, have been made without parties.' Trotsky could not stop himself from shouting out: 'You're forgetting the Jacobins!'

In his reply, Trotsky took up the question of the party, and he was concerned to reply first of all to Paul Levi who, in his usual lofty manner, had declared that for the great majority of European and even American workers this question had been settled long ago, and that a discussion about it would hardly help raise the prestige of the Communist International. 'Doubtless,' said Trotsky, 'if you're thinking of a party like those of Scheidemann and Kautsky. But if what we have in mind is the proletarian party, then it is observable that in various countries this party is passing through different stages of its development. In Germany, the classic land of the old social democracy, we observe a titanic working class, on a high cultural level, advancing uninterruptedly in its struggle, dragging in its wake sizable remnants of old traditions. We see, on the other hand, that precisely those parties which pretend to speak in the name of the majority of the working class, the parties of the Second International, which express the moods of a section of the working class, compel us to pose the question as to whether the party is necessary or not. Just because I know that the party is indispensable, and am very well aware of the value of the party, and just because I see Scheidemann on the one side and, on the other, American or Spanish or French syndicalists who not only wish to fight against the bourgeoisie but who, unlike Scheidemann, really want to tear its head off — for this reason I say that I prefer to discuss with these Spanish, American and French comrades in order to prove to them that the party is indispensable for the fulfilment of the historical mission which is placed upon them — the destruction of the bourgeoisie.

'I will try to prove this to them in a comradely way, on the basis of my own experience, and not by counterposing to them Scheidemann's long years of experience and saying that for the majority this question has already been settled. Comrades, we see how great the influence of anti-parliamentary tendencies still is in the old countries of parliamentarism and democracy, for example France, England, and so on. In France I had the opportunity of personally observing, at the beginning of the war, that the first audacious voices against the war — at the very moment when the Germans stood at the gates of Paris — were raised in the ranks of a small group of French syndical- ists. These were the voices of my friends — Monatte, Rosmer and others. At that time it was impossible for us to pose the question of forming the communist party: such elements were far too few. But I felt myself a comrade among comrades in the company of comrades Monatte, Rosmer and others with an anarchist past. But what was there in common between me and a Renaudel who excellently understands the need of the party?

'The French syndicalists are conducting revolutionary work within the unions. When I discuss today, for example, with comrade Rosmer, we have common ground. The French syndicalists, in defiance of the traditions of democracy and its deceptions, have said: "We do not want any parties, we stand for proletarian unions and for

the revolutionary minority within them which applies direct action."
What the French syndicalists understood by this minority was not
clear even to themselves. It was a portent of the future development,
which, despite their prejudices and illusions, has not hindered these
same syndicalist comrades from playing a revolutionary rôle in
France, and from producing that small minority which has come to
our International Congress.

'What does this minority mean to our friends? It is the chosen
section of the French working class, a section with a clear programme
and organisations of its own, an organisation where they discuss all
questions, and not only discuss but also decide, and where they are
bound by a certain discipline. However, proceeding from the experience of the proletarian struggle against the bourgeoisie, proceeding from its own experience and the experience of other
countries, French syndicalism will be compelled to create the
communist party.

'Comrade Pestaña, who is an influential Spanish syndicalist,
came to visit us because there are among us comrades who to one
degree or another take their stand on the soil of syndicalism; there
are also among us comrades who are, so to speak, parliamentarians,
and others who are neither parliamentarians nor syndicalists but
who stand for mass action, and so on. But what do we offer him? We
offer him an international communist party, that is, the unification
of the advanced elements of the working class who come together
with their experience, share it with the others, criticise one another,
adopt decisions, and so on. When comrade Pestaña returns to Spain
with these decisions his comrades will want to know: "What did you
bring back from Moscow?" He will then present them with the
theses and ask them to vote the resolution up or down; and those
Spanish syndicalists who unite on the basis of the proposed theses
will form nothing but the Spanish Communist Party.

'Today we have received a proposal from the Polish government
to conclude peace. Who decides such questions? We have the Council
of People's Commissars but it too must be subject to certain control.
Whose control? The control of the working class as a formless,
chaotic mass? No. The central committee of the party is convened in
order to discuss the proposal and to decide whether it ought to be

answered. And when we have to conduct war, organise new divisions and find the best elements for them — where do we turn? We turn to the party. To the central committee. The same thing applies to the agrarian question, the question of supplies, and all other questions. Who will decide these questions in Spain? The Spanish Communist Party — and I am confident that Comrade Pestaña will be one of the founders of this party.'[12]

★   In Lenin's view the national question was almost as important as that of the party. The colonial and semi-colonial countries had been aroused by the Russian Revolution. Their struggle for independence was taking place under favourable conditions, since the imperialist oppressors had all come out of the war weakened. This struggle might be decisive, ensure these peoples' liberation and at the same time weaken the great imperialist powers. Lenin was well aware that on this point too, different and sometimes contradictory conceptions would clash at the Congress. He had already had a polemic on this subject with Rosa Luxemburg before the war. For her socialism rose above national demands, which were always more or less contaminated with chauvinism. And he had reason to believe that this would also be the viewpoint of a certain number of delegates. Therefore he had taken it upon himself to draft the theses and presented them to the Congress after the discussions of the commission. In fact it was in the commission that the real discussion took place.

There was a relatively large Indian delegation, with a capable man at its head, Manabendra Nath Roy. His activities in India had led to his being imprisoned and then expelled. At the time of the

12. This optimistic prediction was not to be fulfilled. On his return to Spain Pestaña was one of the syndicalist leaders — the majority — who withdrew the affiliation they had given to the Third International in 1919. But that wasn't the end of the story for Pestaña. He didn't join the Spanish Communist Party, but ten years later he founded a 'Syndicalist Party', which never had more than a few members, more intellectuals than workers, most of them former CNT militants who had broken with the anarcho-syndicalist organisation. He, the anti-parliamentarian, sent to the Cortes in 1936 by the electors of Cádiz, died a deputy two years later in Valencia.

October Revolution he had been in Mexico, and he had come to Moscow, through Germany, stopping and gathering information on the way, so that he arrived at the Congress quite well informed about the revolutionary movement in the world. He had clearly defined ideas on how to carry on the struggle against British imperialism. In his view, it was the Indian Communist Party which would have to take the lead. Of course the Indian bourgeoisie had a programme of national demands. But far from uniting with it in the struggle for independence, it was necessary to fight it as well as the British occupiers, since, inasmuch as it exercised its own power — it already owned important textile and engineering factories — it was the enemy of the workers, as harsh an exploiter as the capitalists of the independent democratic nations.

Lenin replied to him patiently, explaining that, for a shorter or longer period, the Indian Communist Party would only be a small party with few members, having slender resources and incapable of reaching, on the basis of its own programme and activity, any significant number of peasants and workers. On the other hand, on the basis of demands for national independence, it became possible to mobilise great masses — experience had already amply shown this to be true — and it was only in the course of this struggle that the Indian Communist Party would forge and develop its organisation in such a way that it would be in a position, when the national demands had been won, to attack the Indian bourgeoisie. Roy and his friends made some concessions, admitting that in certain circumstances common action might be envisaged; but important differences remained, and presenting his theses to the Congress, Lenin joined his to that of Roy, making a joint report.

The trade-union question was the least fully and the least profitably treated question of the Congress. Not that it wasn't discussed for a long time. The commission was still discussing it when the plenary session was ready to deal with it; and preliminary meetings had taken place, even before my arrival, between Radek and the British trade unionists. Radek had been appointed to give the report, and it was he who had drafted the theses, even though he had no particular competence in these matters. He would have been quite happy to repeat on this matter what his friend Paul Levi had said about the party — such a discussion was humiliating and not likely to increase the prestige of the Communist International.

He got unconditional support from the other social democratic members of the commission, among whom Walcher revealed himself as one of the least understanding, being ignorant of, or not wanting to know about, the features of the trade-union movement in a country such as England, for example, where it had none the less firm traditions and a long history. So on one side were always to be found Tanner, Murphy, Ramsay and John Reed, not in agreement on every point, but agreeing sufficiently to reject as inadequate texts which, essentially, did no more than take up ideas current in the Second International. On the other side stood Radek and the social democrats, confident that they possessed the truth. The discussions went on for hours without getting any further forward.

Yet despite the new importance granted to the rôle of the party, and the recognition of the necessity of a central organism to lead the revolutionary struggle according to the example of the Russian Communist Party, the trade unions still had an important rôle in the capitalist countries and in the building of a socialist society. One couldn't fail to be aware of this in Moscow, for it was common to hear criticisms and recriminations about the Russian trade unions, their inadequacy and the way they carried out their tasks. And the union leaders readily replied to these criticisms. Moreover, new problems had arisen. In the course of the war factory councils had sprung up in many countries. What ought their particular functions to be? What should be their relationship with the unions?

When I came to the commission, it had already held several sessions, but I could easily have believed this was the first. The social democrats were so confident of being the depositaries of truth that they merely set out their point of view, having decided in advance to pay no attention to the remarks of their opponents. Radek listened in an absent-minded manner, while going through the voluminous packets of newspapers brought to him by the couriers of the Communist International. When he had finished the session was closed, to be reopened at his whim. Sometimes it would happen that during a plenary session of the Congress, we were informed that the commission would meet as soon as the session closed — usually around midnight. We recommenced the discussion until about two or three o'clock in the morning, then went to bed, quite sure that we had been wasting our time.

Even the section of the theses on which I was in agreement with Radek — struggle inside the reformist unions and opposition to any split — was formulated so curtly and brutally that it could not convince, only provoke. When the resolution was taken to the Congress, John Reed came to look for me; he was very upset. 'We can't go back to America with a decision like that,' he said. 'In the trade unions the Communist International has supporters and sympathy only among the Industrial Workers of the World (IWW), and you're sending us to the American Federation of Labour where it has nothing but implacable enemies.'

★   Besides the theses on the national question, Lenin had taken responsibility for those on 'The Tasks of the Communist International'. He attributed equal importance to this question, for, in fact, it took up and defined the decisions and conclusions of the Congress, and set them in the context of the situation in the various countries. The commission appointed to study it was so large that its sessions were like a little congress; they took place from ten o'clock to four o'clock, without a break.

One morning, when it was already after ten o'clock, we were still at the hotel when a message reached us saying that Lenin reminded us that the meeting was due to begin at ten o'clock at the Kremlin. There is no need to say that we were somewhat abashed as we sat down round the table. We had acquired bad habits from Radek and Zinoviev. They were always somewhat behind the time-table, and we knew well that for Lenin and Trotsky — in this too they were alike — punctuality was of great importance. So the next day we were all in our places at ten o'clock sharp. But this time it was Lenin who was missing. He arrived a good quarter of an hour late, apologising, for it was his turn to be abashed. He was at the time living at Gorky, some twenty miles from Moscow, and he had been held up by his car breaking down. We continued the discussion at the point we had left it at.

The theses as drafted by Lenin provided us with a convenient way of discussing. We took them paragraph by paragraph, discussing, correcting, amending or merely ratifying the proposed text. The obsession with 'leftism' was present here too. We were asked to condemn by name the organs and organisations afflicted by it, such as the review **Kommunismus** from Vienna, and also the bulletin published in Holland by the Western European Bureau of the Communist International, where 'leftism' had occasionally appeared. I pointed out that we could not put a review edited by Austrian and Balkan comrades and the Bulletin of the Communist International on the same level. If the latter was to be mentioned, it was the leadership of the International which should be censured, since they were responsible for it. This seemed so obvious to me that I didn't imagine there could be any discussion about it; and after all it was only a detail. But Zinoviev insisted, and Paul Levi supported him: the Bulletin must be censured. 'All right,' said Lenin, 'we'll take a vote . . . But where's Bukharin?' he cried, 'he must be found.' Bukharin was brought in — he had a habit of slipping out. Lenin said to him, 'Sit there, next to me, and don't move.' The commission split exactly in half, with the same number of votes for and against. Lenin had followed the operation without taking part, and had reserved his vote; now he cast it on our side.

The next matter to command the attention of the commission was very much more important; it was the Italian question. The Italian Socialist Party was so deeply divided that it is hardly an exaggeration to say that each of its delegates represented a different tendency. Isolated among his delegation, Serrati made vain efforts on his own to hold all these divergent elements together. The right-wing tendency included the best-known, and doubtless the best-informed leaders, Turati and Treves; it was absolutely hostile to the Third International. On the extreme left were Bordiga and his friends, fervent supporters of the Communist International, but abstentionists. Bombacci represented an inconsistent left, Graziadei confined himself to the peaceful theoretical field, and old Lazzari, secretary of the party, was not there. But I had met him on one of his trips to Paris, and had heard him speak unsympathetically of the new International. 'The affiliation is not yet settled,' he said. It was clear that if the Italian Socialist Party had voted for affiliation to the

Third International, it was because its leadership had not been able to resist the strong pressure from the rank-and-file of the party, the workers and peasants. Abandoned by everyone, Serrati was left alone, a victim of blows from all sides.

But there was yet another tendency. It was not represented at the Congress, and it was the very one, according to the theses we were discussing, which, in its publications and activity, expressed the ideas of the Communist International. It was the **Ordine Nuovo** group from Turin, the best-known militants of which were Gramsci and Tasca.[13] When we came to the paragraph dealing with Italy, it was observed that there was no Italian delegate present. None had wanted to come, for precisely because of their differing views, none considered themselves authorised to speak in the name of the party. We had to ask Bordiga to come and present and explain the position of **L'Ordine Nuovo**, which he did very honestly, although as always he began by stating his differences. The details he brought confirmed the drafter of the theses in his intention of giving the 'investiture' to **L'Ordine Nuovo**, and the commission approved unanimously.

Finally came England and the Labour Party. Communists must join, said Lenin, but here he came up against the general and absolute hostility of the British. Zinoviev supported Lenin. Paul Levi did so too in a matter which expressed the scorn of a German both for backward and declining England, and for its tiny communist groups. Bukharin agreed, but with cordiality and understanding towards the British. But all these heavy attacks did not shake the British, who, moreover, found support from the Americans and the Dutch Wijnkoop. As president of the commission, I was due to wind up, but the same arguments had been repeated so often on both sides that I said I would waive my right and we could pass straight to the vote. 'No, no,' said Lenin, 'you must never waive your right.' So I summed up the arguments put forward by the British, which were certainly mine too. Lenin quite clearly had the majority of the

13. 'The **Ordine Nuovo** group constituted an authentic tendency in the Piedmont region. It developed its activity among the masses, able to establish a close relation between the internal problems of the Party and the demands of the Piedmontese proletariat.' Gramsci, **Correspondance Internationale**, 18 July 1925.

commission on his side, but as he felt that there was still serious opposition to his views, he wanted the question to be put to the Congress, and although I had spoken against this particular point of his theses, he asked me to take responsibility for giving the report of the commission to the plenary session.

The Congress followed the debate with great attention and a certain degree of curiosity because the British had decided to have their point of view defended by Sylvia Pankhurst. She was one of the daughters of the famous feminist who had instigated 'revolutionary' agitation to win votes for women, but she was the only one of her family who had developed from feminism to communism. She edited a weekly paper, published pamphlets and showed herself to be a lively and excellent propagandist. The speech she made was suitable for a public meeting rather than for a Congress; it was an agitator's speech. She spoke fierily, throwing herself about dangerously on the narrow rostrum. But she wasn't a good advocate of our viewpoint. Even the sentimental argument of refusing to enter a party discredited in the eyes of the workers, where one would have to meet the leaders who had betrayed during the war — after all not a negligible argument — was drowned in a flood of rhetoric. Lenin's theses won the day, but the minority kept substantial support.

★   I have as yet said nothing about a subject which was to be much discussed later, the 'Conditions for Admission to the Communist International'. There were twenty-one of them. The Russian communists had drawn them up meticulously, intending thereby to anticipate criticism of the method they had followed in establishing the Communist International. These draconian conditions would form such a formidable barrier that the opportunists would never be able to pass through it. They were soon to see that this was an illusion. Certainly they had a good knowledge of the labour movements in the European countries, and they knew the leaders, having encountered them at the congresses of the Second International. But what they didn't and couldn't know, was the lengths to which these men would go with their skilful manoeuvres, for they had received their training in the practices of parliamentary democracy. They could pull more tricks out of the bag than the suspicious Russians could ever imagine. The secretary of the French Communist Party, Frossard, for example, was going to spend two years giving them a lesson in the art of evasion.

Rosa Luxemburg, who knew them inside out because she had spent her life in the German Social Democracy, where she could easily follow the activities of parties in neighbouring countries, had written, as early as 1904, an article published (in Russian) in **Iskra** and (in German) in **Die Neue Zeit**. This article could have served as a warning to the drafters of the theses on the twenty-one conditions if they had had it in mind. 'Above all,' she wrote, 'the idea which is basic to all out-and-out centralism — namely, the desire to stop opportunism with the articles of a statute — is totally false. The articles of a set of regulations may govern the life of small sects and private circles, but a historical current passes through the mesh of the most subtle paragraphs.' A prophetic criticism of which the accuracy was confirmed by the later developments of the Communist International.

★   In the course of one of the sessions of the Congress, a tall youth of about twenty years of age came up to me. He was French, had just arrived in Moscow, and wanted to talk to me. It was Doriot. He told me his story, not a long one. He had been prosecuted for an anti-militarist article and sentenced to some months in prison. Instead of going to prison he had decided to escape, preferring life in Moscow to a cell in the Santé prison. His political education had not been very extensive, but at this time he was reserved, modest and diligent. He spent two whole years in Moscow, and returned to France to become secretary of the Communist Youth. He was elected a deputy in 1924. His break with the Communist International when 'good communist justice' was on his side — he had refused to follow Stalin in his 'leftist' turn in the 'Third Period' of the Communist International — might have allowed him to form and organise a healthy opposition. But, during his short and brilliant career, he had learnt to manoeuvre, having rapidly become a perfect politician, and he had been too seriously contaminated by Stalinism to be able to undertake a selfless task. He wanted to be a 'leader', and it was easy for him, as for so many others, to pass from Stalinism to Hitlerism.

15: Trotsky's closing speech presents the Manifesto

The Congress concluded with the same degree of ceremony with which it had opened. This time the scene was Moscow; the closing session was held in the Great Theatre. The delegates were gathered on the stage. A long table stretched right across it, and behind it sat Zinoviev and the members of the Executive Committee. The huge hall was packed with a joyful and attentive crowd: militants from the Party, the unions and the soviets. After all the meeting was for them. In the Kremlin the discussions had always taken place in German, English or French; now it was time to speak Russian.

The speech was given by Trotsky. It was the manifesto of the Congress, but a manifesto of a different type from what is usually meant by the term. It was divided into five main parts. Trotsky first of all described the general situation in the world, international relations after the Treaty of Versailles. It was a gloomy picture, but it was as the countless victims of the war were beginning to see it. Then he passed on to the economic situation. There was impoverishment and general disorganisation of production, for which remedies were being sought through recourse to state intervention. But in fact state intervention in the economy merely competed with the pernicious activity of speculators in aggravating the chaos of the capitalist economy in the period of its decline. In this period of decline, the bourgeoisie had completely abandoned the idea of reconciling the proletariat to it by means of reforms. There was no longer any single major question decided by popular vote. The whole state machine was more and more clearly reverting to its original form — armed bodies of men. Imperialism must be overthrown to allow humanity to live.

In the face of this régime in its death agony, Soviet Russia, for its part, had shown how a workers' state is capable of reconciling national demands and the demands of economic life, by purging the former of all chauvinism and liberating the latter from imperialism.

On the basis of this broad exposition, Trotsky then summed up the debates and explained the decisions taken, concluding with these words: 'In all his work — whether as leader of a revolutionary strike, or as organiser of underground groups, or as secretary of a trade union, or as an agitator at mass meetings, whether as deputy, co-operative member or fighter on the barricades — the communist always remains true to himself as a disciplined member of the communist party, a zealous fighter, a mortal enemy of capitalist society, its economic foundation, its state forms, its democratic lies, its religion and its morality. He is a self-sacrificing soldier of the proletarian revolution and an indefatigable herald of the new society.

'Working men and women! On this earth there is only one banner which is worth fighting and dying for. It is the banner of the *Communist International*!'

The man, his words, the listening crowd, all contributed to giving this final session of the Congress a moving dignity. The speech had lasted a little more than an hour. Trotsky had spoken without notes; it was wonderful to see how the speaker organised the vast subject, enlivened it by the clarity and power of his thought, and wonderful to watch the passionate intensity on the faces of those following his speech. Parijanine — a Frenchman who had been living in Moscow for some twelve years — came up to me; he was seized by powerful feeling. 'I only hope it's well translated!' he said to me, expressing thereby much more than concern for an accurate translation. He was afraid lest something of this greatness might be lost.

★   The Executive Committee met the very day after the Congress. It was to examine the practical consequences of the decisions and resolutions passed, and to take the necessary measures to put them into effect. The first point on the agenda was the appointment of its president and secretary. There was no disagreement about the re-election of Zinoviev to the presidency but the secretaryship was quite a different story. The Russian delegation wanted Radek to be removed. The first secretary of the Communist International had been Angelica Balabanova, who had been replaced by Radek early in 1920, so he had held the post only for a short time. However, his candidacy, which he persisted with, was supported by some delegates, notably Serrati. A discussion opened, but it was quite short because it simply repeated a debate which had taken place in the Executive Committee a few days before the Congress met.

It was an important, indeed vital, matter, for an unexpected question had been raised, namely: who was to constitute the Communist International? Which parties? Which groups? Which revolutionary tendencies? Who was to be admitted and who rejected? Only the socialist parties which voted for affiliation while keeping within their ranks opponents of the Communist International? Or only the new groupings which had been formed during the war on the very basis of affiliation to the Third International? The Russian Communist Party had adopted an intermediate solution; its theses on admission to the Communist International, involving twenty-one conditions, were to be both a guarantee against opportunists, a barrier forbidding them entry, and a means of allowing necessary selection among the members of the old socialist parties.

Now, to the surprise of everyone, Radek had raised a question which everyone thought to be settled, and he had taken up a position clearly opposed to the decision of the Russian Communist Party. The Congress is going to meet, he said; who can participate? Certainly not those new organisations which, although constituted on the basis of affiliation to the Third International, consist mainly of syndicalists and anarchists; but only the delegates of socialist or communist parties, for only they are competent to appoint delegates. Serrati and Paul Levi immediately supported him. Doubtless the operation had been planned, for the Italian Socialist Party and the German Communist Party were, apart from the Russian Communist Party, the two great parties in the International. Radek may have thought that their intervention in support of him would be decisive. But he had calculated wrongly.

Bukharin reminded him of the position taken up by the central committee of the Russian Communist Party and the text of the appeals issued by the Communist International to the workers of all countries. With the opportunists, he said in effect, we have nothing in common. With sincere and tried revolutionaries who have voted for affiliation to the Third International, we want friendly discussion. We ourselves have made the revisions to our programme that had become necessary; we have, to use Lenin's words, got rid of our dirty social-democratic linen in order to build communism on a new basis. We want to pursue our efforts to induce the syndicalists and anarchists to make the adjustments that are necessary on their side to allow them to join with us in the new communist parties now being formed. Bukharin had concluded by saying that he could not understand why Radek had again brought into question the decisions taken by the Russian Communist Party and by the International. 'What are the British delegates from the Shop Stewards and Workers' Committees doing here? What is Pestaña doing here? And Rosmer? Why should we have called them here if we were determined to close the doors of the Congress in their faces?

It was so obvious that Radek could find no further recruits for his last-minute manoeuvre; he was left with Serrati and Paul Levi. I have spoken about them elsewhere, and what I have said explains their attitude, especially as far as Paul Levi is concerned. He loathed all anarchists and syndicalists *en bloc*; they were elements of an 'opposition' which permanently obsessed him. Serrati's motives were different. He found it unacceptable that the International should cordially welcome anarchist and syndicalist groupings while it continued to formulate various demands as far as a well-established party such as his own was concerned.

At that session of the Executive Committee we had left it there; but of course a conclusion had to be drawn from the debate, and, according to the Russian delegation to the Communist International, this conclusion was the removal of Radek from the secretaryship. The debates had merely underlined the inevitability of this. But the decision was not made immediately. To replace Radek, the delegation proposed a Russian Communist, Kobietsky. We didn't know him. But John Reed, who didn't know him either, asked that the decision should be postponed, saying that he had received information that would have to be checked. There were said to be compromising circumstances in Kobietsky's political past which made him unsuitable, especially for a position of this importance. It was not hard to see where John Reed had got his information from. Radek was still persisting. But Zinoviev commented that nomination by the Russian delegation was a sufficient guarantee, and the matter was settled. After the experience of Radek as secretary, it was necessary to choose someone less brilliant but more reliable.

Another important decision was taken the same day. On the

initiative of the Russian delegation, every delegation was asked to nominate a representative to stay in Moscow and participate directly in the work of the Communist International. This would provide a permanent link, ensuring a satisfactory exchange of information between the Communist International and its sections. For me, this decision was very welcome. I had made the journey, not to attend a Congress, but to study on the spot the Bolshevik Revolution and the Soviet régime it had set up. The Congress had hardly given me the chance to do this, but now I would be able to. Moreover, I was very keen to follow the work of the Provisional International Council of Trade and Industrial Unions. That was where I felt most at home and where I felt confident of doing a useful job. The tactic which Lenin had defended energetically against the 'lefts' in **Left-Wing Communism**, and which had been approved by the majority of the Congress, might seem contradictory. Communists and revolutionary workers were asked to remain in the reformist unions, yet at the same time progress was being made openly towards a Red International of Labour Unions. The reformist leaders of the Amsterdam International Federation of Trade Unions did not fail to point this out, and make a lot of noise about it, and the bourgeois press followed their example. We were denounced as splitters.

But it was only an apparent contradiction. The splitters were not on our side, as events were soon to show. There were indeed splits, but they were provoked by the reformist leaders as soon as they felt the majority slipping out of their grasp. They were not willing at any price to let the mass of union members express themselves and decide freely and in conformity with democratic rules if there was any danger they might lose the leadership of the unions. Their tirades against 'all dictatorships' and in favour of democracy were mere words. In reality they were determined to preserve by all means possible the positions they had only been able to win or keep thanks to the war. I have already had occasion to show just how inflexible Lenin had been on the question of union tactics. It was essential to struggle and remain where the workers were, and almost everywhere that meant in the reformist unions, because the reformist leaders had succeeded in retaining the leadership despite their attitude during the world war. But there, as in the social democratic parties, there were minorities, greater or smaller in numbers, but everywhere significant, fighting under the banner of the Third International to win control of the organisation by getting the majority of the members to adopt the ideas that they were advocating openly.

If our activity did not always develop as we should have liked it to, there were two factors to blame. On the one hand, within the minorities, there were impatient elements and self-styled 'theoreticians' who wanted to have their own unions without delay. Their clumsiness and mistakes only made life easier for the reformists, who were delighted to find themselves faced with such opponents. On the other hand, the precise nature of our task was not always understood in the leadership of the Communist International. Its importance was not grasped, and all the attention was concentrated on the development of the new communist parties. Yet if the reformist union leaders were vulnerable, this was only the case if the blows were struck in the right place, for they were full of guile and deceptiveness. Lies and dissimulation were all on their side. Yet for the most part it was thought enough to hurl insults at them, which they had doubtless deserved, but which were ineffective.

On the occasion of a meeting in London of the General Council of the Amsterdam International Federation of Trade Unions, the Executive Committee of the Communist International had decided to launch, jointly with the Provisional International Council, an appeal to workers in all countries and to British workers in particular. Zinoviev and I had been charged with preparing, each of us separately, drafts on which the definitive text could be based. But our two drafts were so unlike each other in form and content that there was no solution but to adopt one or the other as a whole. I had tried to set out the grievances of workers in an overall scheme which could impress and convince, by recalling the past activities of the Amsterdam leaders, and stressing that this Federation was in no way international — chauvinism flourished in it to such an extent that the affiliated nations were still classified as allies or enemies as they had been in wartime. But Zinoviev merely let fly a broadside of insults, often in pretty bad taste, against 'Messrs. scab leaders', etc. Only someone quite ignorant of the labour movement and of British workers could imagine for a single moment that an appeal of this sort could win us supporters, or even sympathy, and make easier the job of the revolutionary minorities. Zinoviev proposed that we try to combine the two texts, but it was impossible. The appeal reproduced his draft in every detail, and I was very annoyed at having to put my signature to it.

My work at the Communist International was much less interesting, though I had the responsibility of representing Belgium and Switzerland, who had not been able to leave a permanent representative in Moscow. During the course of the Congress I had become friendly with their delegates, of which the main ones were Van Overstraeten for Belgium and Humbert-Droz for Switzerland. Van Overstraeten was serious and able, one of the founders of the Party, who was turned away from communism as early as 1927 by Zinoviev's 'Bolshevisation' of the Communist International. Humbert-Droz did not warrant the confidence that had been placed in him. A pastor in London at the beginning of the world war, he had been persecuted for his opposition to the war. On his return to Switzerland he had helped to regroup the Zimmerwaldians, had organised propaganda in favour of the Third International and edited an excellent magazine. Against all expectations, he approved not only 'Bolshevisation' but the whole of Stalinism, including the 'Moscow Trials'. It was only during the second world war that he was to break with a party which had become entirely different from the one he had helped to create.

★   Like all the Soviet political and trade-union organisations, the Third International had a relaxation centre for its workers. It was a pretty extensive estate — the former property of the Grand Duke Serge, Governor of Moscow — situated at Ilinskoie, about thirteen miles from the city, on the Klin road. The main building was impressive from the point of view of size, but not original in design. Other smaller buildings were scattered throughout the park. The work of the Congress and the long discussion had tired the delegates out, so those who were staying in Moscow went to Ilinskoie for a rest. I had a brief stay there which allowed me to make some interesting observations. First of all I was struck by the contrast between the outside and the inside. For inside the fittings were simple, poverty-stricken even; everything had been taken for the war effort. The bedding consisted solely of straw mattresses, and the food was extremely modest. But the atmosphere was very cordial and agreeable. Everything contributed to making it so. It was summer time, and to save lighting, they had introduced 'double summer time' and so the pleasant evenings lasted longer. In the evening after dinner we got together in the main building. Imagination and the gift for fantasy and artistic creation were so common among the Russians that they were able to improvise the most ingenious entertainments. And above all there were songs, those incomparable Russian folk songs which rose into the night air from the surrounding villages.

One morning I came across M, whom I hadn't seen while I had been on Soviet soil, since that journey from Yamburg to Petrograd when he had tried to persuade me that we ought to use parliament as a platform for communist propaganda. Soon his wife came to join us. As Kollontai's deputy in the section which dealt with activity among women, she was an important person in the Soviet 'hierarchy' (of course at that time no one would have dreamt of using such a term; it took Mussolini's fascism to establish it and Stalinism to pick it up). But for all that she was not inclined to think that all was for the best in the Soviet Republic. Quite the opposite, she criticised widely and without fear or favour. She was a grumbler who insisted on speaking plainly. It is only in the perspective of later events that this seems surprising, for at that time we spoke freely, without embarrassment and in perfect comradeship.

During my stay in Moscow I often saw M and his wife. They had a room at the Hotel Metropole, and however late at night you might be coming home, from a meeting or perhaps from the theatre, you would always see a light at their window. You could be sure of getting a cup of tea from them — even if it was weak — and sometimes a sweet instead of sugar. But you were also sure of hearing a sharp denunciation of the inadequacies of the régime. It was not a good home for wavering communists to go to, but the communists of this time were well hardened.

★   A phone call from Trotsky told me that the French translation of the Congress manifesto had arrived. It would make a thick pamphlet to be published simultaneously in Petrograd and Paris. The translation seemed good to him, but he wanted to go over it with me. The job of revision took several evenings, and on those days he stayed at the Kremlin instead of returning to work at his office after dinner. This gave me the opportunity of resuming my questioning, now concentrating in greater detail on several subjects I wanted to go into in depth, and naturally including the Congress itself. I also questioned him about personalities. Some people I knew very well, but others I knew only by name. He gave me biographies of these, which, when I had the opportunity of checking on them, I always found to be flattering. He had a good knowledge of all those he was working with, on the Party central committee and in the Soviet institutions. If there were several of them whom he didn't like and whom he made harsh judgments of, it was never for personal reasons, but because they were not up to their jobs, or did them badly. But there was never anything petty in his remarks.

'Were you ever worried how things would turn out during all the length of the civil war?' I asked him one day. 'Which was the hardest moment?' 'Brest-Litovsk,' he replied immediately, answering the second question first. 'The Party was deeply disturbed and confused. At the beginning Lenin was almost the only one who wanted to sign the treaty without discussion. We were afraid there would be a split, or bitter internal disputes, which, in the state Soviet Russia was then in, could have been fatal for our Revolution . . . The civil war meant dangers of a different sort. When we were being hard pressed from the East, West and South all at the same time, when Denikin was threatening Tula, then of course we couldn't help wondering if our Red Army might not succumb to this triple assault. For my part, I never lost faith. I was in a particularly good position to judge the situation. I knew precisely what could be asked of our army, and thanks to my endless journeys to the front and throughout the country, I also knew what the counter-revolutionary armies amounted to. They were better equipped than ours, and Yudenich even had tanks for his attack on Petrograd. But I knew their basic weakness — behind them, the peasants could see the owners of the lands they had taken over. In these circumstances even the peasants who weren't very sympathetic towards us became allies we could rely on.'

16: The Eastern Peoples at the Congress of Baku

After the triple blow struck at the interventionist forces, after the destruction of Kolchak, Yudenich and Denikin, the counter-revolution was defeated. Only Wrangel was left trying to scrape together the remnants of Denikin's army, and he could be ignored. After intense discussion the Second Congress had defined the principles on the basis of which communist parties were to be built. The rôle and tasks of the International had been established unambiguously, and great importance had been attached to the national question and the conditions of the colonial and semi-colonial peoples. The 1905 Revolution had had a profound impact among these peoples, in Turkey, Persia and, above all, China. The 1917 Revolution taught them more precisely what tactics they would have to learn and apply in order to liberate themselves. Moscow had just shown them how a people that had undergone relatively little industrialisation, and was mainly composed of peasants, could overthrow its autocratic régime and victoriously resist the intervention of the imperialist powers.

The Executive Committee decided, as a logical follow-up and necessary complement to the work of the Second Congress, to convene the representatives of all the enslaved peoples to a vast conference. The place chosen for this gathering was Baku, on the border between Europe and Asia. Zinoviev, Radek and Bela Kun were to represent the Communist International, and they were to be accompanied by delegates from countries with colonies; these were Tom Quelch for the British Empire, Jansen for Holland, John Reed and myself. Zinoviev told us the journey would involve some risks. It was a long journey, as we had to go right across the country, and although for the moment there was no organised resistance, we might easily run into some bands of rebels on the way. We took five days to get to Baku, stopping in Rostov for a day, then in several Caucasian towns, since we wanted to make the most of this exceptional journey.

The trip was full of interest and without danger. It allowed us to see at first hand the vast extent of damage done by the civil war. Most of the stations had been destroyed, and everywhere the sidings were full of the half-burnt wrecks of coaches. When the Whites had been beaten they destroyed everything they could as they retreated. One of the most important stations in the Ukraine, Lozovaia, had just recently been attacked by a band of Whites, and we had right before our eyes the damage caused by such attacks, which were still frequent in these regions. This helped us to realise the size of the task which the Soviet régime had before it.

On the other hand, in these devastated areas, the food was more varied. On the station platforms peasant women offered us eggs, and even little roast chickens, things which were rare or quite unknown in Moscow. All the length of Caucasia there were appetising piles of fruit — grapes, pears, figs, dates, every variety of melon and water-melon. John Reed often came to talk to us and travelled alongside us. Every time the train stopped, he rushed up to the hawkers with their baskets and came back with his arms laden with fruit. After Petrovsk, the track ran along the side of the Caspian Sea, and if there was an extended stop, he would rush off to swim in the sea. He was enjoying the trip as one would expect from a young American. Once, in his haste to get dressed again, he tore his trousers — a tragic event, since of course he didn't have any others with him.

From the station we went to the theatre where a meeting had been called. By the end of the journey the train was running late, and the theatre had been packed for more than an hour by the time we got there. The auditorium was extremely picturesque. All the Eastern costumes gathered together made an astonishingly rich and colourful picture. The speeches, which had to be translated into several languages, received frenzied applause; they were listened to with passionate interest. John Reed, who was able to stud his English with a few words of Russian, was a great success. He shouted a question to the audience: 'Don't you know how Baku is pronounced in American? It's pronounced *oil*!' The solemn faces were suddenly shaken with laughter.

It was terribly hot. It was a heavy, humid heat, to which we, who had become Muscovites, were not used. Outside the Congress itself there were several demonstrations. The most impressive of these was the burial of the 26 People's Commissars who had been captured by the British and taken across the Caspian Sea to be shot. The coffins were carried by communist militants, singing the beautiful and moving 'Song of the Dead' over and over again.[14]

★   The oil-wells were in a deplorable state. The Revolution had not yet had time or opportunity to get down to the work of restoration, and the installations left behind by Tsarism were far below the desirable standard. The workers — mostly Persians — were housed in wretched huts. The road that led there was broken and dusty, and only a few wells were working. All in all, this exceptional source of wealth offered a pitiful sight. On the other hand, the town was picturesque and highly attractive. The sun, beating down mercilessly, offered extraordinary lighting effects in the alley-ways — black and white were equally vivid. John Reed had found some shops where magnificent pieces of silk could be bought. 'You ought to buy some,' he told us, 'there are some unique items.' 'But we haven't got any money.' 'Ask Zinoviev for some roubles; as a member of the Executive Committee you ought to get them.'

What were the results of this Congress, certainly the first of its kind? We had succeeded in gathering together representatives of all the countries, races and tribes of the East. In the short term it did not have the effects we might have hoped for. In the following months there were no uprisings significant enough to worry or seriously involve the imperialist powers. A deep disturbance had been caused,

14. Discussing a book on the execution of the Commissars, Sosnovsky wrote: 'A. Chaikin, a former member of the Constituent Assembly and a former member of the central committee of the Social-Revolutionary Party, has just published a highly interesting book on the **Execution of the 26 Commissars of Baku** (1919). It is a study in depth of the policy of British imperialism in the Caspian region at the beginning of the civil war . . . When the Georgian Mensheviks granted the Turkish Army the right to pass through their territory in order to beleaguer Baku, the rulers of that city called to their aid the British, of whom they were, of course, the willing tools. The leaders of the pro-Soviet movement were first of all arrested and taken to Kislovodsk, where the British had their headquarters. On 19 September 26 red militants were brought out of prison "to be sent to India via Persia" and to be "kept as hostages", according to the story intended for public opinion. The truth is that these 26 militants were all taken to an out-of-the-way spot and beheaded.' (L Sosnovsky, **Correspondance Internationale**, 18 March 1922.)

but the effects were visible only later on. Time was needed for the debates and resolutions to bear fruit, and for the gathering together of sufficient forces who understood the struggle that would have to be carried on against masters who hitherto had been all-powerful.

Contrary to the assertions of anti-Soviet newspapers, Enver Pasha did not take part in the Congress. He was merely allowed, at his own request, to make a statement in which he confined himself to an expression of sympathy for the initiative taken by Moscow. But we soon saw what game he was playing. A parade was organised during the last days of Congress, a procession in which the delegates and local and regional organisations took part. Enver thought he would take advantage of this to present himself as the hero of the demonstration. On horseback, on a piece of raised ground at the corner of the square round which the procession turned, he was provoking greetings, even applause. His manoeuvre was obvious and he was asked to leave. From then on he came out openly against the Soviet Republic and tried to carve himself out a Muslim State in Turkestan, where he died in 1922.

Many people felt disbelief when they heard the news of his death, but in **Pravda** of 11 October an 'eyewitness' wrote that 'there is no doubt about the correctness of the report'. And he gave the following details: 'On August 4th, about eight miles from the town of Baljuvan, the superior forces of the Red Army surrounded a small contingent of *basmachi* (Muslim insurgents) among whom was Enver Pasha and his collaborator, the Muslim leader Daviet Min Bek. After a fierce struggle, the *basmachi* were crushed. The body of a man wearing an English suit and a fez was found on the battlefield. In his pocket were found two of Enver's personal seals, correspondence with his wife, a letter from his son written in Berlin, a packet of English newspapers from the Indian Empire, and some dispatches in code. Enver was recognised by the people. The *basmachi* who had been taken prisoner confirmed the identification.' (**Correspondance Internationale**, 30 October 1922.)

On the way back there was an alarm. Early one morning, as the train was coming up the edge of the Caspian, we were awakened suddenly. There had been sabotage on the line. The rails had been pulled up, causing the derailment of the locomotive that had gone before ours. The nearby station at Naurskaya where we had stopped had also been attacked. We were stuck. But the band which had organised the incident didn't have the resources to fully exploit the situation produced by the derailment; otherwise it would have been pretty serious for us. The locomotive of our train was unfastened so that a party could go and check on the spot how serious the damage was. When it came back with the search-party on board, we were not surprised to see John Reed among them. For him it was a unique adventure.

Just before we got to Rostov, we were surprised to meet Blumkin, the Social-Revolutionary who had taken part in the attempt on the life of the German ambassador in Moscow, Count Mirbach. At the time the incident had caused grave problems for the Soviet government. They had had to present their apologies to the Berlin government, which was threatening to make even tougher the severe conditions it had imposed at Brest-Litovsk. Later on, Blumkin had come over to Bolshevism, and when we met him he was returning from a mission that the government had entrusted him with. He had lived for some time in Paris and spoke a little French. He asked me about the socialist movement in France and about its leaders, some of whom he had known, notably Jean Longuet, whom he was quite determined to have guillotined. Several times he would interrupt himself, and saying 'Longuette', he would make a gesture in imitation of the blade of the fearful machine coming down on the neck of the unfortunate grand-son of Karl Marx — a quite undeserved fate — and then he would burst out laughing. He was a typical embodiment of the mixture of heroism and puerility which was common among Social-Revolutionaries.

This time we stopped in Rostov only long enough to take part in a demonstration which ended up with a meeting. There was a vast square where rostrums had been put up, and filled with a huge crowd. Blumkin came with me to the rostrum where I was to speak, and he insisted on translating my speech. I avoided any reference to Longuet and he didn't slip him into the translation; but I have always thought that he probably made me demand a few beheadings.

★   In Moscow a sad piece of news greeted us. John Reed, who had returned in advance of us, was in hospital, ill with typhus. No effort was spared to save him, but it was all in vain and a few days later he died. His body was displayed in the great hall of the House of Trade Unions. On the day of the funeral, winter had already arrived and snow was falling. We were overwhelmed. We had got to know him well during the journey to Baku. Before meeting him I had read and translated the articles he had sent from Petrograd, at the time of the Kerensky government, to the excellent American magazine **Masses**, edited by Max Eastman. For us it was an exceptional source of information, of the highest order, shrewd, clear-sighted and picturesque all at the same time. But he had already been in Russia, and travelled throughout Europe, during the imperialist war, together with the artist Boardman Robinson. For a free-lance journalist like him, such trips were adventures which often ended up in prison, notably in Poland and later in Petrograd. So he had plenty to tell us. For us he went over again the accounts he had published in London in 1916 under the title **The War in Eastern Europe**. But he talked to us even more about the October Days, those 'Ten Days That Shook the World', of which he had been an enthusiastic witness, and later, a faithful narrator in the book he wrote on his return to New York in 1919.

His friend Max Eastman once told me that he had hardly taken more than ten days to write it. He had settled himself into a room in Greenwich Village, arranging for all visitors to be kept away. He had accumulated a substantial quantity of documentation, and he came out only to take hurried meals. During the journey we had seen him full of youth and vigour, yet with sudden periods of sadness. He made the first gap in our ranks. His interventions in the Congress, frank, sometimes even brutal, had made him liked by all . . .

A burial place was found for him in the Kremlin wall, in the section reserved for heroes who had fallen in the revolutionary battle. The words of farewell were spoken by Bukharin, for the central committee of the Communist Party, by Kollontai, and by his comrades from the Executive Committee. Louise Bryant, who had arrived only to see him die, was there, completely shattered by grief. The whole scene was indescribably sad.[15]

15. In a letter to Max Eastman, Louise Bryant wrote: 'We had spent only a week together when he was taken ill. We were inexpressibly happy to be

Our return to Moscow was marked by death and distress. The Second Congress had been already under way when three Frenchmen arrived, each of them known as a valuable and serious comrade. Raymond Lefebvre, a talented journalist and writer, was already won over to communism. Vergeat, a mechanic, was a syndicalist. Lepetit, of the navvies' union, was an anarchist. It was an excellent choice, and although this delegation was small in number, it was very much representative of the tendencies present in the French labour movement. Raymond Lefebvre was the most enthusiastic, participating in the discussions among delegates with a youthful ardour, always asking questions and seeking information. 'All we have done so far will have to be begun afresh,' he said to me one day. This was his conclusion from what he had seen and learnt during his stay. Vergeat, by temperament and because he was still outside the party, was more reserved. He was a solid militant who didn't express an opinion without full consideration. He was one of those syndicalists who were wholly devoted to the Russian Revolution, but who still needed to discuss and study among themselves the serious problem of joining a political party. Of the three, Lepetit was naturally the most critical, but the letters he wrote from Moscow, which were published in **Le Libertaire**, showed that even when his criticisms were sharp, they were still combined with sympathy for the new régime.

I had left them in Moscow when I set out for Baku, confident that I would see them again, and that we could have together the useful conversations that the work of the Congress had not allowed us to have earlier. But all three were impatient to return to France to resume their activity as militants. At this time the return route was via Murmansk, from where boats sailed to ports in the West. When they got to Murmansk a storm was raging and the sea was very turbulent. None the less a boat was leaving and they embarked. Since

together again. I found him older, sadder, full of kindness, and strangely beautiful. His clothes were in rags. He was so impressed by the suffering all around him that he quite forgot about himself. I was deeply concerned by this; for I felt incapable of reaching such a degree of fervour. Together we visited Lenin, Trotsky and Kamenev. We went to the theatre to see the Ballet and *Prince Igor*. He was consumed with the desire to return to America.'

then there had been no news of them, and there was deep anxiety, since delegates who had left Murmansk later than they did had already arrived in Paris. We still clung to the hope that they would turn up, and they were looked for everywhere, but in vain. We had to resign ourselves to having lost them. For the French labour movement it was a great sacrifice to the Revolution.

Pierre Pascal had had a particular liking for two of them, Vergeat and Lepetit. While they were in Russia he had helped them and shown them around, letting them benefit from his knowledge of the country, the régime and the men. From Moscow he wrote: 'Vergeat and Lepetit were changed men when they left Russia. Here they learned a great truth which they were not able to see in France. Before, more or less consciously, they imagined that the new society of their dreams, a society without classes and exploitation, could be established in the space of a day, and could be put ready-made in the place of the capitalist régime the day after the revolution. In Russia, on the contrary, they learned that this society must be forged through long years of effort and difficulties . . . Moreover, their education was completed by Lenin himself, through discussion and his writings. They had a long friendly conversation with him, and they read the French translation of his work **The State and Revolution**. It was a real revelation for them to read this . . . It was their feeling of duty which led to their death. They died victims of their haste to return to France bearing the good news of communism.' (**Bulletin Communiste**, 17 February 1921.)

17: The Russian Trade Unions

We had scarcely got back to our rooms at Dielovoï Dvor when we were told that we were going to be transferred to the Hotel Lux. Dielovoï Dvor was so wholly suitable for its purpose that we were unhappy at the thought of leaving it. And our displeasure increased greatly when we were able to visit our new residence. It was on one of the busiest and noisiest thoroughfares in the city, the Tverskaia, a huge monster of a building, where everything was in bad taste — the façade, the furniture, the remnants of the 'luxury' that had given the hotel its name. There were lounges that could not be used, except in the Congress period when they had to put beds everywhere. When Amédée Dunois came to Moscow for a spell, I found him settled in one of these lounges with gilding everywhere. As he had come in a fairly critical state of mind, this accommodation could only increase his reservations. 'Where is the Communist International?' he asked. 'When Zinoviev goes to Petrograd, he seems to take it with him.'

I remained at the Hotel Lux for a whole year, until October 1921, and after that I stayed there for shorter periods, whenever I was summoned to Moscow. I always found it just as unpleasant. However, it was nothing like what it became later, when Stalinism installed suspicion, spying and the permanent use of police methods. There was nothing comparable to the picture painted by Margaret Buber-Neumann in her statement to the Kravchekno trial, which can also be found in her book **Déportée en Sibérie** (pp 8-34). But even if the setting had changed, our life remained the same. There were meetings, discussions, preparation of reports and reading. Newspapers were beginning to come in, although irregularly.

Every day I went to the offices of the All-Russian Central Council of Trade Unions, where quarters had been reserved for the Provisional International Council of Trade and Industrial Unions. Here there was no luxury at all, no trace of luxury of any kind. It was extreme poverty; just the very minimum requirements for work. Little heating or none at all, and above all a terrible smell of fish soup which filled the whole building. It was apparently the only item on the canteen menu. Despite everything the unions were like poor relations. It wasn't that great importance wasn't attached to them (soon they were to be the centre of one of the most serious debates in the central committee and the Party). Quite the opposite; they had been allotted great tasks in the building of communist society. But all the same the main stress was put on the Party, and it had the lion's share of the Republic's resources in men and supplies. And the overriding fact is that there was a shortage of men. The war had wrought havoc among the best, and those who remained could not do everything, despite the long exhausting days they worked. It was necessary to be selective, and the unions came only after the Party (though it should be remembered that the distinction — even the opposition — between unions and party which was made elsewhere was not made by the Russian communists). After a day in those freezing offices we felt rather sluggish and we were glad to get into the keen air outside, even when the thermometer was showing 25 degrees below zero. I used to like to go home by a roundabout route, following the avenues as far as the Pushkin statue. The sun disappearing behind the dark trees still offered a little of its wholesome warmth.

By chance, I had met, among the typists in the office, a Polish girl who had studied in France and who knew several of my friends. She offered to do some translations which would be useful to me, but added immediately: 'But I must tell you I'm a Menshevik.' 'If you promise to work honestly, that makes no difference to me.' Being in contact with her, I was sure to get the other side of the picture. She never failed to stress the inadequacies and weaknesses of the régime; and if she had to translate a text where the Mensheviks were treated badly, she would burst out into a flood of curses, shouting: 'That's untrue! They're all lies!' She was living at Dielovoï Dvor, for our former residence had been allotted to the trade-union officials and secretaries. One evening, needing a translation urgently, I had to go there. A sad sight met my eyes, for everything was in a state of neglect. The house which we had known when it was tidy and pleasant was unrecognisable. An incompetent or negligent caretaker had been enough to bring about such a disaster. There were holes in the floor, the walls were stained, pipes were blocked up and lamps were missing. It was no longer Europe, but the East, where the day-to-day work of maintenance is usually neglected. This oriental lack of concern was one of the negative features in the Russian character, which in so many other ways is appealing.

I had been working with this secretary for some months when one morning she sent a message with one of her friends that she had been arrested by the GPU. I immediately went to Lozovsky to find out the facts. He told me that it was simply an enquiry; they wanted to ask her some questions. She was released the very next day and she came to tell me her story. She had had several meetings with Poles belonging to the Bund (Jewish Socialist Organisation) who could not be said to be friends of the Soviet Republic. Their meetings had taken on a clandestine, almost conspiratorial, aspect. At this point the GPU, which had some reason for keeping a check on these Poles, had proceeded to make some arrests. She was among those arrested. Her tone was calmer than usual, and she spoke of her arrest without anger; this showed that in her own eyes the intervention of the GPU had some justification.

★ The Dutch delegate to the Executive Committee was called Jansen. He was a close friend and admirer of Görter, a vigorous supporter of the ideas of the KAPD, which I have spoken of on several occasions. I had met Jansen in Berlin, when we were both trying to make our way to Moscow. He had been responsible for maintaining contact between Amsterdam and Berlin during and after the war. He knew the German labour movement well, and the men who constituted it, whom he did not like at all. He judged them severely, often with some justice but not wholly justly. His views were partly distorted by a touch of anti-German feeling. We met, exchanged views and discussed, walking through the Moscow night.

One day we made a trip to visit a factory. We were accompanied by a young communist who had spent some time working in Belgium. We had travelled a good way out into the suburbs by tram, but we still had quite a walk ahead of us. The sky was clouded over, but there was no wind and we were warmly dressed, so it was a pleasure to walk. A row of waggons was lined up in front of a shop, and we decided to go in. Perhaps we would be able to get a cup of tea; in any case it would be interesting to see the setting and the people. In town there were still a few cafés, such as that frequented by the 'Imagist' poets, but we never went there. We were brought some lightly coloured hot water; the tea-pot and cups were chipped. But at least it warmed us up, and it wasn't the first time that boiling water had been presented to us as tea.

It goes without saying that our entry had aroused a certain curiosity among the customers, who were anxious to ask us who we were and where we were going. Our young comrade got into conversation with his neighbour and unfortunately he revealed our high function as members of the Executive Committee of the Communist International. 'Then they must be Jews,' replied the other in a tone of utter contempt. 'No, they're not Jews!' After his initial surprise he looked at us insistently, but in the end it proved impossible to get him to abandon his point; likewise his companions who had come to his aid. All the Soviet leaders were Jews, and they didn't hesitate to criticise the régime, even in very crude terms. This was very revealing. Such incidents gave us a valuable means of sounding the mentality of the people. The Revolution had a tough job ahead of it to free these simple brains from the poison poured into them by Tsarism.

For quite different reasons, the visit to the factory was to leave us with a similar impression of the size of the job remaining to be done. But here it was not a question of the people involved. Workers and leaders were wholly likeable. They were entirely devoted to the régime, and they told us calmly of their grievances and of the difficulties they were coming up against. The work was well organised, but they didn't have enough equipment. They were without necessary items which were no longer obtainable.

We were too tired to walk all the way back, and the idea of returning by sledge appealed to us. And to start with it was indeed very pleasant, the cold air lashing our faces. But the pleasure didn't last long. We were well wrapped up, but not sufficiently for a trip of this sort, and we soon decided we had had enough of our first experience of sledge travel.

★   We thought we had exhausted the controversies on what was now the programme of the KAPD — mass parties not parties of leaders, against parliamentarism and against the trade unions; the Second Congress of the Communist International had been, as it were, the epilogue to this debate. However, Hermann Görter, the Dutch communist who was the theoretician of this tendency, had addressed an 'Open Letter to Comrade Lenin', which reopened the discussion. So the leadership of the Communist International had decided to invite Görter to Moscow for a further debate. An extraordinary session of the Executive Committee was arranged. Görter was a poet — a great poet even — and when he was present the discussion inevitably took a literary turn. This his 'Open Letter' ended up with this summary:

'Finally, to put my opinions into as brief and concise a form as possible for the benefit of the workers who need to acquire a clear view of tactics, I shall sum them up in a few theses:

1. The tactics of the revolution in the West must be quite different from those of the Russian Revolution;
2. For here the proletariat is on its own;
3. Therefore here the proletariat has to make the revolution on its own against all the other classes;
4. Hence the proletarian masses are here of relatively greater importance, and leaders are relatively less important;
5. Here the proletariat must have all the best weapons for the revolution;
6. As the unions are defective weapons, they must be abolished or radically transformed, and replaced by factory organisations united into a general organisation;
7. As the proletariat has to make the revolution on its own and has no one to assist it, it has to reach a very high level of consciousness and courage. It is preferable to leave parliamentarism on one side in the revolution.'

As can be seen, this put forward the whole programme of the KAPD. But Görter's principal concern was the trade-union question. When we met, he said to me almost point-blank: 'I hope you are going to revise your theses on the unions.' He seemed surprised to learn that the syndicalists were in agreement with the theses of the Communist International and not at all with his. His position had been sharpened further by this statement against strikes: 'We are still so few, our forces in the KAPD are so small, that we must concentrate them on the revolution, not squander them in strikes.'

The meeting took place on 24 November. Görter gave a long exposition of his views. The previous discussions had been so full that it was impossible to bring up new arguments; everything had been said on both sides. But there was something new from Görter — the actual form of his exposition. It was remarkable, but the substance was not solid. This was very clear at the time, and in retrospect, if one re-reads the summary of his 'Open Letter', one cannot fail to be struck by its naïvety. Trotsky (who was responsible for replying) refuted, in no less brilliant form, the unsure assertions of Görter, and stressed the contradictions, of which the most flagrant was precisely to do with the question of the 'masses'. They reappeared frequently in his exposition, in contrast to the leaders; yet at the same time he criticised the Communist International for 'running after the masses'. Nobody would have dreamt of denying that the revolution would develop differently in the West than in Russia. Lenin had said so time and time again. But for all that, Europe could not be divided, as Görter had divided it, into two quite different worlds. For there were still common features shared by Russia and the West.

At this time Hélène Brion was in Moscow for a short stay. She was an active militant in the Federation of Teachers' Unions, and in France had taken part in the minority wing of the CGT. During the war her actions had led to her being prosecuted and sentenced. She followed these debates with keen interest, and, at the end, expressed her satisfaction at having been able to observe a controversy carried on at such a high level.

18: The Anarchists. Death and funeral of Kropotkin

The Russian anarchists were split into several groups and tendencies, and these divisions had been made even sharper by the war. The spectrum ranged from anarcho-communists to individualists, as in every country, but here the splits were more extensive, as Victor Serge, who was familiar with them, showed in the articles he wrote about them. In June 1920, when I arrived in Moscow, one of these groups, the universalist anarchists, had a huge headquarters at the top of the Tverskaia where they had a permanent office and held meetings. I didn't know any of them, but I knew Alexander Shapiro well. He belonged to the anarcho-syndicalist group. I had seen him several times in London, notably in 1913 at the International Syndicalist Congress. He was then normally resident in London and was in contact with **La Vie Ouvrière**.

I went to see him at the office of his group, *Golos Truda* (The Voice of Labour), which was a shop in the neighbourhood of the Great Theatre. Like most of the anarchists, he and his friends were concentrating on publication. They had a small printing-press which made it possible for them to print a Bulletin and some pamphlets, and on occasion even a book. He gave me several copies of the pamphlets they had just published — texts by Pelloutier, Bakunin and Georges Yvetot. Their ambition was to produce a Russian edition of Pelloutier's **History of the Labour Exchanges**. But their resources were slender, and they didn't have enough paper.

Shapiro was particularly well-informed about what was going on in the world since he worked at the Commissariat for Foreign Affairs, under Chicherin, where he read and translated dispatches. He asked me for details about the trade-union movement in France and about the friends he had there. Then, naturally, we talked about the Soviet régime. He didn't approve of everything; he had many serious criticisms, but he expressed them without acrimony, and he concluded that one could and should work with the soviets. One of his comrades who was present at the discussion was more harsh. He was irritated by what he called the stupid way the Bolsheviks were acting in the countryside, but he none the less came to the same conclusion. We arranged a meeting to discuss with them their problems, their relations with the régime and especially with the Communist Party, and the conditions in which they would be able to carry on their work. Things were to be clearly and honestly defined on both sides.

We had had such a friendly conversation, and the solution seemed so simple that we might have thought the problem was already solved. Among the anarchists there had been different attitudes to the régime according to the different tendencies. These ranged from those who fought against communism and the régime by bomb-throwing and outrages all the way to those who had come over to Bolshevism and joined the Communist Party; among them Alfa, Bianqui and Krasnoshchekov. Yet others held positions of great importance but remained outside the Party — for example, on the railways there was Bill Shatov, who had returned from America. In the reconstruction work ability and devotion could always find employment. An anarchist at the head of an enterprise had enormous possibilities and a great deal of independence. The central authority gave a free hand to initiative, and was only too happy to see an enterprise being well run.

The anarcho-syndicalists were well aware of that, but they wanted something more, namely, the recognition of their group and guarantees that they would be allowed to continue and develop their publishing activity. At the end of our conversation it was agreed that they would draw up a declaration defining their demands and their attitude towards the régime, and that I would submit it to the Executive Committee of the Communist International.

I had undertaken this matter on my own initiative. When I told Trotsky what I had done, he expressed his satisfaction and urged me to continue my efforts towards the establishment of an agreement. I was myself quite confident and anticipated with pleasure an agreement which would have good effects in the syndicalist movement throughout the world. But no one came to the meeting. At the time we had arranged, I received a phone call to tell me that Shapiro and his friend would not be coming. It was Sasha Kropotkin on the phone and she said no more. Why was she given this job? I didn't know her and had never seen her. But it wasn't too hard to imagine what had happened. There had been a discussion, and various view-points and tendencies had come into conflict. Kropotkin's closest friends had particular grievances, which were more or less well-founded. In the end it had been the most narrow-minded, vicious and vindictive who had got their way. It was a stupid decision, since the anarcho-syndicalists were much further removed from the individualists than from the Bolsheviks. If those of the anarchists who, in spite of everything, were fairly close to the communists, and who in any case understood that it was in their interest to contribute to the building of Soviet society, opted out, then they would be lumped together with the individualists and the other sects who deprived the Revolution of valuable assistance in more than one respect, but they themselves suffered even more. In an open struggle they were doomed to defeat from the very start, and that was to no one's advantage.

Kropotkin died on 8 February 1921. He had returned to Russia after the February Revolution to pledge his full support to the Provisional Government, to the feeble régime of Kerensky when it was reinforced by Kornilov. For him this was the logical outcome of the total support he had given at the beginning of the world war to one of the imperialist blocs, the Allies, who claimed to be waging a just war against Prussian militarism. Only a small minority of the anarchists had followed him in this strange evolution. The others, led by Malatesta, denounced Kropotkin and his followers as 'governmental anarchists'. In order to be consistent, or perhaps because he had committed himself so firmly that he could not change camp, Kropotkin, who had supported the Provisional Government and Kerensky's government in everything, declared himself a determined enemy of the Soviet régime.

On that very day Guilbeaux had arranged a meeting with Lenin in the Kremlin. He suggested that I should go with him. Guilbeaux first of all explained his own problem, and then we had a general discussion which led straight to Kropotkin. Lenin spoke of him quite without bitterness. Just the opposite. He praised his work on the French Revolution, **The Great French Revolution**. 'He well understood and demonstrated the rôle of the people in that bourgeois revolution,' he said. 'It's a pity that at the end of his life there was an inexplicable lapse into chauvinism.'[16]

As we were leaving, Lenin asked us, reproachfully, why we weren't sending articles to **L'Humanité**. Then turning to me he said: 'Come and see me from time to time. Your French movement is pretty confusing and often the information we have is inadequate.' 'Oh,' I replied, 'I am already taking up too much of comrade Trotsky's time.' 'Well, you can take a little of mine too.'

Kropotkin's body had been displayed in the great hall of the House of Trade Unions — like John Reed's — and the anarchists kept vigil. The burial was fixed for the following Sunday. The evening before, a secretary from the Communist International came to tell

16. According to Sandomirsky — who, despite his quite different opinions, remained on friendly and intimate terms with him right to the end — it was love of France which drove Kropotkin into the ranks of the Allies, and then put him among the defenders of the February Revolution, hostile to the Bolsheviks and the October Revolution. Yet it was England which had welcomed him warmly and given him asylum to let him work freely, whereas in France he had been imprisoned and then driven out. But all the same, for him France was the land of liberty, and he could not stand the thought that it might be crushed under the Prussian jackboot.

me that I had been appointed to speak in the name of the Communist International. This news seemed unlikely to me, so I went to see Kobietsky, who confirmed the decision. When I observed that I thought some previous discussion, at least an exchange of views, was necessary, he replied that that had been thought to be of no use. He simply said 'We have confidence in you.'

I was perplexed. To speak in the name of the Communist International about a man whom the Bolsheviks had fought against unceasingly, and who, for his part, had been an unyielding opponent of the October Revolution till the day he died. What a delicate task! But two considerations made me realise that it was not such a difficult job as I had at first thought. I remembered the conversation with Lenin (truly a piece of good luck), the tone in which he had spoken of Kropotkin, and his praise of **The Great French Revolution**. And I also recalled something which had surprised me in the early days of my stay in Moscow. On an obelisk standing at the entrance to the Kremlin gardens were inscribed the names of the precursors of communism, of the champions of the working class. What had struck me was the 'eclecticism' with which the names had been chosen. The 'Utopians' were all there, and, more surprisingly, Plekhanov too. Violent polemics and harsh controversies had in no way prevented the recognition of the contribution of doctrinal opponents to the cause of human emancipation. Finally I had yet another example of this unforeseen 'tolerance' on the part of the fierce Bolsheviks. At the beginning of the October Revolution, revolutionary enthusiasm was manifested in every form and in every sphere, notably in painting and sculpture. The painters had occupied a part of the Tverskaia, and in 1920 you could still see engraved on the walls portraits of the great revolutionaries. Kropotkin's was in a prominent position near the Great Theatre.

On Sunday afternoon a long procesion formed up in front of the House of Trade Unions to accompany the body to the Novo-Devichy cemetery, at the very edge of the town. Black flags flew in the air, and there was a series of moving songs. At the cemetery there was a short but sharp incident during the first speeches. A Petrograd anarchist had been speaking for some time when there were muffled but heated cries of protest: 'Davolno! Davolno!' (Enough! Enough!).

On this day of mourning Kropotkin's closest friends were not prepared to be reminded of what most if not all anarchists must consider as his defection in 1914.[17]

Perhaps it was the wrong moment and he should have kept silence? This was a question to be settled among anarchists, but it was also a warning for me, if I had been tempted to allude to that critical period. But I had prepared my short speech on the basis of my personal memories, on what Kropotkin had meant for men of my generation, in Europe, America and throughout the world. I spoke of his contribution to the doctrine of evolution in **Mutual Aid**, and of the character presented in **Memoirs of a Revolutionist**, for whom one could not fail to feel a genuine liking. My words were not interrupted, though I felt that not all those around me were sympathetic. Much later, Victor Serge wrote that I 'spoke in conciliatory terms'. This implies that what I said should be seen as having a precise political meaning, that the content of my speech had been considered by the Executive of the Communist International. As we have seen, this was not so. Yet his interpretation was not purely a personal one, but was an observation he had picked up from those around him.[18]

17. We may recall here the attitude to Kropotkin of Malatesta, who had been his friend for forty years. As soon as he heard that Kropotkin had expressed public support for the Triple Entente in the war, Malatesta wrote an article called: 'Have the anarchists forgotten their principles?' which appeared in November 1914 in Italian, English and French in **Volontà**, **Freedom** and **Le Réveil**. A second article, published by **Freedom** in April 1916 under the headline 'Governmental Anarchists', was a reply to the 'Manifesto of the Sixteen' (the sixteen being Kropotkin and his supporters). On the fact that a break had become inevitable, Malatesta wrote: 'It was one of the most painful and tragic moments of my life (and I would even dare to say, of his too) when, after an extremely distressing discussion, we parted as opponents, even as enemies.' (**Pedro Kropotkine, Recuerdos y criticas de un viejo amigo suyo**. Montevideo, **Studi Sociali**, 15 April 1931.)
18. In the Album devoted to Kropotkin's funeral which was published in Berlin in 1922 by the Anarcho-Syndicalist Confederation, it is stated that I spoke in the name of the Red International of Labour Unions. Doubtless the publishers could not believe that I had been delegated by the Communist International, as my account has shown to be the case.

19: Congress of the French Socialist Party: a majority for affiliation to the Communist International

In one of the sections devoted to the Second Congress of the Communist International, I have spoken of the Independent Socialist Party of Germany, of its considerable numbers and of the tendencies within it. Däumig and Stöcker advocated affiliation to the Third International, while Dittmann and Crispien demanded certain 'concessions'. The reports they gave on their return to Germany aroused lively discussions inside the Party. It appeared that there was no possibility of compromise and that a split was inevitable. An extraordinary Congress was called, and met at Halle from 12 to 17 October. The supporters of affiliation asked Zinoviev to come and speak in the name of the International. The German government granted a visa for a short stay. Zinoviev brought with him the Secretary of the Young Communist International, and Lozovsky as a representative of the trade unions. It was the first time members of the Communist International had been able to leave Russia to take part in a socialist congress, and they wanted to take full advantage of the exceptional opportunity.

These were great and stirring debates! Hilferding led the battle against affiliation and was supported by Martov and Abramovich. Zinoviev gave a brilliant performance and defeated them. He knew and was able to feel that the great majority of the Party wanted to go over to the Third International. This majority was not willing to put up with the hesitations and manoeuvres of the leadership. When it came to the vote, there were 236 votes for affiliation, while the opposition got only 156. Zinoviev came back to Moscow covered in glory, and the Communist International rapidly published his speech in a thick pamphlet called **Twelve Days in Germany**.

During a short stay in Halle, Zinoviev had also been able to deal with matters concerning the French Socialist Party. This party was in a similar position to the German Independent Socialists. There was strong pressure from the base for affiliation to the Communist International, but stubborn constitutionalist resistance from the leadership. Its destiny was linked to that of the Independents and it was to follow the same path. As soon as they learned that Zinoviev was going to make his journey, the supporters of Longuet had sent a delegation to Germany to consult with him. They thought that the twenty-one conditions laid down by the Second Congress for entry to the Communist International were too rigid and would prevent a massive vote for affiliation. Zinoviev agreed to some adaptations, and an agreement was signed.

The Congress of the Socialist Party met at Tours from 25 to 31 December. This time there was no question of Zinoviev attending. The French Government went berserk as soon as Bolshevism was mentioned. But the Communist International found an excellent spokeswoman in Clara Zetkin, who travelled clandestinely to Tours. Her appearance on the Congress platform aroused the enthusiasm of the great majority of delegates. The vote followed the same pattern as that at Halle.[19] There were 285 delegates with 4,575 mandates. The motion for affiliation received 3,028 votes, the opposition only 1,022. The opposition to affiliation was substantial, above all among members of parliament. After a great deal of hesitation, Jean Longuet, Karl Marx's grandson, broke with most of his friends who voted for affiliation.

From Moscow the result seemed even more favourable. There was great satisfaction, even though not so much importance was attached to France and the French Party as to Germany and the German Party — not by a long chalk. For my part, having known well some of the men who supported affiliation, I could hardly fail to remain sceptical as to their sincerity. They were swimming with the stream in order to stay in the leadership of the Party. None the less, having unloaded three quarters of its parliamentarians, and most of those who had been totally compromised in the imperialist war, the new party offered possibilities. There was a clear road ahead for the new elements and the youth who had been thrust into the leadership. It now only remained for them to give proof of their abilities.

★   As a result of the creation of a French Communist Party, section of the Communist International, the Executive of the Inter-

19. The French text reads 'Dresden'. I take this to be a slip. (Translator's Note.)

national decided to appoint me to the 'small bureau' on which sat Zinoviev, Bukharin, Radek and Bela Kun (as I write these names today, I am reminded that I am the sole survivor of this small committee). At the Third Congress this small bureau was to be sharply criticised, especially with reference to the ill-fated March Action in Germany. It was denounced as a thieves' kitchen in which underhand plots were hatched, not only against capitalist governments, but, on occasion, against sections of the International. Nothing was further from the truth. Its main task was to prepare the work of the Executive Committee. Zinoviev normally lived in Petrograd and came to Moscow only irregularly, so that the agenda of sessions was always heavily loaded. As soon as Zinoviev's arrival was announced, there was great commotion. Meetings of the small bureau and the Executive, discussions and decisions — we used to be in non-stop session.

In the small bureau as in the Executive Committee, the tone of the discussions was very friendly, but in the small bureau there was a more intimate atmosphere and the hours spent there were particularly pleasant. Radek was well-behaved as always when he was among men whom he had to regard as his equals. Bukharin always showed the same kindness; he drew witty sketches, and in the course of our meetings he drew countless pictures of Radek in a ballet dancer's skirt; anyone who ever saw Radek can imagine the result . . . On one occasion we had been meeting all afternoon at the Hotel Lux, and we were to meet again after dinner in the Kremlin, in Zinoviev's quarters, to finish off the agenda. When I got there I found Zinoviev stretched out on a divan, and Bukharin lying on the floor, almost entirely hidden in his fur-coat. Like most communist leaders they snatched some sleep when they could. Lenin and Trotsky led better-ordered lives, except of course during the civil war. Even when I was in disagreement with the theses that were put forward and the decisions that were taken, I always felt it was very profitable to take part in these debates. At this time Moscow was the place where it was possible to have the best information on the labour movement throughout the world, and on the general policies of the ruling classes. We got reports, newspapers and verbal communications from visitors, who were now more numerous, coming from all parts of Europe and the world.

20: The French Communist group in Moscow

Dridzo-Lozovsky, who had lived in Paris for a long time, sometimes came to the Hotel Lux to gossip with me. One evening, as he was leaving, I said: 'I'll come down with you, I'm going to the meeting of the French group.' 'I'll come too,' he said at once. The French communist group met in a house which had a thoroughly Western standard of comfort, situated in an alley leading off the Tverskaia, not far from the Hotel Lux. A Scandinavian consul had lived there. Now it accommodated Guilbeaux, his wife and a French engineer. A spacious room, doubtless the consul's office, was a convenient place for meetings. As one may imagine, the group had an odd composition. Most of its members, of very varied origins, had happened to be in Russia at the time of the October uprising, and had then gone over to Communism. Lieutenant Pierre Pascal came from the military mission. He was a fervent practising Catholic, who had come to the side of the Revolution, not despite his Catholicism but because of it. This alone shows that he was no ordinary Catholic; it was precisely the Spartan character of the régime that attracted him. He was a hard worker — he served under Chicherin — who never complained and never asked for anything. During the Third Congress, when we happened to visit him in the room were he worked, we found him so exhausted that we at once thought there was something unusual. What? We couldn't expect to find out from him, but by asking some of the people in his circle we discovered that he had quite simply been forgotten in the distribution of meal-tickets . . . He had had articles published in Petrograd and Paris, and also his **Letters from Red Russia**, which were noteworthy for both their ideas and their style.

René Marchand was the Russian correspondent of the **Figaro** when the war broke out. Both by origin — he was a magistrate's son — and by profession, he was obviously far removed from communism and the socialist revolution. What had brought him over? He had given his reasons in a pamphlet with the long title of **Why I have rallied to the Formula of the Social Revolution**, a strange, rather cautious title. He had been indignant at the machinations, manoeuvres, plots and outrages prepared at the beginning of the Revolution in the embassies of the Entente countries — some of them right under his very eyes. Certainly this had helped to push him over to the other side of the barricades. He too was capable of enormous quantities of work. He had asked me to get him permission to search in the Archives of the Commissariat of Foreign Affairs, in order to find the diplomatic correspondence dealing with the Franco-Russian alliance, particularly the letters and dispatches from Isvolsky, Russian Ambassador to Paris from 1910 to 1916. It was these letters, which he then translated, that we got published in Paris by the Librairie du Travail under the title of **A Black Book** (**Un Livre Noir**, 6 volumes, 1921-34). It was certainly his most important contribution to the Russian Revolution, indeed to history. None the less he tried to repudiate it ten years later, when he had 'rallied' in turn to other 'formulae', even though I had in my possession the translations in his own handwriting. As a man, as a character, as a writer, he could hardly have offered more of a contrast with Pascal. His great hunger was no myth, and he indulged himself by keeping a huge dog in his room in the Hotel Metropole.

Of course it should have been Captain Sadoul that I compared with Pascal. The contrast would have been no less striking, though of a quite different kind. But I have already said everything about Sadoul that needs saying here, for he treated the French group with contempt, and no longer attended it. Besides, he left Soviet Russia pretty soon, since he could no longer find a job at the right level.

Henri Guilbeaux had moved closer to the **Vie Ouvrière** group at the beginning of the first world war. As soon as he had been discharged from the Army, he had been able to go to Switzerland where Romain Rolland had found him work in the International Agency for Prisoners of War. As I have already said, he had left France a disciple of Rolland, but under the influence of the Russian socialists he met at Geneva, he developed quite rapidly towards Bolshevism. He took part in the Kienthal Conference and was finally arrested and expelled by the Swiss authorities, while a French court sentenced him to death in his absence. All this is narrated in various works he wrote between 1933 and 1937, which must be read with care. Although he had often insisted on having it, I had never given him a mandate to represent us at international conferences. I willingly recognised the great merits of the magazine **Demain** (Tomorrow) which he edited and published in Geneva. Every month it provided us with information that was out of the ordinary and extremely useful. Moreover, he showed great courage against the mob of informers and provocateurs who harassed him endlessly. Yet we could not consider him as one of us. He himself demonstrated, by his later evolution, that he was not entirely reliable.

The engineer I have already mentioned was non-political, and Pascal's secretary was politically ignorant. There were also a few supernumeraries who were there only to get the extra food ration granted to members of the group, and in the hope of being able to return to France more easily.

When Lozovsky and I entered the meeting room, the atmosphere seemed so strained, the faces were so contorted, that it was not hard to guess that that evening the discussion had been far from cordial. Lozovsky immediately turned round, saying: 'Typical émigré behaviour . . . I've seen enough of that! Goodnight.' I had to stay, but the evening was unpleasant. Differences of temperament, let alone of political views, were such that mere coexistence was impossible. Anything would serve as an excuse to stir up an old quarrel or to level accusations at Pascal for his Catholicism. In reply, Pascal, wholly dignified, merely read out a text which he considered as a statement of faith. The conflict had been raised with the central committee of the Russian Communist Party, but the compromise solution which had been worked out to deal with it proved to be ineffective in practice. I think this meeting must have been the last one of the communist group in Moscow. In any case, there was no further activity of any sort.

The French communist group in Moscow was indeed as I have described it by 1920; it had outlived its usefulness. But in its early days it had known greatness; two of its members were victims of the counter-revolution. So as not to leave the reader with the impression of its miserable end, I would like to reproduce here a fragment of the historical sketch that Pascal wrote of it:

'On 30 August 1918, **Isvestia** published the following announcement: All comrades speaking English or French and in sympathy with the ideals of the Communist Party are invited to attend a meeting which will take place on Saturday, 31st August at 7.00 pm, Vozdvizhenka No 20. Agenda: report on the situation, in English, by comrade Morgan Philips Price; in French by comrade Jeanne Labourbe. And secondly, the organisation of an Anglo-French group.

'Jeanne Labourbe was a pioneer. She had had a hard-working youth, employed first of all as a shepherdess in a village in Burgundy. Then she went into service in the town, and stayed there until a letter from a friend led to her going to Russia. Installed in a Polish family, she played the wretched rôle of governess and semi-servant; but this none the less permitted her, while teaching her native tongue to her pupil to complete her own education. When the 1905 Revolution broke out in Russia, her big-heartedness and manly courage, and her absolute devotion to all just causes, threw her right into the midst of the movement for liberation. She certainly gave herself to it wholeheartedly; we have seen her live among us only for the group and for communism. It is well-known how she died, on 2nd March 1919 murdered in the night in a cowardly manner, in the depths of a deserted suburb of Odessa, by a group of French and Russian officers, led by General Borius.'

It was also in the Odessa area, where French troops were supporting the White forces, that the second victim was to perish. In his **Memories of the Civil War**, Marcel Body wrote:

'Odessa is blockaded by land and sea . . . there's no more bread, no more water, no more fuel in the town. But on the other hand there are plenty of counter-revolutionaries; the situation is getting worse. At the moment when I am due to make my speech, a comrade passes me a note in which I read: "We expect the town to be occupied tonight. Prepare to take refuge in clandestine lodgings." A few moments later, I see Henri Barberey come into the room, armed and equipped. A few minutes ago he gave a fine speech in Russian. Unless I am mistaken, he is eighteen years old, but in his convictions he is a grown man. He is one of the first Frenchmen who came over to the Revolution.

'At the beginning of the French intervention, the French communist group sent him, with Jeanne Labourbe, to Southern Russia to work there as a militant. His courage borders on recklessness. He was in Sebastopol at the time of the revolt by the sailors of the

French naval squadron in the Black Sea, and he played a major rôle in events which were themselves decisive. Disguised as a sailor, he went on to the French warships to support an agitation which bore fruit . . . On the night of 30th to 31st July Henri Barberey sets out at the head of a small detachment of French volunteers to fight the insurgents who are already masacring communists and Jews in the suburbs of Odessa. He fights with his normal bravery; at times his comrades try, in vain, to restrain him. Setting out alone as a scout — or as bearer of a flag of truce — he is taken prisoner before the very eyes of his comrades, who are powerless to save him. We shall never see him again.' (**Correspondance Internationale**, 11 November 1922.)

21: 'Trotsky's Train'. Wrangel. End of the Civil War

In the fragmentary accounts we received of the civil war operations, there were often allusions to 'Trotsky's train'. It turned up here and there, from the Urals to the Ukraine, encouraging the soldiers of the Red Army, while the very sight of it demoralised the mercenaries of the counter-revolution. Extraordinary exploits followed one another without end; the 'train' became a legendary phenomenon.

Alex Barmin, who himself took part in one of these exploits, has given this account of it. 'A renewed attack by Haller (a Polish general) has enabled him to capture Rechitsa and to cross the river. Gomel was about to fall into the hands of the enemy when Trotsky arrived. Already the evacuation convoys, those wretched convoys of linked vehicles piled with boxes, papers and the remnants of stores, were trailing along the roads of Novozybkov, already the heads of the Executive and the Cheka were moving off by car. Nothing was left at the station but the last armoured train, the train of lost battles commanded by some raving ex-sailor. But suddenly everything changed, and we saw the tide was turning. Trotsky brought with him prepared teams of disciplined organisers, political agitators and technicians, all commanded by an unflagging will. The fifth division, reduced to a few hundred bayonets, had just given ground before the Poles. Our Military College set out at dawn and took up a bridgehead position in front of Rechitsa. It was a lively battle. We charged with side-arms against sharp-shooters sheltering behind a hedge. An intrepid officer, a specialist, led us calmly, revolver in hand. He went through the hedge first. This time we were fighting against soldiers from the Great War, who had learned to fight in France and Germany.

'It was our worst battle. Out of 240 trainee officers more than 100 were killed and we were forced back. But General Haller's infantrymen did not pass. We were told they had sworn to go all the way to Moscow! "They won't even see Gomel," we survivors repeated to each other . . . Trotsky visited the front lines and harangued us. From him came that breath of energy that he took with him everywhere in moments of tragedy. The situation, catastophic two days before, had been put right as if by a miracle. But in reality it was the quite natural miracle of organisation and will. Until recently I still had Trotsky's speech to our Military College, printed on the press of the Red Army train.' (**Vingt ans au service de l'URSS**, pp 111-112.)

I had sometimes got Trotsky to talk about it, but he had never given me any lengthy accounts. In June 1920, when I arrived in Russia, the civil war was virtually at an end, and the train was in the sidings. I could only rejoice at this, but I regretted having arrived too late.

During the autumn it emerged that the remnants of Denikin's army were not so negligible as had at first been believed. A new counter-revolutionary leader, Wrangel, had managed to reassemble them and, with French assistance, to equip them. Britain and America had definitively abandoned attempts at intervention, but France was persisting. Millerand, Poincaré and their 'national bloc' parliament were sending supplies, granting credits, and even recognising Wrangel. The French proletariat had turned out to be unable to prevent this new aggression. Wrangel had set up his headquarters in the Crimea, from where it was easy for him to launch raids on the surrounding area. His columns used surprise tactics, and after each attack they were able to take refuge in the peninsula. The threat became disquieting, for it was feared that he would get bolder and finally attack the Donetz coal basin.

After discussion and study of the situation, the central committee decided to have done with this remnant of counter-revolution, and at the same time teach the French bourgeoisie a lesson; for the latter, hypnotised by the Tsarist loans bonds to which they had subscribed untiringly, were proving to be decidedly pig-headed. So the 'train' was going to set out once more; and before I had time to ask, Trotsky proposed that I should accompany him.

On the morning of 27 October we were at the station. The train was already prepared, and after a brief inspection we set out. The coach of the People's Commissar had belonged to the Tsarist Minister of Railways, and Trotsky had adapted it for his use. The lounge had been transformed into an office-cum-library. The other part consisted of the bathroom, with a narrow room on each side of it with just enough space for a divan. The following coach was for the secretaries; then followed in turn the printing-press, the library, the recreation room, the restaurant, a coach for provisions and spare clothing, an ambulance service, and finally a coach specially fitted up for the two motor-cars. There was all that was necessary for work, for defence, and even for attack . . .[20]

At all times the train was a hive of activity. There was a newspaper **V Pouti** (On the Way), which appeared daily with leaders, a commentary on events, and the 'latest news'. As soon as the train stopped, we plugged into the cables to get into contact with Moscow immediately. At the appropriate times, the radio would pick up foreign broadcasts. 'Your French radio is completely stupid,' Trotsky said to me: 'Berlin and London give interesting news, but your radio is nothing but rubbish.' Trotsky always had some work in preparation, and when military operations permitted, he would set his secretaries to work, dictating and revising the typed sheets. 'I acquired this habit of dictating during the war,' he told me, adding immediately that before 'there wouldn't have been any secretaries'. One should not draw the conclusion that the work done in this way was skimped or neglected. No one made greater demands on himself than Trotsky. He had a horror of carelessness in style, just as in dress and behaviour. He would go over the dictated pages again, re-read them, correct them, rearrange them; a second and a third copying

20. On the 'train', consult Trotsky, **My Life**, Grosset & Dunlap, 1960, pp 411-422.

became necessary. But sometimes the enemy didn't leave enough time for such polishing, and certain texts were left with a rhetorical turn to them.

The work-table took up almost the whole of one side, on the wall of which was hung a huge map of Russia. On the two walls at right angles to this were book-shelves weighed down with books, encyclopaedias and technical works. Other books on the most varied subjects bore witness to the new occupant's universal curiosity. There was even a French corner where I found the French translation of the Marxist studies by Antonio Labriola. But I was very surprised to see Mallarmé's **Verse and Prose Works** in the blue-covered edition of the Perrin academic library.

We stayed for two days in Kharkov, where the headquarters of Soviet Armies was situated. It was Frunze, later to be Commissar for War, who was directing operations. But our first visit was to Rakovsky, at that time President of the Ukrainian Council of People's Commissars. He was Trotsky's closest friend. The two men had met at the time of the Balkan War, when Trotsky was following operations as a war correspondent, then again later at Zimmerwald, and in Russia after the October Revolution. We spent these two days on long meetings where all sorts of questions were examined. Rakovsky took advantage of the presence of a member of the Political Bureau to settle some outstanding difficulties. When he brought Trotsky back to the train, his face, always cordial and kindly, was beaming: 'What a lot of work we've been able to get through!' he said.

The train continued its journey southwards. Trotsky had conferred with Frunze, and he outlined to me briefly the plan of operations, the last phase of which was due to begin. The Red Army had captured Nikopol, on the Dnieper, an essential position, and had dug itself in there firmly. Based on this stronghold, which Wrangel had attacked in vain, the Soviet forces were going to compel the enemy to withdraw all his troops into the Crimea. Then they would cross the Perekop Isthmus, and chase any who resisted into the sea. This time it would be the end, but how many more valuable lives would be lost? The isthmus was a narrow strip of land, scarcely four kilometers across. It would be easy for the enemy to organise a resistance which could not be smashed without heavy losses.

The train stopped and was placed in sidings at Alexandrovsk. There a Red Army commander was awaiting Trotsky. He gave him a report on the situation. We could continue by car as far as the Army headquarters, for the road had been cleared. But enemy patrols were still reported in the locality.

It was very cold. Night had fallen, and the car was travelling over a snow-covered plain. No sign of the road was visible, and I wondered how the driver could find his way. Trotsky promised me a glass of tea at the priest's house. 'Why the priest's house?' I enquired in surprise. 'Because there is scarcely ever any other house capable of accommodating the headquarters.' Yet when the car stopped, it was outside a very modest house. In a room quite cluttered up with furniture, Trotsky conferred with the Red commander and his staff officer. A map had been spread out on the table; the only light was provided by a candle.

There was a conflict between the two men. The former explained his position with fierce impatience, almost with anger; the staff officer was much calmer. The affair was soon settled, for Trotsky had seen hundreds of similar disputes. There were frequent clashes between a man moved into a commander's position, and a technician. Here the young commander was a Petrograd worker, and as was often the case, he was brave and bold, but impatient and unwilling to put up with the comments of the staff officer who had to come to grips with the detailed problems of food supplies. 'A classic dispute', Trotsky said to me, 'an obstacle we have often had to overcome. But without this collaboration between revolutionary enthusiasm and the technique of the professional, we could never have been victorious.' It was an illustration on a small scale of the serious problem posed at the time of the creation of the Red Army. Trotsky, who advocated the use of officers from the Tsarist Army who promised to serve loyally, came up against an opposition which got more and more aggressive when there was a setback, or when one of these officers betrayed.[21]

We climbed back into the car. It was very cold, the wind was shaking the car and blowing right through it. 'Well,' I said to Trotsky, 'you promised me a comfortable priest's house and a glass of tea.'

21. On this question, see Trotsky's book **Stalin**, Chapter 9.

'It's true,' he replied with a smile, 'in war you must be prepared for surprises.' At Alexandrovsk we rejoined the train. Trotsky studied some dispatches which had arrived during his absence, and then we set out for Moscow again, this time without any stops. Trotsky talked to me about the war at greater length than he had done hitherto. 'The battle must have been joined now,' he said. 'It'll be a terrible fight. We've got to capture positions which are easily defended. What a horrible thing war is!' Then he recalled some episodes from the war, among them the battle outside Kazan which had settled Kolchak's fate. The siege was dragging on, and the commanders decided that a feint was necessary to deceive the enemy, to destroy his flotilla by night, attack the shore batteries and provoke panic among the troops. Trotsky decided that he would himself take part in the operations which were to be directed by Raskolnikov. The strategem was a total success. But what a risk! I felt bound to reproach him in retrospect. 'Had you any right to expose yourself like that?' There was no hesitation about the brief and unanswerable reply. 'If you have to ask men to risk their lives, you have to show them that you're not afraid of risking your own.'

The train continued its journey steadily but at a moderate speed. It was heavily loaded, and needed two locomotives to pull it. When we got to Moscow, they had just received word that the soldiers of the Red Army had captured the last defences closing the Perekop Isthmus. Wrangel fled, abandoning the men he had dragged into his adventure with him. Poincaré's France had played its last card and lost. The civil war was over.[22]

---

22. But France had not finished with Wrangel. For in **Europe Nouvelle** of 10 December 1921 this letter from Constantinople was published: 'Since Wrangel's army evacuated the Crimea, France has spent more than two hundred million francs on the maintenance of Russian officers and soldiers in Turkey. To begin with, it was thought that this army in exile could still render services in the struggle against the soviets. But soon the French High Commissioner at Constantinople realised that, in its present state and with its present leaders, this military agglomeration no longer had the unity of spirit on which any armed force must base itself, and was doomed to disintegration. There followed a prolonged struggle between the French Government and general Wrangel, who, for his part, wanted to preserve his army as a military force, but was still clinging desperately to his supreme command, which he was not willing to abandon at any price.'

1921

1: The Trade-Union question provokes a great debate

SOON AFTER my return to Moscow I met Lozovsky, who told me an important trade-union meeting was due to take place that evening. He explained the subject of the meeting in such vague terms that it was difficult to know what it was really about. But it reminded me of a conversation I had had in the train with Trotsky, when he had referred to the Party leadership's preoccupations with the organisation of production, and especially with the rôle of the unions in this field. This meeting was rapidly followed by several others on the same theme, and the newspapers published accounts of them. The question rapidly took on extraordinary dimensions; various groups were formed inside the central committee, publicly opposed to each other. From this time on it was possible to grasp the precise nature of the question being asked, and to follow a discussion which was to have deep repercussions and would mark an important date in the life of the Party.

The régime which bore the name of 'war communism' had been born with the war and should have died with it. It survived because there were hesitations as to the sort of organisation which ought to replace it. People were groping, searching and failing to make decisions. It is only fair to add at this point that after the exhausting effort that the war had demanded, there was felt, in every stratum of Soviet society, a legitimate wish for a breathing-space. But this survival presented serious dangers. War communism was communism in name only — for communism supposes abundance and this was scarcity — but it had been a necessity of the war imposed on the Soviet Union by the Whites and by the Entente. To resist the thrust of counter-revolution, continually renewed for three years, and the interventions of the French, British and Americans, it had been absolutely necessary to equip the Red Army. And however scanty this equipment was, it absorbed an enormous share of the country's resources. In production, everything was oriented towards the war effort, and to nourish the army and the factory workers, agricultural products were requisitioned in the countryside.

This requisition was brutal by its very nature. It irritated and at the same time demoralised the peasantry, because they were left no more than what was required for subsistence. Sometimes it was more brutal than necessary because of the stupidity or complacency of the young Bolsheviks who were intoxicated by having power suddenly thrust upon them. The peasants had none the less put up with it, but by now their patience, or their good will, was running out. The problem that the Soviet Republic had to solve was what was called after the second world war the reconversion of the war economy into a peace economy; but at that time this would have seemed a very ambitious formulation. The time had come to relax the grip.[23]

Speaking to the central committee, Trotsky had summed up in a striking image the excess of centralisation to which the civil war had led: 'We have erected an enormous inkwell in Red Square, and everyone has to come and dip his pen in it in order to write.' An organism had indeed been created to manage the economy of the country. This was the Supreme Council of National Economy, but for various reasons it carried out its rôle badly, and the unions, which had a dominant place in it, didn't do their job properly. Seeking to discover the reason for this, Trotsky — at the time he was a Commissar for Transport, and a trade unionist by virtue of being a worker in the industry — had had himself appointed as union

23. On this question, see Trotsky's **The New Course**, Ann Arbor 1965, pp 69-70. In a proposal made to the central committee of the Party in February 1920, Trotsky said: 'It is clear that the present policy of the requisition of food products according to norms of consumption . . . threatens to disorganise completely the economic life of the country.'

delegate to the General Council of the General Confederation of Trade Unions, and thus was able to take part in its meetings.

The first thing that had struck him was the careless approach to preparation and methods of work. No one turned up at the proper time; members drifted in one after another so that meetings started very late. Since he was accustomed to punctuality by a natural disposition which had been reinforced by the experience of war-time discipline, he was shocked by these things. If such carelessness existed at the top, then it could easily be imagined what would be discovered if one moved down towards the lower-level organisations. While this experience was brief, it was decisive in his eyes, and it had led him to propose modifications in the trade-union structure which were embodied in a plan which he submitted to the central committee.

Nobody basically disputed that the unions were in a state of semi-lethargy; the only difference of opinion was on the causes and the cures. There was undeniably a crisis; a solution had to be found. Now, the Red Army was being demobilised, and Trotsky asked: 'What are we going to do with all these young men of great merit, who have had their training there? They are capable organisers and administrators, accurate, punctual, knowing how to work and used to team-work. Are we merely going to fling them into Soviet life without trying to make the best use of their capacities?' Replying to this question, he proposed that they should be incorporated, in proportions to be fixed, into the trade-union leaderships where they would provide a stimulus and valuable methods of work. This was the basis for the discussion. Certain members of the central committee, led by Tomsky, secretary of the Trade Union Central Council, were violently hostile and denied that there was any crisis. Others hesitated, looking for a compromise. The problem was so important and complex that the central committee decided that a broad public discussion would take place in the press, where every tendency could present and defend its theses, and in public meetings.

At the beginning there were five tendencies: those of Trotsky, Bukharin, Shlyapnikov (almost syndicalist, though a Party member and very attached to the Party), and Sapronov (democratic central-ism); while the *status quo* was defended by Tomsky, Zinoviev and Kamenev. In the course of the campaign, the intermediary positions disappeared. Trotsky recognised the correctness of certain criticisms which had been expressed of his plan, and modified it, but he stood up vigorously to those who claimed to see in it a militarisation of the unions. During one meeting I attended, Ryazanov thought he could give a humorous interpretation of the plan by imagining an arrogant young soldier with his military cap over his ear bursting into a trade-union office and claiming to dictate decisions. Trotsky had been angered by this, and a good part of the audience had protested with him. Trotsky, Bukharin and Sapronov came together on a common platform in face of the defenders of the *status quo*, who were supported by Lenin, though he didn't commit himself too deeply. (Shlyapnikov's tendency was too weak to carve itself out a place between these two blocs.) It was later known and understood that Lenin's main criticism of Trotsky's plan was that it was inopportune. He had in mind another solution, immeasurably more far-reaching, since it would modify the very structure of the Soviet régime in several important respects. This was the solution the Party was to adopt some months later — the New Economic Policy.[24]

2: The Kronstadt Rising

The discussion was continuing, and the Party Congress was about to meet, when the Kronstadt rising broke out. It was terrible news; at first we couldn't believe it. Kronstadt, the most enthusiastic centre of the October Revolution, rising up against the Soviet Republic — could it be possible? The Party leaders themselves were taken by surprise. We were dismayed. As always in difficult and dangerous situations, it was Trotsky who was sent to Petrograd by the central

24. At the Tenth Congress of the Russian Communist Party, at the session held on 8 March, he spoke of the great debate in these terms: 'I shall now pass to another point, the trade union discussion which has taken up so much of the Party's time. In my view this was a quite impermissible luxury, and we certainly made a mistake in allowing the discussion to take place. We have given first place to a question which, for objective reasons, could not occupy this place. And we got involved in it without realising that we were diverting attention from real and threatening problems which were so close to us.'

committee, which thereby took the risk of attributing to him responsibilities which were not his.[25]

It is essential to study in detail the nature of the movement, and above all its causes, for some of these were obvious. The Kronstadt of 1921 was no longer the Kronstadt of 1917. The transfer of the Soviet government to Moscow had led to the syphoning off of a large number of militants, and the civil war had taken many more. The working-class suburbs had provided their contingents. The Petrograd of the October insurrection, the Petrograd where all the phases of the Revolution had developed, now gave the impression of a city that had lost its rank, that was no longer a capital. Zinoviev was responsible for it, and he was the man least capable of methodical administration, apart from the fact that his attention was now required by the Communist International and its sections. The town and region had been left in total neglect, and the conditions of workers and the organisation of labour had been so disregarded that strikes had broken out. Situated at the very extremity of the country, Petrograd was also in the worst possible position for food supplies when Russia was cut off from the outside world. Its position, which was advantageous in peace-time, became the most exposed in war.

That counter-revolutionary elements should have tried to exploit the situation was nothing unusual. It was their job to stir up discontent, to inject poison into grievances, to draw the movement towards them. What was the source of the slogan 'Soviets without Bolsheviks'? It isn't easy to pin it down, but it was so suitable for rallying everyone, all the opponents of the régime, in particular the Social-Revolutionaries, the Cadets, the Mensheviks, eager to take

25. Trotsky knew Kronstadt and its militants well. In his **History of the Russian Revolution** (Volume I) he speaks of it in these terms: 'Despite merciless repression, the flame of revolt was never extinguished in Kronstadt. After the insurrection it flared up threateningly . . . On 13th May 1917, the Soviet took this decision: "The sole power in Kronstadt is held by the Soviet of workers' and soldiers' deputies." Exemplary order was maintained; haunts of vice were closed down . . . The Kronstadt sailors constituted a sort of "Militant Order of the Revolution" . . . Among the top leaders it was decided to teach the people of Kronstadt a lesson. It was Tseretelli who made himelf the prosecutor. Trotsky took up their defence.'

their revenge, that it is permissible to suppose that it was they who first had the idea. The propaganda they made around this demand was able to have an impact on the sailors and soldiers, mainly young recruits coming from the countryside, already disturbed by the bitter complaints they read in letters from their families, who were irritated by the brutal requisition. Such were the conclusions of the investigation carried out by the Party leaders. Writing a year later on the 'anniversary' of the event, Andrés Nin, who had spent the past year in Russia and had had the possibility of getting information and checking it, gave identical explanations and evaluations. (**Correspondance Internationale** 12 April 1922.)

The position of the opponents of the Bolsheviks has been set out in various pamphlets, usually written by anarchists. It can be found in what I think is the most recent, published in 1948 by Ida Mett (Editions Spartacus), with the title **The Kronstadt Commune, Bloody Twilight of the Soviets**. The author's conclusion is already clearly indicated by this title, yet he declares that he undertook his research purely in order to establish the historical truth on this painful event. Did he succeed? He recognises that there is still not enough evidence for a definitive analysis, since the archives of the Soviet government and the Red Army cannot be consulted. None the less he reproduces and comments on many important documents. But what a lot of contradictions there are among the evidence and opinions he quotes, usually coming from conscious opponents of the Bolsheviks.

On the question of the origin and cause of the rising, one of the leaders of the insurrection, Petrichenko, wrote in 1926 that it was the continuation of the régime of war communism after the civil war had finished which irritated the workers and drove them to rise up against the Soviet government. But this government desired no less than they to pass from a war régime to a peace-time régime. Was it too slow in doing so? Could it have brought into application any earlier the new economic policy which had been preoccupying it for months? Study and research were going ahead; the great debate on the trade unions must be seen in the framework of this research. Only someone very rash would believe that he could give an answer to these questions, while it is difficult, if not impossible, to make an exact reconstruction of the general situation existing at that time.

Even if one concedes that the rising was carried out by workers and sailors acting in full independence, on their own initiative, and without any relations with counter-revolutionaries, it must be recognised that from the moment the rising was launched, all the enemies of the Bolsheviks hastened to join it: Left and Right Social-Revolutionaries, anarchists, Mensheviks. The foreign press was exultant; it did not even wait for the active phase of the conflict before drawing attention to it. It was not interested in the programme of the rebels, but it understood that their revolt might accomplish what all the bourgeoisies together had failed to do — the overthrow of a detested régime whose collapse they had been anxiously awaiting for years.

Among the leaflets distributed at Kronstadt, one, signed by 'a group of Mensheviks', ended with the words: 'Where are the true counter-revolutionaries? They are the Bolsheviks, the commissars. Long live the Revolution! Long live the Constituent Assembly!' According to the **Socialist Messenger**, the official organ of the Russian social democrats, published abroad, 'the slogans of Kronstadt are Menshevik', while Martov denied that the Mensheviks and Social-Revolutionaries were participating in the movement. In his view, the initiative was taken by the sailors, who were breaking with the Communist Party on questions of organisation rather than on principles.

The facts reported in the pamphlet show that it was the Provisional Revolutionary Committee which took the initiative for the military measures. On the basis of a false report, it hastened to occupy strategic points and take possession of state establishments, etc. These operations took place on 2 March, and it was only on 7 March that the government, having exhausted all possibilities of conciliation, had to decide to order the attack. The Social-Revolutionaries had done their best to prevent a peaceful solution to the conflict. One of their leaders, Chernov, a former minister of the coalition cabinets which had led the February Revolution into the hands of Kornilov and Kerensky, exclaimed: 'Don't let yourself be deceived by engaging in negotiations with the Bolshevik authorities; they are doing it only in order to gain time.' When action became inevitable, the government undertook it reluctantly, as is shown by the evidence of Lutovinov, one of the leaders of the 'Workers' Opposition'. On his arrival in Berlin on 21 March, he declared: 'The news published in the foreign press about the Kronstadt events has been greatly exaggerated. The Soviet government is strong enough to deal with the rebels; the slowness of the operations is due to their concern to spare the population of the town.'

Lutovinov had been sent to Berlin in disgrace, and the fact that he belonged to the 'Workers' Opposition' gives special value to his statement.

While it is possible that the Soviet government made mistakes, what can be said of the rôle of a man like Chernov, who saw the whole thing simply as an opportunity for revenge against the Bolsheviks because they had removed him from his presidential chair when they dissolved the Constituent Assembly? Knowing that the insurrection was doomed to failure, he did all he could to whip up the sailors, thus helping to increase a pointless sacrifice of human lives. Given the situation, once the fight was engaged, it was bound to be a desperate one. Losses were heavy on both sides, among the rebels and among the trainee officers of the Red Army.

At various times the Kronstadt sailors had shown that they were prone to give way to impatience. Under the Provisional Government, on 13 May, they had proclaimed that 'the sole power in Kronstadt is the Soviet'. Then it was Trotsky who took up their defence against the Menshevik Minister Tseretelli, as we have seen in a note above. Two months later, during the period of great disturbance known as the 'July Days', following the unfortunate offensive which Kerensky had decided on under pressure from the Allies, the Kronstadt sailors came to Petrograd in a mass. After having demonstrated through the town, they proceeded to the Tauride Palace where the Soviet was sitting, and, in an imperative tone, they demanded that the socialist ministers should come and give them an explanation. Chernov was the first to appear. 'Search him! Make sure he isn't armed!' came the shouts on every side. It was not a friendly welcome. 'In that case, I've nothing to say,' he declared, turning his back on the crowd, as if to return to the Palace. However, the tumult died down. He was able to make a short speech, to try to appease those who were protesting. When he had finished, several sailors, tough elements, took hold of him and pushed him towards a car, taking him hostage. This unforeseen action produced total confusion, with some approving while others protested. While the discussion continued, some workers rushed into the Palace, shouting: 'Chernov has been seized by hotheads! We must save him!' Martov, Kamenev and Trotsky hurried out of the session. Not without difficulty, Trotsky obtained Chernov's release, and, taking him by the arm, brought him back to the Soviet. In 1921, Chernov had completely forgotten this scene of four years earlier. His only thought was to stir up in a criminal way the brothers of those sailors who had treated him more harshly than the Bolsheviks did.

3: Lenin presents the New Economic Policy (NEP) to the Third Congress of the Communist International

The Third Congress of the Communist International was called for 22 June 1921, in Moscow. The founding congress of the Red International of Labour Unions was to be held at the same time. During the year which had gone by since the Second Congress, there had been no lack of important events. New communist parties had been formed or developed according to the tactics and rules adopted by the International. What stage were they now at? The Congress would certainly discuss this, but the debate which would undoubtedly overshadow all the others would be that devoted to the March Action in Germany.[26]

The failure of this action, but even more its nature and the way it had been carried out, had produced serious repercussions, above all of course in the German section, but also in the other sections of the Communist International. For the Red International of Labour Unions, there was clearly a difficult Congress ahead. Among the syndicalists and anarcho-syndicalists, both those who had affiliated formally and those who were sympathetic, it was possible to observe a marked aloofness, all kinds of reservations, even distrust. Moreover, the Soviet Republic as it was in the early summer of 1921 — when

26. For details on this, see later in this chapter.

the memory of Kronstadt was still alive, and when serious changes in economic policy (liable to produce criticisms from left and right alike) were imminent — would certainly not offer the delegates a picture that would get rid of their doubts and overcome their distrust. I don't know if Zinoviev didn't appreciate that or didn't want to appreciate it, but he decided to ask all sections of the International and the trade-union organisations to send large delegations. And after having taken this decision of which the consequences were soon obvious, he didn't worry about accommodating them. When the first delegates arrived scarcely anything had been fixed up, and the comrades in charge of lodgings were in a ludicrous situation. They asked me to intervene with Trotsky — always the final resort.

But if I could see the necessity and urgency of rapid action, I refused to bother Trotsky with this matter of accommodation for delegates. I knew how careful he was not to infringe other comrades' responsibilities, especially when it was a case of 'old Bolsheviks' like Zinoviev who resented the fact that he had acquired a leading position. But time was short, so I agreed to explain the situation to him. As I had foreseen, his first impulse was to refuse, which I was expecting and was therefore not surprised at it. But the matter was worrying him, and he asked me several questions and finally decided to telephone Zinoviev. The latter was surprised to learn of difficulties he had known nothing about, and consented quite willingly to the setting up of a commission to be presided over by Sklyansky, Trotsky's assistant at the Commissariat for War. With Sklyansky, you could be sure things would be dealt with promptly; buildings were prepared, supplies gathered together, and the delegates were able to be accommodated when they arrived.

With the French delegation there was a small incident, but one that was not without significance. To facilitate their work, it had been decided to accommodate all the delegates, and only them, in the Hotel Lux. In Paris a woman translator had been attached to the delegation; on the journey one of the delegates had picked her up — and in addition he wanted to bring with him an American journalist — it was a real retinue of attendants. He knew the regulation that had been adopted but he considered it was not for men of his sort. Infuriated at the calm resistance he came up against, he appealed to various 'authorities' . . . (the American journalist was Lewis Gannett, then on the staff of the liberal weekly **The Nation** and today literary critic of the **New York Herald Tribune**).

The French delegation was led by Fernand Loriot and Boris Souvarine. They had just been released after ten months in the Santé prison, accused of 'plotting against the security of the state'. In each grouping of communists or sympathisers, the government had selected the two most prominent militants, so that altogether ten had been accused. For the syndicalists it had been Monatte and Monmoussseau. The jury had declared them not guilty.

Paul Levi, who had led the German delegation at the Second Congress, was not there this time. He had been expelled for having criticised in an impermissible manner the 'March Action' which he described as a *'putsch'*. Clara Zetkin had not followed him, but had stayed in the Communist Party though her criticisms were scarcely less severe. Although Trotsky had been made responsible for giving the main report on 'The World Economic Crisis and the New Tasks of the Communist International', the Congress, dominated by this German question, was centred on the tactics of the Communist International. In fact the two questions were closely linked.

At the beginning of the year Trotsky had been visited by Bela Kun, who had come specifically in order to discuss with him the tactics which in his view the International ought to adopt. He said that it was absolutely necessary and urgent to be thoroughly committed to a systematic offensive strategy, making use of all the resources the Soviet Republic had at its disposal. For the bourgeois régimes, especially that in Germany, were still feeble. Now was the moment to attack them remorselessly, with a succession of uprisings, strikes and insurrections. Any later would be too late. Such was his thesis. Trotsky refuted it in a somewhat brutal manner, for he had been astonished to hear it put forward. But it had been useless for him to remind Bela Kun that it is an elementary truth of revolutionary action that one doesn't launch an insurrection just when one wants to, whatever the cost, and that a movement embarked on against the stream of events or in unfavourable circumstances can have fatal consequences for the working class. He failed to convince him. And worse, Bela Kun had won over to his views important militants from several sections of the International, notably the German and Italian.

To understand the meaning of the March Action and its consequences, which were grave, it is necessary to recall the military rebellion, which had taken place a year earlier, in March 1920, known as the Kapp-Lüttwitz putsch or simply as the Kapp putsch. Some of the members of the General Staff had then allied themselves with the 'free corps', composed of former German officers who had been demobilised as a result of the reduction in forces imposed by the Treaty of Versailles. They had planned to strike a decisive blow against the Weimar Republic. The two main leaders of the movement were General von Lüttwitz and the leading civil servant Kapp. On 10 March Lüttwitz issued an ultimatum to President Ebert. The President was to immediately replace the Socialist government with a government of 'neutral experts', that is, former high civil servants of the Empire. The Reichstag was to be dissolved, Ebert would retire, and the new President would be selected by a plebiscite. Finally the conspirators offered to make a dictator of Noske — the Socialist leader who had savagely repressed the workers' insurrections in November 1919. When the ultimatum was rejected, armed forces marched on Berlin on 13 March. Ebert summoned the generals von Seeckt and Schleicher, but they would not come, being unwilling to march against the rebels. The government fled to Dresden, then to Stuttgart.

It appears that in these grave circumstances it was the president of the General Confederation of Labour, Karl Legien, who was the most perceptive and who best saw the danger and how the rebellion could be broken. Although he had always shown himself to be one of the most prudent and moderate elements, he did not hesitate to call a general strike, the ultimate weapon of the working class which he had always condemned. He set up a general strike committee with representatives from all the workers' organisations, including the communists. This first general strike was a master blow. The German economy was instantly and wholly paralysed, and ordinary life was suspended throughout the country. The rebels, dismayed by this unforeseen response, were obliged to give up by the third day.

The memory of this impressive movement, this general mobilisation of workers which had so quickly overcome the attempted coup by the top military in alliance with the supporters of the Hohen-zollern, remained very much alive in the minds of workers, and for a time it dominated German politics. Just because of that, the March Action, dispersed, unclear, worrying, and ending up with a humiliating defeat, gave the impression of an artificial movement, badly prepared and badly carried out. It had originated in the Mansfeld coal-field, in central Germany, which was in a state of permanent upheaval; these were suitable conditions for launching a general strike, and here indeed it was effective. But the strike was only partial at Chemnitz, in Thuringia and Saxony. Bombs had exploded in several towns, such as Breslau and Halle, and other incidents which had been planned didn't even begin to go into operation. The movement miscarried. Reprisals were harsh.

The failure of this unprecedented movement allowed the bour-geois newspapers and the social democratic press to affirm from the very first day, though without any evidence, that it had been ordered and directed from Moscow. But they were not alone in this. Certain leaders of the Communist Party thought so too, among them Paul Levi and Clara Zetkin. Levi described it as an anarchist action in the tradition of Bakunin rather than of Marx. Levi's friends Malzahn and Paul Neumann, leaders of the Berlin metalworkers' union, had opposed solidarity strikes. Outside Germany there were communists equally eager to denounce what they described as an intolerable intervention by the Communist International. They were to be found even in the leadership of the French Communist Party, and also in Czechoslovakia.

Until the Third Congress of the Third International — called for 22 June — there were furious polemics among the leaders of the German Communist Party. Most of them were proud of the rôle played by the Party, and demanded the expulsion of their opponents. Paul Levi attacked them in public, and was expelled. Clara Zetkin remained silent and agreed to go to Moscow to confer with Lenin and Trotsky, who were known to be quite unwilling to give un-reserved approval to the tactics responsible for this adventuristic movement. The pre-congress discussions and conversations showed that they were confronted with a very strong opposition. Perhaps they would find themselves in a minority. The German delegation was systematising and generalising its March tactics, and advocating a 'revolutionary offensive'. They were sure to get the support of the Poles, the Austrians and the Italians. But Lenin and Trotsky were in full agreement on the need for unyielding resistance to such a fatal strategy for the labour movement, and they accepted that they would appear as 'right-wingers' and even run the risk of seeing a majority of the Congress declare against them.

The March Action had been a stinging defeat for Bela Kun. He knew well that the Russian delegation would attack him mercilessly, Lenin even more than Trotsky. He had found willing listeners to his loathsome theory in Germany, for both the Communist Parties were in agreement for once; but he remained the initiator and principal advocate of this tactic of the 'revolutionary offensive'. But he knew he had support and was preparing his defence. During this period he came to see me quite often — normally we met only infrequently — carrying **L'Humanité**, to ask me for details about men, articles and facts. His manoeuvre, which he left me to guess at, was to neutralise in advance, or at the very least embarrass, delegates who would be inclined to condemn him; and he was well aware that the French would be among these. He was collecting arguments to use against them. He chased after delegates as soon as they arrived, and he succeeded in mobilising against the French Communist Party and **L'Humanité** the parties of Belgium and of Luxembourg, whose spokesman was Ed Reiland, founder and chief inspiration of the Party. These were excellent communists, and not supporters of the 'offensive', but they had many grievances with regard to their French neighbour, and they were quite unaware of Bela Kun's plans. They had the opportunity to intervene during a meeting of the extended Executive Committee, which it had been decided to call because so many delegates had already arrived. Now the French delegation had arrived with the clearly determined intention of demanding from the Executive a full explanation of the German events. Some had been alarmed by an action with suspect motives, while the opportunists, those who were in the International despite themselves, were happy to have an opportunity to denounce an alleged interference by the International in the life of the German section. The interventions by the two numerically weak parties irritated them, and were one reason more why they persisted in their demands.

Before the general discussion, there was a serious squabble. The discussion had been opened in the normal fashion with Zinoviev's report on the activity of the International during the past year. Delegates would intervene, discuss, give explanations, reply to criticisms, and finally the report would be approved. But as I have said, the French delegation had arrived in an excited state of mind, for they were convinced that the March Action had been ordered by the leadership of the International. So they wanted the leadership to explain, to give an account of itself, straightaway, before everything else. This was the point to start with. They refused to accept the report. This produced stupefaction. Such a demand, and the tone in which it was expressed, was so out of proportion to the — pretty meagre — prestige and authority that the French Communist Party enjoyed within the International. Moreover it was absurd. Everyone knew that the March Action would be thoroughly discussed and would lead to wide-ranging debates. This is what Zinoviev explained. The French remained obstinate. The Germans said some unpleasant things to them. Radek got angry, and in passing referred to the French Communist Party as being social democratic and opportunist . . . Hereupon the French delegation announced that it was withdrawing and left the congress hall.

This was ridiculous, for Radek was a delegate just like the rest, and like the rest he had the right to express his opinion, a right considered at that time to be both necessary and legitimate. While the session was suspended, I ran into Zinoviev. 'Your friends think they're in parliament,' he said. 'They're a real nuisance with their procedural points.' 'But it's not my fault, and I can't do anything about it,' I replied, 'they don't consult me before they make fools of themselves.' The delegation seemed to have come with an exorbitant but detailed mandate with regard to the leadership of the International. And they feared that my participation in that leadership might prevent them penetrating the secrets of the International — if there were such secrets. I let them manoeuvre to their heart's content; the Congress of the Red International of Labour Unions was giving me enough worries and was quite enough to keep me busy.

When, later on, the Congress came on the real substance of the question, the German delegation submitted to the Congress and bitterly defended the thesis they had developed on the 'revolutionary offensive'. They argued that it was necessary to keep the masses on the alert, to fight the passivity that they were liable to let themselves slip into, by means of actions that were more or less imposed on them, but were repeated again and again. For Trotsky this was not a new thesis. It was the one Bela Kun had come to propound to him, and which he had vigorously rejected, as I have related in the preceding pages. But events revealed that it was not peculiar to Bela Kun, but had numerous supporters in almost all the sections of the International. It was defended heatedly and insistently by men like Thalheimer; the German Communist Party and the KAPD, rarely in agreement, were entirely united on this; it found support within the delegations of important sections — all these facts sufficed to prove that it was not just an improvised theory made up after the event to cover up for a failure and an outside intervention.[27]

The theses on tactics submitted to the Congress, on which Radek gave the report, recognised that the March Action had been a step forward by the Communist Party after its unification with the majority of the Independents. But they went on to insist on the necessity of basing actions on a serious study of the situation and of preparing them with scrupulous care. An offensive was not always and in all cases the correct tactic. The German delegation and their allies were not satisfied. They demanded that the Congress should recognise that the March Action had been a mass action forced on the working class by provocations from the employers and the

27. Moreover, Thalheimer remained faithful to Bela Kun, and several months after the Congress he had this note published in **Correspondance Internationale** (4 January 1922): 'At the Third Congress of the Communist International, the opinions of Bela Kun were severely criticised by Lenin. But to cut short all slanders about Bela Kun's personal character, Lenin felt he should end the discussion by recognising, explicitly and unreservedly, the personal integrity, courage and revolutionary devotion of Bela Kun and his friends. He did this in the commission.' Throughout the debates, Lenin had covered Bela Kun with sarcasm; expressions such as 'stupidity of Bela Kun', 'foolishness of Bela Kun' recurred time and time again.

government; that the Party had taken on the leadership of it and had fulfilled its rôle courageously; and that it had thereby demonstrated its capacity to guide the working class in its struggles all the way to revolution.

This is what Trotsky declared he could not concede to them. To establish that the necessary study of the situation had not been made seriously before the action, it was enough for him to draw on the contributions made by the supporters of the offensive. One of them had affirmed that in March the situation was clear and extremely acute. The reparations, the threatened occupation of the Ruhr, the question of Upper Silesia, the economic crisis and unemployment, the strikes, all these factors made it particularly favourable. For another of them, the situation was as confused as could be imagined: the workers were not interested in Upper Silesia, the unions were 'against us', the degree of passivity of the workers was unbelievable; hence it was necessary to shake them up with a revolutionary initiative. A third was in agreement as to the 'unbelievable passivity' and also in agreement with the conclusion the preceding speaker had drawn: 'we had to push forward at any price'.

Trotsky summed up: 'After all that, when you ask us here for total approval, when you ask us to give up any discussion or analysis of the facts, you must understand that we cannot concede that to you. Your primary concern is to be able to go back to Germany with a resolution which doesn't contain even the appearance of a criticism. You want the approval of the International to protect you from the mass of the Party. But the criticism emerges of its own accord from your own statements when, after speaking of a thick wall of passivity, of general stagnation, you proclaim: "Therefore let us go forward!" It is the duty of the Communist International to warn its sections against artificially provoked actions. The Congress must tell the German workers that a mistake has been made and that the Party's attempt to take the leading rôle in a great mass movement has not been successful.'

Trotsky also replied to the Italians who supported the tactic of the 'revolutionary offensive' by saying: 'Now we are free; we have got rid of the reformist leaders, and we can fulfil our tasks. We are in a position to launch mass actions.' He answered: 'The opportunists aren't the only problem in the world. You have excluded them from your ranks and that is a good thing. But there is still capitalist society, the police, the army, definite economic conditions, a whole complex world . . . one must combine the icy language of statistics with the passionate will of revolutionary violence.'

These basic truths were not very well received at the time, but they did not take long to establish themselves; and the fact that they had been insisted on bore fruit. In a study on **The Class Struggle in Germany during 1922** Thalheimer wrote about the March Action: 'Launched by the vanguard, it was only a skirmish, an anticipation of the battle which only the whole class is capable of joining. It ended with defeat and the momentary weakening of the vanguard elements. The majority of the working class was not yet ready . . . even in pursuit of immediate and well-defined aims. The wave of combativity continued to weaken. Capitalism and its agents in the working class wanted to take advantage of their victory. They sought to discredit and isolate the vanguard elements within the proletariat . . . they directed their offensive against the eight-hour day, wage-rates and the right to strike . . . The Communist Party, having recognised that the March Action was premature, pulled itself together and launched a new action.' (**Annuaire du Travail,** pp 363-364.)

The debate on the March Action, despite its great importance, was only an application of the theme Trotsky had developed in his major report on 'The World Economic Crisis and the New Tasks of the Communist International'. The analysis in depth he had carried out revealed clearly the characteristics of the present situation. 'Germany of 1921 bears no resemblance to Germany of 1918,' an acute observer of German affairs had remarked. In France, **Le Temps** could assert that 'the coming crises will be surmounted'. To conclude his analysis, Trotsky said: 'History has granted the bourgeoisie a breathing space . . . The triumph of the proletariat immediately after the war was a historical possibility, but it was not achieved . . . Basically, perspectives remain profoundly revolutionary. The situation is becoming more and more favourable for us, but it is also growing extremely complex. Victory will not come to us automatically. We must take advantage of this period of relative stabilisation to extend our influence in the working class, and to win a majority before we are confronted with decisive events.'

The advocates of the offensive made their criticisms in a very forceful manner. Germans, Hungarians, Poles and Italians alike, they showed the same juvenile but dangerous impatience, with such expressions as: 'we will make the revolution with sword in hand and not with statistics'; 'we don't need to show that the revolution is necessary but to make it'; 'since the NEP Soviet Russia is able to act as a safety valve for capitalism . . .' Thalheimer accused Trotsky of 'putting the revolutionary energy of the proletariat in cold storage'.[28]

Trotsky replied to each of them with explanations and further details, concluding in the same way as on the tactical question. In the course of his exposition, he had insisted on what was the principal fact, but which was then generally left unnoticed or denied, namely that America had now assumed a preponderant role in international relations. He stressed that it had taken over the place formerly occupied by Britain. 'The Dollar has become the "Sovereign" of the world financial market.'

★ On 7 July Lenin presented his report on 'The Internal Situation in Soviet Russia and the Tasks of the Russian Communist Party'. He had prepared for the Congress a pamphlet entitled **The Tax in Kind** in which he took up several of his articles written at different times. Some of them were devoted to the régime he described as 'state capitalism', which he said was a half-way house to a socialist régime. In spring 1918 he had written an important pamphlet on the same subject, called **The Chief Task of Our Day**, of which he recalled the significant passages:

'State capitalism would be a step forward as compared with the present state of affairs in our Soviet Republic . . . No one, I think, in

---

28. Two years later, Trotsky wrote about these discussions: 'It would not hurt to recall also the principal disagreement that appeared at the time of the Third Congress of the Communist International. It is now obvious that the change obtained at that time under the leadership of Lenin, in spite of the furious resistance of a considerable part — at the start, of a majority — of the Congress, literally saved the International from the destruction and decomposition with which it was threatened if it went the way of automatic, uncritical "leftism".' (**The New Course**, Ann Arbor 1965, p 48.)

studying the question of the economic system of Russia, has denied its transitional character. Nor, I think, has any communist denied that the term Soviet Socialist Republic implies the determination of the Soviet power to achieve the transition to socialism, and not that the existing economic system is recognised as a socialist order.

'But what does the word "transition" mean? Does it not mean, as applied to an economy, that the present system contains elements, particles, fragments of both capitalism and socialism? Everyone will admit that it does. But not all who admit this take the trouble to consider what elements actually constitute the various socio-economic structures that exist in Russia at the present time. And this is the crux of the question.

'Let us enumerate these elements:

1. patriarchal, i.e. to a considerable extent natural, peasant farming;
2. small commodity production (this includes the majority of those peasants who sell their grain);
3. private capitalism;
4. state capitalism;
5. socialism.

'Russia is so vast and varied that all these different types of socio-economic structures are intermingled. This is what constitutes the specific feature of the situation . . .

'State capitalism would be a gigantic step forward . . . because it is worth paying for "tuition", because it is useful for the workers, because victory over disorder, economic ruin and laxity is the most important thing, because the continuation of the anarchy of small ownership is the greatest, the most serious danger, and it will *certainly* be our ruin . . . whereas not only will the payment of a heavier tribute to state capitalism not ruin us, it will lead us to socialism by the surest road . . .

'In the first place *economically* state capitalism is immeasurably superior to our present economic system.

'In the second place there is nothing terrible in it for the Soviet power, for the Soviet state is a state in which the power of the workers and the poor is assured . . .

'To make things even clearer, let us first of all take the most concrete example of state capitalism. Everybody knows what this example is. It is Germany. Here we have "the last word" in modern large-scale capitalist engineering and planned organisation, *subordinated to Junker-bourgeois imperialism*. Cross out the words in italics, and in place of the militarist, Junker, bourgeois, imperialist state put also a state, but of a different social type, of a different class content — a Soviet state, that is, a proletarian state, and you will have the sum total of the conditions necessary for socialism.'

Lenin would not have dreamt of denying that the NEP was a retreat, but it was a retreat which brought Russia back on to the road she would have taken as a deliberate decision if the civil war had not forced her to submit to various measures which constituted what was called 'war communism'. The delegates had had the opportunity of becoming familiar with these definitions and explanations. Lenin therefore needed only to stress the principles on which the working out of the tasks of the Communist Party had been based. 'We have always considered,' he said, 'that our revolution was a forerunner in Europe. We counted on world revolution, and so we envisaged our historical task as being the preparation of this revolution. But the consciousness of the revolutionary masses did not come up to the level of this hope, and so it was unable to unleash revolution elsewhere; yet in the end it proved strong enough to prevent the bourgeoisie from attacking us.

'Already there are some lessons to be drawn from our experiences. They have demonstrated that the peasants, by their very essence, can exist only under the leadership of the bourgeoisie or of the proletariat. The alliance that the proletariat has contracted with the peasants is purely military in nature. The peasants support the workers above all because, behind the Whites, they can see the old landlords anxious to take back their estates. The proletariat has given the land to the peasants, because even where the peasants had driven out the landlords and occupied the land at the beginning of the Revolution, it was only because of the October rising that they were able to keep what their spontaneous risings had given them. But in return the peasants had to provide food supplies for the towns; that was the requisition. With the end of the civil war, a new situation emerged with new tasks. The New Economic Policy has been elaborated in order to fulfil them.'

Replying to the criticisms expressed by several delegates, Lenin dealt in particular with Terracini, who had juxtaposed the formula of 'winning the majority of the working class', to the rôle of active minorities, and had taken up the thesis of the 'offensivists' in favour of the endless repetition of actions. 'The Congress,' he said, 'must wage a vigorous offensive against such "leftist" stupidities. Terracini says that we Bolsheviks were not very numerous in October. That is true, but we had won the majority of the Soviets of Workers' and Peasants' Deputies, and at least half the army was with us. The necessary precondition of our victory was ten million armed workers and peasants.'

Alexandra Kollontai had presented the usual criticism made by the Workers' Opposition: too much importance was being given to technicians at the expense of the initiative and capacities of the working class. It was Trotsky who replied to her. Lenin had asked him to so as to indicate their complete agreement on this question as well as on those the Congress had already discussed. 'From the principled standpoint,' he said, 'it is undeniable that more than ample power and initiative are inherent in the proletariat and we hope that all mankind will considerably change its aspects thanks to the power of the working class. But we never claimed that the working class is from its birth capable of building a new society. It can only create all the necessary social and political preconditions for it. More than this, through the direct seizure of power it is enabled to find all the necessary auxiliary forces.'

A long report on 'the Structure, Methods and Action of the Communist Parties', presented by the German Koenen, was discussed amid the apathy normal at the end of congresses. The aim was to give very detailed instructions to assist the young communist parties in their difficult task. They had many devoted members and the rank and file were impelled by deep and sincere revolutionary feelings. However, the inadequate number of cadres and their inexperience prevented them from making the best use of the forces at their disposal. But the presenter of the report confined himself to proposing a simple slavish imitation of the Russian Communist Party. This was a lazy answer, evading the real difficulties and papering over real problems. The results were bound to be harmful, and Lenin condemned it at the next Congress.

★ Those delegates who had taken part in the preceding Congress could not help making a worrying observation. There was not much left of the revolutionary fervour which had been the dominant feature of the Second Congress. Zinoviev had wanted large delegations, and in these delegations there had been journalists, teachers and writers, some of whom said openly that they were not communists, and they they had come only in order to study some particular branch of Soviet activity. The differences which had emerged over tactics, the serious failures in Poland, Italy and Germany, encouraged among them a sort of dilettantish attitude, which was expressed in remarks and observations in a remote, condescending tone. This helped to create an atmosphere of easy-going scepticism. These people ran no risk of being carried away by revolutionary passion.

4: The Red International of Labour Unions holds its founding Congress

For reasons of a different kind, the Congress of the Red International of Labour Unions was held in unfavourable conditions. The preparatory work over the previous year had aimed at achieving the programme settled at the time of the setting up of the Provisional International Council — namely, to unite in the same International both those union bodies which were already in a position to affiliate as a whole, and minorities which had been established within reformist unions on the basis of the principle of affiliation. The constant progress of these minorities, which had continued to grow in numbers and influence, encouraged us to hope that they would soon be capable of overcoming the resistance of the reformist leaders and bringing the whole organisation into the new trade union International.

But things worked out quite differently. Soon after the Second Congress of the Communist International, Pestaña, delegate from the CNT (Spanish National Confederation of Labour), and Armando Borghi, secretary of the Italian *Unione Sindacale*, broke from the Third International. Their criticisms of the Soviet régime became increasingly harsh. But these two organisations had voted for affiliation to the Third International, and without them and the revolutionary syndicalist elements they represented, there would be an important gap. And that was not all. Inevitably the attitude of Pestaña and Borghi had serious repercussions in syndicalist circles everywhere, notably in France. The question of the relations between the Communist International and the Red International of Labour Unions, and that of the relations between party and unions came to the fore.

Nothing but this was discussed now, and it was discussed interminably, as though it was a question of knowing which, party or unions, would dictate to the other. Yet already before the war, in France for example, the CGT had agreed to meet the Socialist Party, and to organise great national and international demonstrations jointly with it in face of the threat of war. During the war friendly contacts had been established spontaneously between the socialist and syndicalist minorities, and including the anarchists too, when the CGT and the Socialist Party leaderships had lined up with the government's war policy. There had been the Zimmerwald Conference, then the Committee for the Resumption of International Relations, which had brought socialists, syndicalists and anarchists together in joint work on a common programme. We therefore seemed to be justified in thinking that if this question of the relations between unions and political parties still presented difficulties, it would be possible to overcome them.

Contrary to these optimistic forecasts, the question was presented in a very unfortunate manner. In the course of the discussions and controversies, the expression 'organic link' between the two Internationals had emerged, and this formulation became the pivot of the polemics. In France, the so-called 'pure syndicalists' attributed to this the meaning of a subordination of the unions to the party, something absolutely unacceptable to revolutionary syndicalists. They happened at this time to be in the leadership of the CGT minority, and for the Congress they constituted a delegation where the various tendencies of the minority were represented, but which set out with a formal mandate to oppose any proposal calling for the 'organic link'.

On the agenda we had fixed for the Congress, the question of the relations between the two Internationals had been given an important position. Zinoviev was due to give the report, and I was to give an associated report. Although we would not have differed in our main conclusions, we would have approached the question in different ways. I felt that people talked too much, and not always intelligently, about 'syndicalist prejudices', and I intended to recall that these 'prejudices' had not stopped syndicalists being in the front line of the resistance to the war and of the defence of the October Revolution. At the last minute we had to change our plans. Zinoviev, who had been so imperceptive when the Kronstadt rising had broken out at the very gates of Petrograd, had likewise failed to understand developments in syndicalist circles. Only just before the Congress did he notice that there wasn't much affection for him there; rightly or wrongly the syndicalists didn't like him. As a result he decided to abandon his report and to withdraw from the Congress.

Lozovsky communicated this decision to me, saying: 'Instead of two reports there will be one only, yours.' I replied that that was impossible, for at one blow it would ruin my personal work, and make vain the efforts I was intending to make to reach a reconciliation of opinions which were not all that divergent, and which in any case ought not to prevent coexistence within the same International. We should be able to find a basis for collaboration between men who had come from different political traditions, but were equally devoted to the Revolution and to communism. But Lozovsky insisted, and brought me to see Tom Mann and Trotsky, whom he had already informed. The three seemed to be competing as to who could insist the most strongly. I had to submit.

The French delegation seemed determined to make my job more difficult. Among its members were some excellent friends of mine, who were fully in agreement with my position and the views I wanted to defend. But they were not in a majority, and though they were the most qualified they did not make the most noise. The others, putting their confidence in what they considered to be the imperative mandate of the delegation, chose as their spokesmen a versatile and whimsical anarchist and a man, hitherto unknown, who was a self-appointed theoretician of revolutionary syndicalism. They too began by raising a point of procedure; they wanted the problem of the relations between the two Internationals to be discussed first at the Congress of the Communist International. A strange attitude from men who claimed to want to know nothing about political parties. As their demands were overruled, they withdrew. They repeated the scene the French Party delegation had just enacted at the Congress of the Communist International. It must be a French idiosyncrasy! Really it was something quite different, but I myself only discovered this later on; I shall discuss it below.[29]

The vast majority of the Congress was beginning to find the French quite unbearable. When these 'pure syndicalists' wanted to present themselves as mentors, to teach the delegates a lesson and give a learned formulation of the true principles of trade-union action, the Congress became angry. 'You're always talking about the general strike,' they shouted, 'but you never make it. It's us who do that.' They had no answer to that. In the turbulent post-war period the French had to their credit only two big railway strikes, the second of which was to spark off a general strike in solidarity which Jouhaux and the CGT leadership had been able to sabotage without difficulty. And on the debit side of the account was the shameful capitulation of 21 July 1919.[30] Those former social democrats who had retained a certain hostility towards the syndicalists were aroused by what they called the intolerable attitude of the French. One of them, the Bulgarian Dimitrov — who was in Moscow for the first time, and participating in his first Congress — quite simply demanded that they be excluded from the Congress.

In contrast, the Spanish syndicalist delegation was a great consolation to me. It had four members, young, eager and enthusiastic, very likeable on a personal level. Nin and Maurin came from Catalonia, Arlandis from Valencia and Jesus Ibañez from Biscay. They had a mandate from the CNT. Pestaña had been arrested in

29. See below pages 198-9.
30. On this date an international action by workers against the Allied policy of intervention and support to the counter-revolutionary generals was due to take place. In France and Italy a general strike was planned. In face of threats from Clemenceau, Jouhaux and the CGT the leadership capitulated. The Italians were left on their own, but their strike call was followed throughout the country. Serrati never failed to remind the French of this when they criticised him.

Italy and had not returned to Spain. The CNT was sending this delegation but was reserving its decision, and would make a definitive decision only after the Congress, on the basis of the delegates' report. I was pleasantly surprised to learn that they shared my position, the one I had defended to the Congress. Only Arlandis, who was easily influenced, sometimes let himself be persuaded by the 'pure syndicalists' and caused us some anxiety. He ended up a Party member and a Stalinist — just as Pestaña finished up as leader of a 'syndicalist party' which he had founded himself. The anarchists had added a fifth member, G Leval, to the delegation. We didn't see much of him, for he left the other delegates immediately to unite with the opponents of affiliation.

Lozovsky submitted to me the text of the resolution which was to be the conclusion of these wretched debates. It had already been signed by all the members of the Bureau, including Tom Mann. One of the paragraphs called for the 'organic link' between political parties and unions. It was a response to the irritating attitude of the 'pure syndicalists' of the French delegation. In other circumstances I would certainly have managed to get a more flexible text accepted, for this one might seem uselessly and dangerously provocative. It gave Jouhaux and the other reformist leaders a weapon against the minority which they would not fail to use. This was perfectly clear to me and my friends, but the only concession I could get was that the organic link was not made absolutely obligatory, but was merely recommended as 'highly desirable'.

Despite this tiresome debate and the time it wasted, the Congress was able to complete its agenda and to do some useful work. It drew up an overall programme and studied in depth the question of tactics in the dual struggle — firstly, the defence against the capitalist offensive, for the bourgeoisie was trying to take back the reforms granted in face of the threat of revolution; secondly, the necessary action to thwart the reformist leaders' desire to split. In some countries unemployment was taking on a new aspect by being at an exceptionally high level and was tending to become permanent. Great masses of workers could no longer get employment in their industries, and it was vital to maintain through the work of the trade unions the links they had with their comrades still at work.

★ Earl Browder, then an associate of William Foster in the Trade Union Educational League, was sent to Moscow to represent the League at the Congress. He arrived some weeks before it opened, and so was able to take part in the preparatory meetings where the delegates compared their points of view. I didn't know him, but I knew Foster well. An active militant in the IWW, he had come to France to study the revolutionary syndicalist movement to which the IWW was allied. He had become friendly with the CGT leaders, particularly Pierre Monatte who also helped him to pick up a bit of French. What he saw and learned in France led him to modify his ideas on tactics. He became convinced that the activity and devotion expended on the IWW organisations would be used more profitably for the working class in the unions of the American Federation of Labour, whose reformism could be combatted more effectively from inside than from outside. This was the position he advocated on his return to America.

In these small meetings, Browder's attitude surprised me. He never spoke except to express his complete approval, in as few words as possible, of Lozovsky's opinions. Yet these were not the opinions of his League, which supported revolutionary syndicalism. I pointed this out to him several times, hoping to provoke a discussion; but all in vain. He clearly wanted to confine himself to these expressions of approval which he didn't even take the trouble to give reasons for. I understood later that Foster had sent him on in advance to prepare the ground. Foster's recent past was an eventful one. During the war he had become a supporter of the Allies, had made propaganda for American entry into the war, and had sold 'Liberty bonds'. After the war, with the assistance of the AFL, he had organised a great steelworkers' strike. In the metal industry the employers were then all-powerful. Not only did they succeed in overcoming the workers' resistance, but they had legal action instituted against the 'ringleaders' of the strike. Foster had been acquitted, but his attitude in face of the judges had been so unsteady that it had aroused the mockery of the reformist leaders. He came to Moscow only several weeks after the Congress, and his visit was notable for its discretion . . . in the course of time, Foster and the man whom American militants called his 'office boy' were each to replace the other as leaders of the Communist Party of America.

One of my friends in the French delegation was Victor Godonnèche. He had been one of the first to join the Committee for the Third International, and he had taken over the secretaryship when Pierre Monatte was imprisoned for 'conspiracy'. After the split in the trade unions, he was assistant secretary of the Printers' Federation of the Confédération Générale du Travail Unitaire. One afternoon when he had come to the Kremlin on his own he suddenly heard a voice asking him: 'French?' It was Lenin hurrying after him, wanting to start a conversation. The discussion continued as far as the congress hall, where, before entering, Lenin held Godonnèche back for a moment to ask him about the labour movement, to enquire what he thought of the Congress, and what his impressions were. Godonnèche came to tell me about what he thought was an extraordinary adventure. Lenin's simplicity, his cordial manner, the fact that the conversation had been started and continued as if between two friends who usually gossiped when they happened to meet, all that had made a striking impression on him. For 'old Muscovites' there was nothing unusual about it, but I could appreciate my friend's feelings when he told me his story. I got him to write it down, and I would have quoted it here, for I kept it, never having had the opportunity to publish it. But it was destroyed during the war, by the occupying forces, along with many other things.

5: Balance-sheet of seventeen months in Russia

When the congresses were over, most of the delegates did not hurry away; in particular those who were merely sympathetic or curious found life in Moscow of great interest. They discussed the debates and decisions of the congresses in a detached manner, as mere spectators. They made gentle fun of Zinoviev's falsetto voice; the leaders had disappointed them, especially Lenin, who, in his dress and his eloquence, was so different from the type of 'Russian revolutionary' they had been able to meet in the West and whom they would have liked to find in Moscow. But they had to go. When the special congress menu gave way to the standard diet, there was a sudden rush at the office which arranged outward journeys.

★   I extended my stay somewhat. During these seventeen months I had accumulatd a quantity of notes and documents which I had to put in order, and I also had to wait for Marchand to finish his translations of the diplomatic dispatches and reports which were then to be taken into France. On the afternoon of the day fixed for our departure, Trotsky came to the Hotel Lux. He had planned to be at the station to see the train leave, but that evening there was to be an important meeting of the Council of People's Commissars which he could not really get away from. I was quite insistent that he shouldn't put himself out in any case. None the less I wasn't too surprised when, at the station, someone announced that he was there. Among other things, he asked me to give his greetings to Pierre Monatte — he greatly regretted that he had not come to the Congress — and to all those he had worked with in Paris, during the war, on the Committee for the Resumption of International Relations. The attitude of the French delegation at the Congress of the Red International of Labour Unions had annoyed him. The syndicalist minority of the CGT had published a statement in Paris, renouncing for the present advocating affiliation to the Red International of Labour Unions as a result of the decision on 'organic links'; it was signed not only by pro-communist syndicalists but also by members of the Communist Party. In his view this was a grave error on the part of the former, and worrying attitude on the part of the latter. But all this in no way shook his confidence in the French proletariat.

The train took us as far as Reval where we boarded a pleasant little boat which was to take us to Stettin. There were about ten of us delegates. After the austerity of Moscow, we enjoyed great luxury; the cabins were comfortable, there was plenty of food, with a varied menu and some rare items. The sea was calm and the boat slid gently across it; we were relaxing in this peaceful setting when a gloomy rumour began to spread: 'We've been spotted!' We clustered in tiny groups to discuss, wondering what we should do, what measures could be taken. If we were going to be arrested at Stettin, then we should make preparations immediately. One among us, a Pole, was particularly worried. He was like a smaller version of Radek. Suddenly he lost his temper as if he had found the cure for his worries and the key to his misfortune: 'It's Trotsky's fault again,' he said, turning towards me; 'what did he need to come to the station for?' I could only hang my head, for I was responsible . . . In fact our anxiety did not last long. We continued eating well and rapidly regained our good humour, except for the unfortunate Pole . . . And we landed at Stettin without let or hindrance. But who had alarmed us for his own amusement? There was a Communist International courier travelling with us. I knew him; he was a man who enjoyed life, did his job well and was something of a sceptic. Now among the Russians the 'delegates' were far from popular. There were for this reasons both general — the passivity of the Western proletariats leaving the Russian communists isolated — and particular — the incredible demands of certain delegates. It was easy to see that our courier had enjoyed himself at our expense.

6: Return to Paris — a different world

I had returned to France in October 1921. As early as February 1922 I was recalled to Moscow to take part in an extended Executive Committee meeting of great importance, to discuss the tactic of the 'united front'. I had had only just enough time to observe that the situation in France was even worse than I had imagined. After a long stay at the very heart of the Revolution, I found myself in a country where the revolutionary spirit, so strong at the end of the war, had been greatly dampened down. On all sides there were reservations and a passivity which held back the thrust towards communism. Strange to say, it was in the leadership of the syndicalist minority that I found the most loathsome 'politicians', in the derogatory sense that they themselves gave to the word. They wrote and chattered interminably about the correct way of making the revolution — for to them October was not a true revolution. They constructed the communist society in words alone, but behind the mask of a sickening hypocrisy. And while they chattered in a complacent and self-satisfied way, the CGT leadership was preparing to split.

In the Communist Party and on **L'Humanité** most of the leaders and editorial staff had remained in the Party out of self-interest rather than conviction. They complained — in private —

about 'Moscow', finding its calls unacceptable. They cheated the Communist International instead of having things out in an open manner. Of the twenty-one conditions of admission to the International and the various decisions of the Second Congress, the ones that had been most willingly acepted were those dealing with participation in elections and parliamentary activity. A parliamentary seat was desired, not as a combat position, as much in the front line as any other, but because it was a comfortable position with many advantages. All too often the old Socialist Party was simply continuing under a new name. They plotted in corners when they knew they were among cronies and could speak their mind. They strove to find ingenious ways of 'seeming' to be in agreement with the decisions of the Communist International. Here too hypocrisy was normal currency. For the mass of the membership remained attached to the Russian Revolution and the Communist International. They stood up to the endless criticisms made of these by the agents of the counter-revolution, the bourgeois press and the reformist leaders of the CGT. Mensheviks and Social-Revolutionaries now settled in Paris did their best, through mutilated and faked information, to turn them away from the Soviets. But criticisms, accounts of events and insinuations coming from syndicalists and anarchists disturbed and worried them.[31]

31. Even in February 1922, you could read in **Le Populaire**, the daily paper of the Socialist Party, edited by Léon Blum and Jean Longuet, an article headed 'Trotsky excommunicated by his father', in which, giving a full ration of stupidity, the writer concluded with the remark: 'Moreover, Trotsky has abandoned the Jewish religion by marrying a Russian woman.'

1922

1: Return to Moscow; the United Front; Shlyapnikov and Cachin

THE THIRD CONGRESS of the Communist International had given the communist parties the slogan 'Go to the masses', in order to win the majority of the working class. It was thus hoped to forestall the danger that the communist parties would turn in on themselves in a sectarian way, and to warn them against ill-prepared actions. 'Moscow', which was often accused of failing to recognise certain features of the policy of the democratic nations, was better informed, followed more closely and understood better the fundamental and secondary changes which affected the world situation and the situation in each country. Early in 1922, it was observed that revolutionary possibilities had become more remote. A certain hesitancy was obvious among the workers, whereas the bourgeoisie, virtually moribund at the end of the war, had gained sufficient self-confidence to attack, and was already doing so with some success. The appropriate tactics required a stress on the workers' immediate demands; this would mean that the communist parties need not fear being isolated among the working class. Quite the opposite, it would enable them to regroup the great majority of workers on their programme.

The Congress had given only some general indications as to the application of these tactics, and they risked being misunderstood or neglected altogether. Anxious to have a practical result from the decisions of the Third Congress, Lenin considered it was necessary to indicate in detail the form of their application. He called the new tactic the 'united front of the proletariat'. Henceforth the bourgeois offensive would come up against the whole body of the workers, hitherto dispersed by political and trade-union splits.

The tactic of the united front was adopted by the Executive Committee of the Communist International at its session of 4 December 1921. Zinoviev explained and defended it in an important speech, but it was Radek who gave an excellent exposition of the meaning and origin of the tactic in an article which he wrote at the time:

'Shortly after the Congress of Halle, which led to the split in the Independent Socialist Party and the formation of a united German Communist Party, the latter addressed an "Open Letter" to the two Social Democratic Parties and to the central trade-union body, inviting them to common action in defence of the immediate interests of the working class. Most of the members of the Communist Party found these tactics excellent, but some Party militants, and even militants of the Communist International, were shocked. "What! After splitting, after calling these men traitors to the proletariat, we should propose common action to them!" They were no less shocked by the demands formulated in the "Open Letter'. There was not a word about the dictatorship of the proletariat. It was written in a moderate and reasonable tone, avoiding any propagandist type of exaggeration . . . In the face of the employers' offensive, the masses considered any new split as a crime. The communists had to come closer to them. But how? By affirming the necessity for the dictatorship of the proletariat? But was it not the case that many workers remained in the Social Democratic Parties just because they still put their trust in the old methods? So the only way to approach these non-communist masses was to start from their present sufferings and to support them in their short-term demands.

'By taking on this task the Communist Party would demonstrate more effectively than it had been able to do hitherto, the necessity for fighting for the dictatorship of the proletariat. In view of the present disintegration of the capitalist régime, the launching of action by the broad masses for wage increases in order to partially make up for the endless rise in the cost of living would finally bring out the irreconcilable antagonisms between the proletariat and bourgeois democracy, showing the urgent need for much more vigorous demands, for example workers' control of production. At the same time it would compel the social democratic and trade-union leaders to move to the left for fear of revealing their bankruptcy. And this would not be over the question of the dictatorship of the proletariat, where it would not be difficult to play on ambiguities, but over the question of daily bread and working hours, much clearer in workers' minds.

'The bitter resistance of the social democratic and trade-union leaders to the German Communist Party's tactic was the best proof of its correctness. It is true that the Communist Party was confining itself to proposing an action on the basis of the most immediate demands. Far from being decreased thereby, the Party's power of attraction was visibly increased. The Social Democrats managed to ward off the first blow, but the Party extended and consolidated its positions in the trade unions. Its "Open Letter" overcame the damage caused by mistakes during the March Action . . . Like any tactical turn by a great party, this one was not born out of the theoretical meditations of a few men. When the central committee of the Party proposed it to a meeting of representatives from the branches, it turned out that a considerable number of provincial bodies were already working in this direction. The tactic was born from the practical needs of the German movement. It was soon recognised that it also fitted the needs of other countries.'

This long quotation was necessary. It is valuable because it gives a precise description of the meaning of a tactic which was to be fully discussed later, for months on end. We need merely note here that it had nothing in common with the 'Popular Front', a Stalinist invention of much later on, nor with Dimitrov's 'Trojan horse' (an invention of the same brand), simply a device for infiltrating among the enemy. The united front presents itself openly and honestly for what it is: namely, a means of grouping the working class starting from its short-term demands, but without concealing the final goal of socialist revolution, towards which the tactic will lead by means of the normal development of the movement, by arousing the class's self-confidence and faith in revolution. If it was a threat to reformist leaders, it was only to those of them who had finally gone over to collaboration with the bourgeoisie, those who today wanted to confine the action of the working class to the framework of the existing régime and of the unviable Europe of the Treaty of Versailles, after having accepted the division of workers into allies and enemies during the war. The united front would help to unmask these, but this would be only a secondary and subordinate result of the tactic.

The united front tactic got a very poor reception from the leaders of the social democratic parties and those of the reformist unions. Sometimes they denounced it as a retreat by the Communist International, and hence as a confession of weakness; sometimes they denounced it as a manoeuvre. But it was always with the same acrimony. Their hostility came as no surprise. What was more surprising was the response given by the communist parties to the International's appeal. Besides its intrinsic value, the tactic also had an important but unforeseen effect inside the International itself. It was an acid test which tore away the façades and revealed the true state of the communist parties, and more particularly of their leaderships.

To what extent were these new parties, formed in different ways and scarcely two years old, really sections of an International, component parts of one big party, with the same programme and identical activity?

Much stress had been put on the distinctive character of the new International. It was a highly centralised party, which discussed its problems at congresses which met every year, or oftener if necessary, where the debates were free and extensive, but where decisions taken were binding on all. It had nothing in common with the Second International where every party remained free to act as it pleased. The scorn felt for that traitors' International seemed to suggest that all who came to the Third International were in agreement on this basic idea. As soon as the tactic of the united front was presented to the communist parties, it revealed that this was far from being the case.

It provoked a broad spectrum of responses, going from approval with reservations (the tactic was inopportune) to outright rejection. In the latter case it was denounced as a retreat and a repudiation of communism. In Germany, where it had been first applied, where the Party had a good working-class base, and where the influence of the Spartacists, of Rosa Luxemburg and Karl Liebknecht still survived, it developed without too many obstacles. None the less it aroused an active and voluble opposition, especially in Berlin, which made itself heard outside Germany.

The most novel position towards the united front was that of the Italian Communist Party. Its origins were also novel, different from those of the other communist parties; it had not been shaped in the same mould. None of the former leaders of the Socialist Party were in its leadership, which was entirely in the hands of the Bordigists, or at any rate clearly dominated by them. Quite unencumbered by any right or centre tendency, Bordiga and the communists around him put their own stamp on the programme, and activity of the Party. They were young, well-educated and brilliant, but above or marginal to the labour movement. For them the communist party constituted the shock-troops of the revolution, and its leadership was the great general staff. So they thought they could easily respond to the appeal of the International. 'A united front in the unions? We have nothing against that; contacts can be made between communists and reformist trade-union leaders concerning common action for their demands. But for the Party nothing of the sort. It must jealously safeguard its revolutionary purity, and cannot involve itself with the old socialist leaders it has got rid of.'

It was inside the French Communist Party that the greatest stir was created. The united front caused a crisis in the Party. Almost the whole leadership declared that it was unacceptable, and saw it as an opportunity to stand up openly against the leadership of the Communist International. The Party which was indisputably the least communist showed itself to be the most demanding. An examination of the composition of its leadership made it easy to see what was behind this paradox. It consisted mainly of journalists and deputies, several of them from the old Socialist Party, and its links with the trade-union movement were weak. The most sincere were much given to phrase-mongering, and most of its members found it hard to put up with the criticisms of the Communist International. They thought that the tactic would give them an easy revenge, for in the debate it would be they who were denouncing the 'opportunism' and inconsistency of the leadership of the Communist International. The Party press overacted enormously. There was no honest exposition of the tactic, but criticisms of every kind, ironic or indignant. The central committee met to discuss the question. The resolution which was adopted did not merely declare that it was 'impossible' to apply the tactic in France, but 'considered' that it presented to the International 'dangers against which safeguards would have to be taken'. Thus assured of substantial approval, the Party secretary, Frossard, convened an extraordinary conference of federal secretaries, which was held in Paris on 22 January 1922.

There was in the Party a left-wing tendency, composed mainly of new recruits, which was sincerely attached and devoted to the Russian Revolution. It was this tendency which had enforced affiliation to the Communist International, and it was always ready to approve its decisions, but this time it did so without enthusiasm. None the less one of its members came to the rostrum to defend the tactic which, one after another, the federal secretaries were condemning (46) or approving feebly (12). But he did it in such a way that his intervention was a catastrophe pure and simple. He was the one who on this occasion launched an expression destined to become famous — 'plucking the chickens'. He couldn't understand why the united front was arousing such feelings, and he went on to explain that it was no more than a subtle manoeuvre which made it possible to strip the Socialist Parties and the reformist unions of their members who would be taken one by one like the feathers from a chicken. As may be imagined, the 'chickens' thus warned became excited, jeered and shouted, to the great joy of the gallery and the consternation of the frank 'plucker'.

In face of this disorder provoked by genuine or pretended misunderstanding, a general discussion was necessary. The leadership of the Communist International had decided in advance to convene an extended Executive Committee. These extended committees which became a regular practice were, in fact, small-scale congresses. To the regular members of the Executive Committee were added delegations sent specially by the sections, making a total of about a hundred participants. This one took place from 21 February to 4 March 1922, in the Kremlin, in the Mitrofanovsky Hall, where, in March 1919, the First Congress, which had proclaimed the International, had met. The debates were very interesting, for their setting and character ruled out all rhetoric and all gossip. You had to be precise and capable of advancing serious arguments to justify the positions that had been taken up, the interpretations that had been formulated and above all the accusations that had been made. The French, who had been particularly aggressive, were not slow to notice this. Those among them who were most willing for a reconciliation, at least formally, put forward the thesis that for France the united front tactic had no point. They claimed that the 'dissidents' — i.e. those who had left the Party after the vote of affiliation to the Third International — were now only a tiny group. All that they had managed to take with them was the great bulk of the members of parliament; their paper had only a very low circulation, 'whereas we, with **L'Humanité**, touch the whole working class'. The same was true in the unions; the split, desired by the reformist leaders, had been fatal to them.

There was some truth in these claims, but the picture was still much too optimistic. The split in the unions, which had become final at the beginning of the year, had revealed amply that Jouhaux and his friends had remained in the leadership of the CGT only by means of manoeuvres and deceptions. The forces they had kept were small, but not completely negligible. And the unity of the proletarian front was no less necessary, since it would also make it possible to bring back to the unions and into action those workers who, out of impatience and discouragement, had left the unions altogether. Already these amounted to more than a million.

Those who remained obstinate formed a strange group who presented an inconsistent and mainly verbal leftism. They were very embarrassed when Trotsky — who had been appointed to give the report — showed, by means of quotations from their articles, written in Paris but which they had not dared to lay claim to in Moscow, that their so-called revolutionary intransigence revealed nothing but their remoteness — whether voluntary or involuntary — from the labour movement, a false interpretation of the proposed tactic, and a fundamental hostility towards the Communist International.

The Italians provided them with support they could not have expected, for their position, as we have seen, was quite a different one. They for their part never complained of 'dictatorship from Moscow'; they would more probably have wanted it to be strengthened. Bordiga had not come. It was Togliatti — then under the name of Ercoli — who was leading the delegation. He had doubtless received formal instructions, for he stood up to attacks from all sides. The Russian delegation put Lunacharsky up against him. He had never yet intervened in the congresses of the Communist International, but he spoke Italian fluently, and so was able to speak to the Italians in their own language. Ercoli remained unmoved, and even agreed, at the end of the debates, to sign a joint statement with the French.

The resolution adopted by the Committee noted that the debates had shown that the united front tactic in no way meant a relaxation of opposition to reformism; it rather continued and developed the tactic worked out at the Third Congress of the Communist International, and provided a detailed application of its slogan 'Go to the masses'. The bureau of the Committee was made responsible for deciding, in collaboration with the delegations, 'the practical measures which should be taken immediately in the various countries to apply the tactic, which, needless to say, must be adapted to the situation in each particular country'.

The minority issued a statement, the Italians and French being joined by the Spanish (the party delegates from Madrid, though they, unlike the French, could hardly claim to be faced with only the skeletons of unions and a socialist party). The minority accepted the majority decision, ending up with these words: 'You may be assured that, in this instance as in every other, we remain disciplined and faithful to the resolutions of the Third International.'

★   The Executive Committee did not confine itself to the discussion of this tactical question. Its agenda contained several other matters, and it also had to deal with an internal question of the Russian Communist Party. A letter signed by 22 members of the Workers' Opposition referred to it the situation imposed on their tendency. They wrote that they had decided to turn to the Executive Committee of the Communist International precisely because the question of the united front was to be discussed there, adding: 'Supporters of the united front as interpreted in the theses of the Communist International, we appeal to you in the sincere desire of putting an end to all obstacles to the unity of this front within the Russian Communist Party . . . The joint forces of the Party and union bureaucracies are abusing their power and disregarding the decisions of our congresses which require the principles of workers' democracy to be put into practice. Our fractions in the unions and even in the congresses are deprived of the right to express their will in the election of the central committee . . . Such methods lead to careerism and servility.' Among the signatories were some very old members of the Party — two had been members since 1892 and almost all before 1914.

The letter was passed on for study and investigation to a commission in which Clara Zetkin, Cachin and Terracini took part. In a unanimous resolution, they declared that they could not 'consider the grievances of the 22 comrades to have any basis. The leadership of the Russian Communist Party has never been unaware of the dangers they point out, and the best way to fight them is to continue to act as disciplined militants within the Party.' Cachin was appointed to report back to the Committee. It was far from a happy choice; no one was less qualified than he to reprimand and advise old Russian revolutionaries. He was well known for his dealings with Mussolini at the beginning of the first world war, for his squalid chauvinism, his attacks on Bolshevism and his remarkable tendency to swim with the stream. Shlyapnikov, who had lived and worked in France, saw this choice as adding insult to injury. Leaving the committee with me, he said angrily: 'You couldn't find anyone better than that wretch to condemn us!'

★   Three years of imperialist war and three years of civil war had produced an accumulation of ruins. Soviet Russia had only just been able to start on the reconstruction of a devastated country, by mustering her resources to organise a peace-time economy, when a new calamity befell her. An exceptional drought had started in the springtime and continued throughout the summer, destroying the harvests. A merciless sun burned up all vegetation. At any time the consequences of such a scourge would have been terrible, but coming after six years of destruction it was an enormous disaster. Whole regions were ravaged by famine. This was not a new thing in Russia — famine had raged more than once in Tsarist Russia, most recently in 1891. But that did not stop the enemies of the Soviets making the Bolsheviks responsible. And this, moreover, gave them an argument for remaining deaf to the appeals that Soviet Russia addressed to the whole world, asking assistance from all who still had a sense of human solidarity. These were not in the majority. Those who had relied on armed intervention to overthrow the régime and had failed now rejoiced; they saw the famine as a belated ally which would bring them their revenge.

Even among those who were not blinded by hate and were simply waiting for the moment when the Soviets would be forced to deal with the West on its own terms, there was open talk of 'the death agony of Russia'. Thus **Europe Nouvelle** published a major article under the headline: 'The West Confronted with the Death Agony of Russia'. The author, having affirmed that the Western world wanted to overcome the famine, added: 'An overall plan must be drawn up. The West would have to go to Russia as an explorer goes to the depths of the colonies, with railway apparatus, medical teams and light equipment. Only then would its work be lasting. And, of course, guarantees will have to be given.'

In plain language, that meant colonising Russia. But these people were in too much of a hurry. Soviet Russia was cruelly wounded but it was not in its death agony. It had already passed through hard trials; this one was more painful than those that had preceded it, and it emerged with the flesh of its children mutilated.

2: World economic crisis. Lloyd George proposes a Conference. Cannes.

Soviet Russia had its internal difficulties. The Communist International was not being built without obstacles — all this was only to be expected. But in these first years of peace, the great powers didn't have a smooth road ahead of them either. After the short period of artificial prosperity which had followed the end of hostilities for the Allies, an economic crisis was developing, more or less severe according to the country concerned. The new Europe as created by the peace treaties offered France the possibility of once again becoming the great power on the Continent. The possession of iron ore in Lorraine allowed her to impose her own conditions on Germany in order to obtain the necessary coal from the Ruhr. The Little Entente (Czechoslovakia, Yugoslavia and Rumania) and Poland guaranteed her security by blockading an amputated Germany. At the same time, because of these countries, her political and economic hegemony in Central Europe and the Balkans was undisputed.

But the French bourgeoisie was no longer of the stature to take on such a rôle. Perhaps the bloodshed of the war — 1,500,000 dead — had weakened them too much, perhaps they no longer found in themselves the vigour and drive necessary for great ventures. But they scorned vast plans and became hypnotised by a stupid and obstinate concern for revenge on Germany. Their professional nationalists were incapable of thinking in any terms except those of territorial demands — Alsace-Lorraine, the Saar, the left bank of the Rhine where they vainly tried to produce 'quislings'. And above all, 'Germany must pay'.

Some statements made to Robert de Jouvenel by some very varied individuals are illuminating. First of all Rathenau: 'The French don't want such a system (German participation in co-operation on major enterprises). They are small shop-keepers who live in terror of seeing a great enterprise carried out, even to their own advantage, if those in charge should seem to be making a profit.' (**La Politique d'Aujourd'hui**, p 219.) Then Barrès, a literary man and president of the League of Patriots: 'They have tried to force our industrial development, to turn the best of our activity towards economic expansion. French happiness is distorted thereby.' (*Ibid.* p 68.) Finally Tardieu, certainly a surprising view: 'These problems are above all moral ones.' (*Ibid.* p 82.) 'Our grouping of natural forces is the Little Entente, Italy and Belgium.' (*Ibid.* p 86.)

This short-sighted policy doomed to failure the frequent conferences at which the Allies tried to resolve the problems of the post-war period. Invariably France found herself isolated. She was in opposition to America, who reminded her of her debts; to England, who was anxious to see the revival of the large-scale international trade her economy depended on; to Italy, who was in dispute with her over Syria. For Syria had been granted to Italy in London in May 1915 by the Allies, as the price of her entry into the war on their side.

Faced with the threat of a vast permanent army of unemployed,

England was getting impatient. She proposed the holding of a conference, to which all nations would be invited, to study the reconstruction of the European economy. A preparatory meeting took place at Cannes. Towards the end there was a dramatic event. Briand — then Prime Minister — was suddenly called back to Paris and obliged to resign. In his absence Millerand and Poincaré had organised a plot against him. Poincaré returned to power, took the Foreign Ministry, and made Barthou his second-in-command, as deputy Prime Minister. Briand had brought off an amazing feat by governing for nearly a year with the nationalist Chamber of Deputies of the *bloc national*. Poincaré would have liked to impose conditions on the admission of Russia to the conference. Here again it was a question of money. Like Germany, Russia would have to pay, pay the debts of the old régime, pay the war debts, and even the sums spent by France in supporting counter-revolutionary enterprises and the support given to their unfortunate generals. A liberal English newspaper, **The Daily News**, at this time asked Poincaré if he was willing to give his English and American creditors the guarantees he was demanding from Soviet Russia. At the end of the Cannes meeting, Soviet Russia was officially invited to participate in the international conference to be held in March at Genoa.

Radek stressed the meaning and importance of the change in policy of the great powers towards Russia. They were implicitly recognising the definitive failure of the counter-revolutionary campaigns. 'Incapable of defeating her by armed force, the bourgeois governments were forced to tolerate Soviet Russia and to try to trade with her.' For its part, **Le Temps** had to recognise this in the following melancholy lines: 'Despite its crimes, the régime defends national independence and speaks in the name of the Russian people.'

★   If President Wilson had been able to get his opinions accepted, there would have been a general conference, with the Bolsheviks participating, right after the end of the war, early in 1919. His proposal for this came up against the hostility of Pichon, Clemenceau's Foreign Minister, who, rather than wanting to discuss with the Bolsheviks, was contemplating their overthrow by armed intervention. Better informed and more far-sighted than his opponents,

Wilson tried in vain to make them understand that Bolshevism could not be defeated by armed force. He found support from Lloyd George, who at that time faced the threat of a revolutionary movement in Britain. To save face, Lloyd George declared that the Bolsheviks should not be put on the same footing as the other members of the conference, but would be summoned 'according to the tradition of the invitations that the Roman Empire sent to the leaders of the neighbouring states, its tributaries, to give an account of their actions'. In the end the Bolsheviks were invited, but not as 'tributaries', which would have been somewhat ridiculous. The conference was to be held on the island of Prinkipo in the Sea of Marmara. But it didn't take place; the representatives of the other so-called Russian governments apart from the Bolsheviks refused to meet the Bolsheviks. And Clemenceau only needed to gain time for the whole idea of the conference to be abandoned.

3: The delegates of the three Internationals at Berlin

Thus the great powers were impelled by the difficulties of their internal situations to try to resolve the fundamental problem of the reconstruction of the European economy and even of the world economy. But did the workers' organisations have nothing to say? Were they once again going to let the representatives of the capitalist powers act alone? At the end of their conferences they had managed to do no more than dislocate the European economy. Having recognised their failure, would they not be tempted to reconstruct this economy at the expense of the working class? The International Union of Socialist Parties, which was known as the Two-and-a-half International because it placed itself between the Second and the Third, did not think the working-class organisations should stay silent. It took the initiative in calling a conference of the representatives of the three Internationals to be held at the same time as the international conference of governments (this was the suggestion of the Danish Socialist leader Stauning) which would follow its work and elaborate its own parallel programme for the reconstruction of Europe.

After preparatory meetings at Berne and Innsbruck, an 'International Union of Socialist Parties' had held its first conference at Vienna from 22 to 27 February 1921. Its programme was based on the 'revolutionary class struggle'. It proclaimed the need to defend Soviet Russia and to launch a general action against the imperialist excesses of the Entente, 'an aim which can be achieved by the proletariat only if it unites on the basis of the principles of revolutionary socialism, with the unshakeable will to continue the struggle, and groups all its forces in a powerful international organisation'.

This organisation could not be the Third International, 'since it claims to submit all the parties to an all-powerful committee'. Even less could it be 'the so-called Second International', since it is 'unable to unite within it the living forces of the proletariat' and 'is from now on no more than an obstacle to international socialist unity'.

At its foundation the Union consisted of the Social Democratic Parties of Austria, Yugoslavia, Latvia, Russia (Mensheviks), the German Independent Socialist Party, the Socialist Parties of France and the USA, the British Independent Labour Party, the German Socialist Party of Czechoslovakia, one faction of the Swiss Socialist Party, and the Jewish Socialist organisation 'Poale Zion'. It claimed that it was not an International but a 'Union which will be the means of creating one'.

The Socialist parties it brought together were those that had not been willing to join the Second International. They felt they could not go to Moscow, but refused to join up again with the parties of men like Noske, Scheidemann, Vandervelde and Henderson. They made very firm and relevant criticisms of them, and yet, when it came to it, they lined up with them every time an important decision was necessary. They spoke well and acted badly or not at all. This was the personal tragedy of the Menshevik leader Leon Martov.

The extended Executive Committee, having learned of the initiative by the Vienna International, decided to support it and send a delegation to the proposed meeting. It added that, for its part, it would propose participation in the conference by all the trade-union confederations and centres, national and international — the Amsterdam International Federation of Trade Unions, the Red International of Labour Unions, the CGT, the Italian *Unione Sindacale*, the

American Federation of Labour, the anarcho-syndicalist organisations, the IWW and the factory committees. It also proposed to add to the agenda 'the preparation of the struggle against future imperialist wars, the reconstruction of devastated regions, the revision of the imperialist treaties made at Versailles and elsewhere. In this vast field the tactic of the united front is necessary.' The capitalists of the whole world, said the Executive Committee resolution, 'have gone over to a systematic offensive against the working class. Everywhere wages are being cut, the working day is being lengthened, the suffering of the unemployed is increasing. Capitalism is trying to place on the shoulders of the working class the burden of the financial and economic consequences of the world slaughter.'

As the Second International also accepted the proposal by the Vienna Union, the meeting was called for 2 April in Berlin.

The delegation of the Communist International was led by Radek and Bukharin, for the International and the Russian Communist Party. Vuyovich was representing the Young Communist International, and Clara Zetkin the German Communist Party. Bordiga and Frossard were invited and were to travel directly to Berlin to represent the French and Italian Parties. Šmeral came from Prague. As for me, I had the mandate of the Red International of Labour Unions.

The German Social Democratic parliamentary group had put at our disposal the vast hall in the Reichstag which they used for their deliberations. The delegates were seated around tables in the form of a T. Fritz Adler, who was chairman, sat in the centre with the delegates from the Vienna Union, while at right angles to them sat, on the one side, the representatives of the Second International, and on the opposite side, well away from them, the delegates of the Third International. Adler gave an optimistic opening speech, and then Clara Zetkin read the statement which she had been instructed by the Executive Committee to submit to the conference at the opening of the discussion. It was a commentary explaining the resolution adopted at the Executive Committee.

The Second International still had some big battalions — the German Social Democracy and the Labour Party, plus a party of smaller size, the Belgian Workers' Party, which had, however, among its leaders De Brouckère, Vandervelde and Huysmans, the last two having been the president and secretary of the Second International before 1914. Ramsay MacDonald was the first to speak for it. The tone of his speech was moderate, rather like a sermon, and yet scarcely encouraging because he wanted to impose conditions on the presence of the Communist International and the continuation of the work of the conference. He said that the Communist International must abandon its attacks on the leaders of the parties of the Second International; the practice of creating cells in other organisations must stop; and finally socialists imprisoned in Russia must be released. Then Wels, now appearing as leader of the German Social Democracy, and Vandervelde spoke in the same vein, the latter also opposing the proposal of putting on the agenda the question of the revision of the Treaty of Versailles. 'We should,' he said, 'run the risk of playing Stinnes' game.'

Radek stressed the unusual nature of these claims. We have responded to the Vienna appeal. We are not imposing conditions on anyone; our sole concern is to organise the defence of workers against the capitalist offensive. But 'if you want a conference of polemics and arguments, we are ready for it; then, however, our meeting becomes pointless.'

Liveliness, and even brutality in polemics was nothing new. They had already been very sharp within the parties of the Second International. In Germany they were directed against Bernstein and his revisionist supporters. In France, during the Dreyfus affair, and again when Millerand entered the Government, the Guesdists attacked their opponents with insults that were often crude. At the congress held on the eve of the first world war, Guesde accused Jaurès of 'socialist high treason' because he had approved the motion put forward by Vaillant and Keir Hardie calling for a general strike against the war. As for creating cells within other organisations, the reformists had never hesitated to do this if they thought it necessary to defend their positions, but they did it without admitting to it.

When the chairman closed the session, Serrati could be seen in heated discussion with Otto Bauer. Serrati was in an uncomfortable position in the Italian Socialist party, which had lost its whole left wing. He was now very isolated and was still looking towards Moscow.

His little group was said to be the Two-and-a-three-quarters International. As they were about to part, Otto Bauer raised his voice and he could be heard saying to Serrati 'I don't agree with you' in a tone which allowed no possibility of a reply.

During a translation a little old man, all pink and white, ventured into our part of the hall. It was Kautsky. Those among us who had never seen him before were astonished; they hadn't imagined that the 'pope' of the pre-1914 **Neue Zeit**, the defender of orthodoxy, was like that.

Radek drew up on his own the definitive reply of our delegation to the various motions submitted to the Conference. It looked as if there could be no disagreement among us. He called us together to read it to us before sending it to Fritz Adler. We were surprised to see that by his text we were committing ourselves on a question which was not within our competence. As delegates of the Executive of the Communist International we were quite free to pronounce on the first two conditions and to reject them. As for the third, concerning the imprisoned socialists, only the Soviet Government was in a position to decide. Bukharin pointed this out. It was self-evident, and I supported his remarks, but Radek immediately lost his temper. He threw his file down on the table, and, addressing Bukharin, who had been very friendly in his manner, he said in crude fashion: 'Since you're criticising what I've done, you take on the job of replying.' We calmed down Radek who took back his text. Then there was only Bordiga who asked that his reservations about the united front tactic should be noted. His obstinacy, decidedly unshakeable, was verging on mania.

As could have been all too easily foreseen, when we returned to Moscow we were criticised by Lenin. In an article called 'We have paid too much' he formulated his estimation of the Conference and its results. He asked:

'What conclusion should be drawn from this?

'First, that Comrades Radek, Bukharin and others who represented the Communist International acted wrongly.

'Further. Does it follow from this that we must tear up the agreement that they signed? No. I think it would be wrong to draw such a conclusion. All we have to do is to realise that on this occasion

the bourgeois diplomats proved to be more skilful than ours . . .
The mistake that Comrades Radek, Bukharin and the others made is
not a grave one, especially as our only risk is that the enemies of
Soviet Russia may be encouraged by the result of the Berlin Conference to make two or three perhaps successful attempts on the lives of
certain persons: for they know beforehand that they can shoot at
communists in the expectation that conferences like the Berlin
Conference will hinder the communists from shooting at them.'

The agreement provided for the setting up of a commission of
nine members — three for each International — which would follow
the deliberations of the Genoa Conference and would then convene a
world labour congress. The delegates of the Second International
had signed it only as a matter of form, for they did not want such a
congress at any price. They had finally made their choice, namely, to
work with the bourgeoisie. They manoeuvred to prevent the commission from meeting. There was no need for its death to be recorded,
for it had never really lived.

4: Genoa and Rapallo

The International Conference at Genoa took on considerable importance from the very fact that it was held at all. It was the first time
since the war that representatives of all nations were gathered round
one table. The classification into allies and enemies was finished
with. But this still did not mean that any area of agreement would be
found, that even a minimum of agreement would be achieved. The
little political operation that had brought the preparatory meeting at
Cannes to a close indicated that France was intending to harden in
her attitude of unyielding creditor which was making her appear to
the world in the unenviable rôle of Shylock. From the very day that
it had become clear that, whatever the result of the war, France
would come out of it exhausted, Briand, perhaps because of his
origins in revolutionary socialism, showed an understanding of events
and of the European situation that was rare among French political
leaders. He had proposed making a favourable response to the peace
proposals of Austria and even of Germany. Later he outlined a

proposal for a European federation which came up against the narrow nationalisms that the war had awakened. So Poincaré had good reason to be distrustful of him, and to be sure his presence would be felt at Genoa he had sent Barthou, with the same political background as himself — the same career, the same lack of understanding of economics, the same anti-German feelings, the same hatred of Soviet Russia.

It quite rapidly became plain that the participants in the Conference would constantly find their road blocked by a France whose mind was deliberately closed on the question of a sound European economy. England insisted; more than ever she needed the re-establishment of large-scale international trade. She too had come out of the long war exhausted, and the fruits of victory were indeed bitter. With her allies she had defeated her continental rival, but only in order to see America rob her of the pleasant and profitable rôle of arbiter that she had long played in Europe. She was more willing to face reality, and her politicians had always shown themselves capable of adapting to changing situations. Italy, likewise incapable of providing work for a considerable part of her labour force, supported the attempts at reaching agreement. France demanded the imposition on Russia of draconian conditions, worse than those imposed on Germany by the Treaty of Versailles. She thought Russia was so exhausted she would be forced to accept. The result was quite different. Germany and Russia were both treated as pariahs, one because she was Germany and had been defeated, the other because she was socialist. So they concluded an agreement, the Treaty of Rapallo.

The French chauvinists were furious; now their defeat was complete. The representatives of the other nations were angry with France because her obstinacy and foolishness had prevented even a minimal agreement. Radek took a malicious delight in reminding Barthou, who had written a book on Mirabeau, that the orator of the Constituent Assembly had once said: 'The sovereignty of peoples is not committed by treaties signed by tyrants.'

America had disowned Wilson. She had not wanted to join the League of Nations, but she had not lost interest in European affairs or the policies of the European states. She followed these questions all the more closely because most of the states were in debt to her, and she was not slow in showing her dissatisfaction with France. Early in January 1922, Senator MacCormick 'requested Secretary of State Hughes to inform the House as to the expenses of the European countries which owed money to the United States and as to the causes of their chronic deficit. In particular, what sums these nations are devoting to military expenditure, and what is the total of interest due annually to the United States from each of its European debtors.' And he declared: 'If in the last fourteen months France has been largely isolated from its European allies as a result of its policies, these same policies have astonished and disillusioned the people of the United States during these last weeks.'

★   The communists had hoped that the Genoa Conference would make easier the formation of an international workers' united front, and would produce a mobilisation of workers' and socialist organisations which would reinforce the action of the Soviet delegates to the Conference in putting before the world the only possible sure foundations for a reconstruction of the European economy. Nothing of the sort happened. The working class followed the Conference as a passive spectator. In France, the communists opposed to the united front hotted up their campaign against the Communist International, despite the undertakings they had just given to the Executive Committee. Their unscrupulousness went so far as to attempt to enrol Clara Zetkin in their clique. When the old militant learned what was being done, she protested indignantly; but her letter, published in **L'Humanité**, offered the opportunity for a fresh wave of attacks against the Communist International. The Amsterdam International Federation of Trade Unions was just then holding a meeting at Rome. It confined itself to a dubious verbal gesture, adopting a motion calling for the general strike as a weapon against war.

5: The Trial of the Social-Revolutionaries

The trial of the Social-Revolutionaries which had been discussed at Berlin opened in Moscow on 23 May. Clara Zetkin, writing on 8 May in the name of the Communist International delegation, announced it to Fritz Adler in the following terms:

'I have to make the following statement in the name of our delegation:

1   The six counsels for the defence named in your letter will be admitted in this capacity to the trial of the Social-Revolutionaries in Moscow. The three Social-Revolutionaries mentioned by you will be likewise admitted. The Soviet Government will do everything in its power to facilitate their entry to Russia. The travellers will obtain the necessary visas at the Russian Embassy in Berlin. The trial is fixed for 23 May. You are requested to communicate this date to those concerned urgently.

2   Our delegation requests you to communicate to the delegates of the German Social Democracy on the commission of nine the following information: the freedom of action of our delegation in Germany is being restricted by the German authorities. The Prussian Minister of the Interior has just forbidden comrade Radek to speak in public in Düsseldorf, whereas he gave the permission refused to him to Mr Vandervelde, signatory of the Versailles Treaty. The Foreign Minister has gone further by forbidding comrade Radek to go to Düsseldorf.

3   A warrant has just been issued for the arrest of the secretary of our delegation, Felix Wolf, who is accused of having taken part in the March Action in 1921. We expect the delegates of the German Social Democracy on the commission of nine to intervene immediately with all necessary vigour to obtain the revocation of these measures. If they are not revoked, our delegation would have to consider the possibility of a transfer of the meetings of the commission of nine to Moscow, where the representatives of all tendencies would enjoy full and equal liberty.'

To allow the defence to prepare its case, the first hearing was put off until 8 June. The defence for the accused consisted of Vandervelde, Rosenfeld, Theodor Liebknecht, Moutet, Wauters, and several Russian lawyers including Zhdanov, Muraviev and Tager.

The indictment was formidable. Having decided to carry on a merciless war against the Soviet régime, the Social-Revolutionaries had sought collaboration with and had collaborated with Admiral Kolchak in the Urals and with Denikin in the South, supporting all the counter-revolutionary efforts. They had sought and accepted aid from foreign embassies, and at their instigation had committed criminal sabotage. They had attempted to kill Soviet leaders. Among other things, they were responsible for the assassinations of Uritsky and Volodarsky, and for the attempt to kill Lenin. All the accusations against them were so firmly based that they could not hope to refute them as a whole. None the less, they defended themselves extremely vigorously, raising procedural points and disputing secondary details. And they gave a general justification for their actions. The war they had declared on the régime was their response to the dissolution of the Constituent Assembly by the Bolsheviks. They presented themselves as political opponents, firmly determined not to withdraw any of their ideas.

At the outset, Vandervelde disputed the impartiality of the court. Pyatakov, who was presiding, replied: 'Socialist have always rejected the gross falsehood that the courts are impartial. In the bourgeois countries, the courts are the intruments of prosecution used by the possessing classes. In Soviet Russia they defend the interests of the working masses. None the less they know how to examine objectively the cases brought before them.'

I cannot give my personal impression of this trial, the first of the political trials. I had had to return to Paris before it began. But all the accounts are in agreement. The accused defended themselves energetically throughout the trial and were given complete freedom to do so. Their capabilities might be disputed, and their political ideas are open to discussion, but no one would have dreamt of denying their personal courage, their spirit of self-sacrifice, nor of denying or even forgetting the heroic past of their Party. There was no question of reviling them, even less of making them revile themselves. They were before the court in full strength, with every means at their disposal and not making any concessions as to their convictions. The one who appeared as their leader was Gotz.[32]

32. 'A considerable rôle, though rather in the wings, was played within the Social-Revolutionary fraction and the leading cell of the Soviet by Gotz. A

A great impression was made by the statement of Pierre Pascal. Belonging to the French military mission, he had had an inside view of the clandestine activities of his bosses in favour of the counter-revolution. 'I myself,' he said, 'deciphered a telegram which dealt with the use of terrorism. I can categorically affirm that the French Mission encouraged attempts at murder in Russia. The day after the attempt on Lenin's life, as I was on my way to the mission, General Lavergne came up to me, carrying a newspaper. "Have you seen what they are saying about us?" he asked me. I did not reply. He went on: "I don't know if Lockhart[33] is involved it it, but it's nothing to do with me." But seeing my boss's state of excitement I had a very clear impression that his denials, which would have been superfluous in my presence if they had been sincere, could be explained by nervousness springing from guilt.' (**Correspondance Internationale**, 23 June 1922.)

As for the attempt on Lenin's life, this is how the matter was dealt with in the central organ of the Party, appearing in Samara where the majority of the members of the central committee of the Social-Revolutionary Party were to be found. The article was headed 'Punishment and not Vengeance'.

'A terrible blow has just been struck against the Soviet Bolshevik power. Lenin is wounded. The all too famous president of the *Sovnarkom* (Council of People's Commissars) has been eliminated for some time, if not permanently (the bullet having passed through his lung).

'It is a blow against Soviet power. Without Lenin this power is impotent. Without Lenin this power is cowardly and stupid.

'Who are the two men who fired on the head of the Workers' and Peasants' State? We don't know. But since the act took place as

terrorist coming from a well-known family, Gotz was less pretentious and more active than his closest political friends. But being designated as a "practical man", he confined himself to intrigues, leaving the great questions to others. It must also be added that he was neither a speaker nor a writer, and that his main asset was a personal authority won through years as a convict.' (L Trotsky, **History of the Russian Revolution**, Volume I.)

33. Bruce Lockhart, Lloyd George's personal agent in Russia. See his book **Memoirs of a British Agent**.

he was leaving a workers' meeting we may imagine that, like Volodarsky, Lenin has been punished by workers. In any case, this was an action on the part of democratic circles.'

In an article published just before the trial, Trotsky had written a brief history of the Social-Revolutionary Party. He wrote:

'Once again the Russian Social-Revolutionary Party has become the object of general attention, but in a quite different way than during the February Revolution. It often happens that history thus summons up a party or a man after having buried them. In 1917 the Social-Revolutionary Party spread all over Russia in a few months, in a few weeks even. Then it disappeared just as quickly. The present trial gives us an opportunity of glancing at the surprising fortunes of this Party.

'Back in the first years of this century Plekhanov called the Social-Revolutionary Party the Social-Reactionary Party. But in the struggle against Tsarism and serfdom, this party played a revolutionary rôle. It incited the peasants to rebellion, called young students into political activity, and brought together under its flag a large number of workers who were linked morally or materially to the countryside, and who considered the revolution, not from a proletarian class standpoint, but from the point of view of the vague notion of "labour". The terrorists sought out individual combats, and they gave their own lives in order to take those of the Tsar's dignitaries. We criticised this method; but in demonstrations it often happened that the most devoted Marxist workers found themselves standing up to the police and the Cossacks side by side with the "Narodnik" workers. Later they were united again in prison, travelling across Siberia, in exile . . . Already a deep gulf lay between the young Social-Revolutionary weaver from Petrograd, ever ready to give his life for the working class and intellectuals like Avksentyev, students from Heidelberg or elsewhere, followers of Kant and Nietzsche, who were in no way different from the French pettybourgeois radicals, except that they were less cultured and had bigger illusions.

'The war and Revolution led the Social-Revolutionary Party to rapid disintegration. The political collapse of the Party's leaders was particularly rapid because the great events demanded clear and precise responses. At Zimmerwald we saw Chernov suddenly line up with the extreme left, thus breaking with the "national defence" of bourgeois democracy. Later the same Chernov, member of a bourgeois government, supported the July offensive in agreement with the Entente countries.'

The end of this process of disintegration was the split in the Party. The leaders went over to Kolchak and Denikin, while masses of the workers joined the defenders of the Soviet régime.

At the end of the discussion, fourteen of the accused were condemned to death, but a decision by the All-Russian Central Executive Committee of Soviets specified that 'the punishment would be carried out only if their Party continued its criminal policies towards Soviet Russia by risings in the countryside, by espionage and attempts at murder that are later disowned, by calumny and poisoning of minds.'

6 Fifth anniversary of the October Revolution. Fourth Congress of the Communist International

In accordance with the rule adopted by the Communist International — a congress every year — the Fourth Congress ought to have been held in July. It was postponed for a few months so that it would coincide with the fifth anniversary of the October Revolution. It was held in Moscow from 9 November to 15 December 1922. But for the fifth anniversary, the Congress was transported once again to Petrograd, where the new régime had been proclaimed. The inaugural session took place on 5 November, at nine in the evening, in the House of the People. Zinoviev gave a review of the events of the past five years. On 7 November meetings were organised in all the districts of the city, more than two hundred in all.

I was selected to go to Kronstadt with Lozovsky. We were first of all taken to the Navy Club. Here we saw various objects recalling the Franco-Russian alliance — some 'Kronstadt sailors' had been brought from Toulon to Paris when the Russian fleet was visiting its ally in order to arouse popular enthusiasm for an alliance that was far from popular. This offered a ready-made theme for our speeches;

yesterday the alliance of governments for war, but today the alliance of proletariats to liberate the world. Our brief visit did not allow us to ascertain whether the painful events of the previous year had left feelings of resentment. We were merely able to observe that the audiences for the meetings were very receptive.

It was late evening when we returned to Petrograd. We had had a tiring day, and when we got back to the hotel we had no thought but to rest. But it was a national celebration. An anniversary celebration was proceeding upstairs, in the state apartments. A formidable band was thundering away, crude and noisy. We were ill-prepared for such enjoyment, and having made a token appearance at the banquet, we were glad to be able to get away.

These receptions and banquets were always a serious problem for the Russian Communists, especially when entertaining foreign delegates. Should they get a Soviet Russian diet, or should they be treated according to traditional Russian hospitality? The question had come up for the first time in the spring of 1920, when an important British Labour and Trade Union delegation was due to make a visit. The central committee deliberated as to whether the menu should include wine . . . Once however we did have the traditional feast. Certain questions on the agenda had brought an exceptional number of Russians to the Executive Committee of the International, which had been sitting since morning; then Zinoviev announced that the session was suspended. We went into a neighbouring room, where, on tables covered with fine white tablecloths, there was an enormous selection of hors-d'oeuvres. We thought it was the whole menu, but it was only the famous Russian hors-d'oeuvres, and the real meal began when they were finished. We found ourselves at Kollontai's table; we had already had the chance of seeing her, but it was the first opportunity for a real conversation. We interrogated her about the 'Workers' Opposition', which she had led in struggle together with Shlyapnikov — rather a curious turn, for nothing in her origins and previous activity seemed to have prepared her for this semi-syndicalist position. But we couldn't get anything out of her. The Workers' Opposition had been condemned by the Russian Communist Party, and the decision had been ratified by the International. Events were moving faster and faster and it was now an affair of the past.

★ On the morning of 13 November, before the session was opened, the hall in the Great Palace where the Congress was being held was packed out. All the delegates were in their seats, and spectators were piling up in the space reserved for them. The preceding sessions had been devoted to Zinoviev's report and the discussion on it. Now Lenin was due to speak. He had been laid low by his first attack of arteriosclerosis earlier in the year, at the beginning of May. In the Party and the government people were overwhelmed. Lenin had held such a position that they couldn't get used to the idea that they would have to carry on the Revolution without him. They hoped, they wanted to be able to hope, that his robust constitution and the exceptional care his doctors were taking of him would enable him to overcome the illness. When the news reached us, Lenin was already said to be in a state of convalescence,[34] and when the delegates arrived in Moscow they were inclined to think it had only been a false alarm since Lenin was going to present his report to the Congress.

Usually, although he followed the debates closely, he did not spend a lot of time in the sessions. He came and went, always with the same discretion, often without being noticed. This morning he was to speak first. The delegates waited for him, gripped by deep emotion. When he came in, they all spontaneously stood up and sang the *Internationale*. As soon as he had taken his place at the rostrum, he began his report with these words: 'Comrades, I am

34. Zinoviev gave the details anxiously awaited by communists in an article published by **Correspondance Internationale** in its issue of 7 October 1922, under the title: 'Lenin's recovery'. 'Lenin,' he recalled, 'had always been a great worker; but he knew how to relax. He loved nature, and used to go for walks and bicycle rides in the country. In Switzerland we climbed mountains, and we skated in Galicia. But during the first five years — and especially the first four — the tasks had been so enormous that there was no possibility of rest. In 1918, after the attempt on his life, he had spent two weeks fighting against death. In the end, his strong constitution triumphed. Now it has triumphed again. The captain's convalescence is over, and he is returning to his position of command. The whole crew of the ship, from the first to the last, are taking fresh heart . . . The conscious workers of all countries will rejoice with us.'

down on the list as the main speaker, but you will understand that after my lengthy illness I am not able to make a long report.' Those who were seeing hin for the first time said: 'It's still the same Lenin.' But the others could not allow themselves such illusions. Instead of the alert Lenin they had known, the man they had before them was deeply marked by paralysis. His features remained fixed and he walked like a robot. His usual simple, rapid, self-confident speech had given way to a halting, hesitant delivery. Sometimes he couldn't find the words he wanted. The comrade who had been sent to assist him was doing the job badly, so Radek sent him away and took his place.

None the less his mind remained unshaken, and the main ideas were presented and developed with skill. He was forced, he said, to confine himself to an introduction to the most important questions, and the most important was the NEP. It had been in existence for eighteen months, and it could be judged by results. What Lenin said then is so essential, so characteristic of the man, his technique and his method — a total absence of chattering or bluff — that I felt it was necessary to quote his conclusion in full as an appendix. This was also his last intervention in the life of the Communist International. In this respect, his speech is a document of exceptional value. So I shall limit myself here to a brief outline of the ideas he put forward.

First of all, the general meaning of the NEP as a retreat, for as such it is valid for everyone, and it will confront everyone. Therefore it must be considered, foreseen and prepared everywhere. If we examine the results, we can say that we have undergone the test successfully. We have stabilised the rouble — now we need a currency for our commercial transactions. The peasants are paying the tax in kind — the risings produced by their discontent have almost completely disappeared. In light industry the upsurge is general, and workers' conditions are improving. Only with large industry is the situation still difficult — that's the great problem. But it must be solved because large industry is indispensable for the building of our socialist society. The concessions we have made to private capital, which had worried many of our comrades — here and elsewhere — have found few takers. The capitalists approach but go away again because they don't find what they're looking for here, namely an immediate cure for their present difficulties. This is the situation. 'Of course we have done a host of foolish things. No one knows that better than I do.' Then after a sharp criticism of the state apparatus, he spent a long time attacking the resolution passed by the Third Congress on the structure, methods and tactics of the communist parties. 'The resolution is an excellent one, but it is almost entirely Russian . . . we made a big mistake with this resolution.' And in conclusion this pregnant comment: 'We have not learnt how to present our Russian experience to foreigners.' A final warning which was to remain a dead letter. The men who took his place did not correct this 'big mistake'. On the contrary, they took it as their starting-point, repeated it and amplified it.

Trotsky had been chosen to complete the report of which Lenin, as he declared at the beginning, was able to write only the introduction. He spoke a week later; the official report of the session begins by stating: 'the chairman opened the session at 6.15 p.m. and invited comrade Trotsky to speak. The delegates rose to their feet and greeted comrade Trotsky with enthusiastic applause.'

Trotsky first of all recalled how and in what conditions the October rising had been launched. If the prolonged civil war only came later, it was because our job had been too easy: 'No one wanted to take us seriously,' he said. 'They thought that passive resistance, sabotage and a quick intervention by the Allies would soon deal with us. When they realised that things would not turn out like that, all the forces of counter-revolution were mobilised against us. Then we were forced to expropriate more than we would have wished, much more than we were in a position to turn to account. These facts allow us to formulate a first law. We can assert that, for the Western parties, for the labour movement in general, the task will be much more difficult before the decisive insurrection, but much easier after it. Our war communism sprang from the civil war itself. It was above all a need to provide food for the workers and the army, and to squeeze from an industry that was disorganised and sabotaged by the bourgeoisie everything that the army needed to carry on the war . . . If the European proletariat had taken power in 1919, it would have taken a backward country in tow. All the substitutes we had to have recourse to were of value only to satisfy the needs of the war industries.'

This war communism had given way to a state capitalism. Trotsky did not like using this expression, which might lead to confusion; reformists can make state capitalism by partial national-isations. But Lenin had made clear the meaning it had for him and for us. Trotsky went on to analyse the complexities of the new régime. 'We have a total of a million workers. How many are there in the leased enterprises? 80,000. And even then, out of this figure there are only 40 or 50 thousand in purely private establishments, for some of them have been allocated to Soviet institutions.' As for the great concessions, destined for major foreign firms, of which a list has been drawn up, the situation can be summed up as: lots of discussions, but few concessions.

Dealing with the question of the productivity of labour, Trotsky said that the superiority of socialism must be proved by superior productivity. 'It's a proof we are not yet in a position to give because we are still too poor. But our Soviet Russia is only five years old, and if we compare the situation to that in France, for example, in the first years of the great Revolution, we can see that the picture we present is not so gloomy. Let us borrow some comparative data from the French historian Taine. In 1799, ten years after the outbreak of the Revolution, Paris was still only getting a third, sometimes even a fifth of the amount of flour that was normally necessary. In 37 *départements*, the population was declining because of famine and epidemics.'

As far as the perspectives for world revolution were concerned, there was a remarkable display of that foresight which he revealed many times in his life, starting with his famous essay entitled **The Proletariat and the Revolution**.[35] It was 1922. Poincaré was in power

35. A biographer writes: 'Although living outside Russia, Trotsky felt the pulse of the masses beating with exceptional acuteness. His description of the course of a revolution, the rôles he attributes to the workers, to the non-proletarian urban population, to the intellectuals and to the Army; his evaluation of the influence of the war on the mentality of the masses — all that corresponds precisely to what happened during the risings in 1905. When a historian of Russian political life reads **The Proletariat and the**

in France; in Britain, the Liberal-Conservative coalition was governing. He foresaw a period in which peace and reformism would inevitably flourish. 'After the illusions of the war and the intoxication of victory, France will see a flourishing of the illusions of pacifism and reformism, which will come to power in the form of a "left bloc" . . . In Britain, I foresee a parallel development; the replacement of the Conservative and Liberal government by a democratic government favouring peace. So then in France we shall have a "left bloc" and in Britain a Labour government. Under these conditions, what will happen in Germany? The Social Democratic lungs will get some big puffs of fresh air. We shall have a new version of Wilsonism, on a broader basis but even more short-lived than its predecessor. That is why it is necessary that we should prepare for this period firm and strong communist parties which are capable of standing firm in this phase of pacifist and reformist euphoria. For when the illusions collapse, the workers will turn towards them. They will appear as the only parties of truth, of cold brutal truth, parties which do not lie to the working class.'

The question of the programme of the Communist International was on the agenda. Various proposals were put forward and defended by their authors. The discussion led to a sharp clash between Bukharin and Radek. Radek had given a report on the offensive by capital; he painted a very gloomy picture. Some left-wing elements criticised him for a complete absence of revolutionary perspectives, which the centrists would not fail to use in their attacks on the communists. Bukharin came into conflict with Radek on the question of workers' immediate demands. Was there a place for them in a programme for the Communist International? Bukharin declared vigorously against, while Radek advocated their inclusion no less energetically. It was clear that the question required further study. In the end it was decided to refer all the proposals to a special commission which would report to the next Congress.

Revolution, he feels that the essay must have been written *after* the Revolution, for it follows the course of events so closely. But it appeared before 9 (new style 22) January 1905, that is, before the great rising of the St Petersburg proletariat.' (**Our Revolution**, pp 26-27.)

7: The French Communist Party and its difficulties

If the delegates' attention had been seized by the grave matter dealt with by Lenin and Trotsky and the long discussion arising from it, their curiosity was aroused by another question, of less importance, and certainly less encouraging. Once again the French Communist Party was on the agenda. It had made wretched progress. As we have seen, the old Socialist Party had voted for affiliation to the Communist International by an enormous majority at the Congress of Tours at the end of December 1920. The Communist Party thus found itself composed of a very large proportion of the old Party. The 'dissidents' had kept above all the majority of the members of Parliament and some of the cadres — the 'ornaments of the Party' as Jean Longuet said. The rank-and-file, healthy and enthusiastic, consisted of new elements, the youth, ex-servicemen, syndicalists and a small bunch of anarchists; they went over to communism eagerly.[36]

However, as we have seen, the delegations sent to Moscow in July of the following year, to the congresses of the Communist International and the Red International of Labour Unions, had a strange attitude. The First Congress of the Party, held at Marseilles in December 1921, had revealed something confusing and worrying in the functioning of the Party, unpleasant underhand manoeuvres. Without any prior discussion to justify or explain the action, Boris Souvarine, then in Moscow as the Party's delegate to the Executive Committee of the International, had not been re-elected to the central committee. Whereupon the comrades of his tendency gave their resignation on the spot. This was the first crisis. The Communist International censured those who resigned for withdrawing. It censured more strongly the leadership for its manoeuvre and demanded that those who had resigned should be reinstated.

Then came the tactic of the united front. I have shown how it was greeted. But at the extended Executive Committee the opponents of the tactic had declared that they would submit to the decisions of

36. At the end of the war, the Socialist Party, which had a mere 34,000 members as against 100,000 in 1914, went through a period of intensive growth. Within a few months it gained 150,000 members.

the International, and some months later Frossard, who this time had agreed to make the journey to Moscow, declared at the end of the discussion: 'It is . . . for these reasons . . . that the delegation of the majority of the French Party commits itself to report to the Party the resolutions that are going to be passed, to explain them, give a commentary on them, defend them, and ensure that in the shortest possible time they will be confirmed in practice. And in conclusion I hope that at the Fourth Congress of the Communist International it will not be the French question which will attract the particular attention of the International.' And he returned to Paris with a motion for the next Party Congress signed by Frossard and Souvarine. So there was agreement between left and centre, the axis of the combination on which the French Communist Party was built.

The Second Congress of the Party was due to meet in Paris on 15 October, just before the Fourth Congress of the Communist International, which, Frossard hoped, would no longer have to deal with the eternal French question. The International's representative was Manuilsky. To put a final seal on the agreement, he arranged meetings with the representatives of the two tendencies. He proposed equal representation of the left and centre tendencies on the central committee, the delegate of the International intervening to help resolve conflicts if the members of the two tendencies should stick to firm and unyielding positions. The centre refused. It claimed that this would mean that the Communist Party was no longer independent. The representative of the International would become the arbiter and would make the decisions. The left claimed the right to a majority. Manuilsky's prestige and authority were so weak that the Congress opened without him being able to get an agreement.

After the opening debates the scandal broke. Frossard's second-in-command in the secretariat, Ker, was at the rostrum to give his report. He was a good worker, competent, likeable and conciliatory. To the atonishment of everyone, he launched into a violent indictment of the left, describing the negotiations with the representative of the International as a plot hatched in secret. It was a declaration of war, but the most surprising thing was that it was he who had been given the responsibility for it. All the debates were to be dominated by this attack. What did the centre want? It already occupied the commanding positions. Frossard was secretary, Cachin editor of **L'Humanité**, and the great majority of the central committee was in its hands. But the affiliation to the Communist International was a drag on it; it was constantly in disagreement with its decisions. None the less it took good care not to stand up openly against the International. On the contrary, after having shown an inclination to resist, it yielded, humbly protesting its undying loyalty. Did it now want to go further? At the end of the debates, it got a small majority of the votes, 1,698 against 1,516 for the left. A large number, 814, abstained, thus indicating their discontent. None the less the centre claimed all power. It would govern alone 'in agreement with the International' — although it was in disagreement with the man who was representing the International here.[37]

What exactly did this complicated game mean? There was no need to share the secrets of the leadership to imagine what was going on there. We knew the men who found it hard to accept the authority of the International. Some even admitted it. But the man who was preparing and guiding all these manoeuvres, a past-master at subterfuges and evasions, was the secretary of the Party himself, Frossard. He wasn't yet forty, but he was already an old stager in the Party. During the war, he had moved towards the Zimmerwald tendency. Merrheim, who had had the chance to get to know him well, considered him as an unreliable colleague. Besides, he hastened to join up with Longuet as soon as the latter had organised his minority tendency in the Socialist Party. This included plenty of deputies; they criticised the government's war policy, but voted for the war credits. It was in a position involving no danger and no risks, and it became advantageous when the minority won the day and had party positions at its disposal. Cachin became editor of the daily paper and Frossard secretary of the Party.

I had met them both in Moscow, at the time of the Second Congress of the International when they had been sent there to 'get information'. Frossard took refuge behind Cachin, whom he let expose himself to rebuffs alone. Later the same game continued when

37. It was Cachin who came to the rostrum to say so. 'In the name of the centre, I declare that we alone will take the leadership of the Party.'

the Executive summoned them to Moscow. Both began by vigorously refusing to make the journey. When the messages took on an urgent tone, Frossard let Cachin flounder about, knowing that he would yield and that he, Frossard, would thus be able to evade the issue. In fact Cachin, after having screamed and protested that he would not go, set out, already preparing sentimental tirades to soften his critics, which would be delivered with a tear in his eye.

It was Frossard who, by accident, revealed his technique to me. During the only trip he made to Moscow as Party secretary, he had given a firm undertaking about the founding Congress of the *Confédération Générale du Travail Unitaire* which was due to be held at Saint-Etienne. He would call a meeting of delegates belonging to the Party before the Congress to work out a programme and tactics together; and he himself would intervene in the Congress. He did all that, prudently as ever, but he did it. The debates were pretty harsh. Knowing that they would not win a majority, the anarchists and 'pure syndicalists' who, by chance, had control of the secretariat and the executive commission of the CGTU, were aggressive, and attacked the Communist Party and its members.

One of them, the secretary of an important departmental union, was standing up to them, though rather ineptly. While he was speaking, Frossard approached me and said: 'I've wound the brother up too much!' At the time his confidential remark — which I was surprised at because there was no intimacy between us — amused me. But later, trying to get an overall assessment of the French Communist Party, in so many ways disappointing and even pitiful, I found in the remark the key to repeated incidents and successive crises. Frossard, remaining in the background, 'wound up the brothers'. He had wound them up for the Third Congress of the Communist International and for the First Congress of the Red International of Labour Unions. He had 'wound up' Ker, usually too submissive, for the Paris Congress. Above all he 'wound up' the new leaders of the CGTU, communist sympathisers who wanted to affiliate to the Red International of Labour Unions. But they were easily confused and worried by the idea of *ukases* from Moscow. This was his main trump card. A hostile CGTU would make the formation of a true communist party difficult.[38]

This time the crisis was of such an acute nature that it became necessary to put a stop to the manoeuvres and evasions which were creating an intolerable situation. To prepare for the Congress debates, a commission was formed which was exceptionally weighty in numbers and composition. The delegations were represented on it by their most qualified members. The Russian delegation had set an example by appointing Lenin, Trotsky, Zinoviev and Bukharin. Lenin did not attend, but he followed the debates closely. It was within this commission that the fate of the French Communist Party was settled. The Party came before it in fragments. The centre brought its claim to govern on its own, a claim loosely formulated in Paris and already seeming ill-founded in Moscow. The left was deeply attached to the Communist International, but was too weak to take over the leadership as the Italians had done. Finally the 'right wing', whose verbal leftism I have already alluded to with reference to the discussion on the united front. It was no less hostile than the centre to the International, and in fact was following the same line.

Since I had only joined the Party after my return to France in the last months of 1921, I was able to judge them all with a degree of detachment. The dangers of the methods adopted in 1920 for creating communist parties was evident. Even Zinoviev could see them and pointed them out in his report. 'In our Party we have all the more centrism, all the more social democracy, because we took into our ranks numerous fractions from the old social democratic movement.' So the French Communist Party was not the only one in this situation, but what gave its case an unpleasing character was the hypocrisy of a number of its leaders.[39]

On the day when I was due to speak to the commission, we had

38. In an article on the Paris Congress published in the **Bulletin Communiste** of 9 November 1922, M Chambelland wrote: 'I remembered that before Saint-Etienne, Monmousseau could not be hard enough against Frossard, who, by using third parties, tried to turn the trade-union movement against Moscow for the purposes of his own policy. And I wondered whether Monmousseau and his friends were going to agree to play the same rôle under the same influence, here and in Moscow.'

39. 'The centre tendency in France is a survival of the old social democratic

just received the latest number of the **Bulletin Communiste**, in which, at this very moment, they were impudent enough to take up the old criticisms of the International's tactics. This gave me an introduction to the subject which dealt with the rightists at one blow. While I was reading it, they all hung their heads, feeling the unanimous disapproval of the commission. To the representatives of the centre, I asked the question. 'You claim to exercise the leadership on your own and in agreement with the International. But who can put any trust in your declarations?' At this point some of them grunted. Speaking at the end of the session, Trotsky took to task by name Ker, whom he had just learnt to be a freemason — something many of us did not know. 'How can you be a communist and a freemason?' Trotsky asked. For him the two were absolutely incompatible.

The discussion continued for several sessions. I will pick out just one brief but important incident which marked the last session. The centre delegation was, in fact, quite heterogeneous. Besides those who were old stagers in politics and the Party, there were new elements who had come to socialism after the war and because of the war. The most remarkable of them was Renaud Jean, who tried to remain unaligned with any tendency. He had gone to war as a peasant, and was incapacitated by a serious wound. During his convalescence he had read and learnt a great deal. He wrote well, giving a powerful expression to the anger of the men who had suffered in the trenches and had come back determined to drive out their rulers and overthrow the régime responsible for the futile slaughter. His peasant origins led him, in part unconsciously, to draw a contrast between the peasants who had fought the war in the trenches and the factory workers, who had been able to take advantage of deferment of conscription. The fact that he could claim a personal and independent position showed clearly that he did not adhere to communism and the International without reservations. Finally, he wanted to present ostentatiously the image of himself as the irreproachable militant.

mentality, but it conceals itself behind a mask by accepting all that is asked of it.' (Bukharin's speech to the commission.)

All these details are necessary to understand an incident which flared up at the end of a long session. The agenda had been completed when a delegate from the Communist Youth asked to be allowed to put a question. 'Our Federation,' he said, 'receives subsidies from the Young Communist International. It seems normal to us that a section of the International should be assisted by the centre or by other sections. Now some comrades, especially comrade Renaud Jean, are attacking us about this. I would ask that, in this commission, qualified speakers should remind him that this is a perfectly normal expression of solidarity in an international organisation.'

The question had hardly been stated when Renaud Jean stood up and strode towards the table where the bureau were sitting, and launched into a tangled explanation. Trotsky rather harshly interrupted him to say that the Communist International had nothing in common with a market-place full of sly, haggling peasants. Renaud Jean withdrew nonplussed. The session was closed amid a certain embarrassment. Doubtless Trotsky could have made his point more calmly — as he did the next day in a private interview. But it was two o'clock in the morning, and an expression of impatience was understandable, for everyone was anxious to get away. Moreover it was the worst possible time to choose to raise a matter that was certainly of some importance and merited discussion. Renaud Jean was not alone in thinking that in this respect the Inernational should act with discrimination and closely supervise the use of funds put at the disposal of sections. Yet he was much less scrupulous later on, for he endorsed all the follies and crimes of the International under Zinoviev and then Stalin, the 'zigzags', the 'Moscow Trials', the purges, the famine that was provoked in order to defeat the Ukrainian peasants, the murders of the killers themselves. Perhaps he sometimes found it a bit much to take, for from time to time the rumour would spread that Renaud Jean had left the Party. But there was no truth in it. Renaud Jean's resistance was limited to a few grimaces before he swallowed the bitter potion.

In the public session, Trotsky gave his report. He did not try to minimise the difficulties of the task facing the International. 'We now have before us,' he said, 'an important and very difficult question.' Examining the internal struggles of the Party, and the polemic between factions, he referred to the speech he had given eighteen months ago to the enlarged Executive. Nothing had changed; the most striking thing was that 'we are still marking time on the same spot.' And he in turn was led to observe that too much of the old Socialist Party had survived in the young Communist Party. 'At Tours we dragged along with us many habits and customs which are unwilling to give way to the attitudes and customs of communist action.'

A particularly difficult problem was the relationship of the Party with the trade unions. Revolutionary syndicalism had deep roots in the French labour movement. It had required the October Revolution and the creation of the Communist International to get rid of the syndicalists' principled opposition to political parties. But if opposition had disappeared, there was still a certain distrust which the policies of the Party leadership were not likely to dispel. Quite the opposite. So even among those syndicalists who had joined the Party there were reservations about the Party's intervention in strikes. On the other hand, if strikes and working-class action were going to take place without the participation of the Party, then it could never become a communist party. For various reasons, the Party leadership followed the line of least resistance on this question, that is, it completely withdrew in face of the unions. This could not be a solution. No one knew better than I did that it was a peculiarly tough problem. I could see the syndicalists who were most favourably disposed to the Party moving away when they observed that too often it was behaving like the old Socialist Party, when they saw that young militants were abandoning union work in favour of electoral activity which would get them a seat in parliament.

The Party's policy was not just passive. Instead of trying to tone down the divergences, reconcile the differing viewpoints and find a basis for common action, it preserved and sharpened the differences in order to be able to put pressure on Moscow. But it could hardly be claimed that, thanks to this division of labour between party and unions, all was for the best in the French working-class movement. Trotsky listed examples of defeated strikes and serious failures which it would have been possible to avoid.

After long deliberations, involving examination and discussion of the Party's activity, peculiarities of the labour movement, factional struggles, the press, the peasant question and colonial policy, the commission drew up a programme of action. This recognised unanimously that Party members belonging to the freemasons and the League for the Rights of Man should immediately break with 'these bourgeois instruments created to lull workers' class-consciousness to sleep'. As an exceptional measure, to enable the Party to get out of the dead-end it had got into, it was proposed that the central committee should be constituted proportionally on the basis of the votes at the Paris Congress, with the delegations themselves selecting office-holders. Representatives of the three tendencies then declared that they accepted the resolution unconditionally. All of them protested their attachment and devotion to the Communist International.

8: Frossard resigns — Cachin remains

While the Congress was deliberating and making its decisions, Frossard, who had remained in Paris despite the repeated appeals of the International, was plotting, uniting and organising his followers in case the Congress should take a decision which would make all evasions henceforth impossible. The plotters included the majority of the members of the central committee and a large part of the editorial board of L'Humanité. Since they controlled the secretariat through Frossard and the daily paper through Cachin, they were convinced they could stand up against the International. The decisions taken in Moscow put them in a difficult situation. Everything was settled — the composition of the central committee, of the editorial board and the board of directors of L'Humanité. But they did not give up hope. The delegates of the centre had not been able to stand up to the pressure put on them by Moscow by the unanimous will of the Congress. On their return to Paris, they would pull themselves together and, according to their usual habit, they would find pretexts to delay putting the decisions into practice. 'Gain time': that had always been Frossard's tactic. He had admitted it publicly in a meeting of the Seine Federation. But just because he was an expert at this tactic, he soon understood that it would no longer be possible. A choice was necessary. He hesitated. He valued a position which made him the effective leader of the Party. But he was torn between the International and his friends; the latter put pressure on him; feeling himself beaten, he resigned.

Everything was settled rapidly. Humbert-Droz, the delegate of the International, and I went to see Cachin to draw up the list of the editorial staff of **L'Humanité**. All those who had plotted with Frossard were eliminated. Cachin defended some of them rather weakly, but he showed passion only in opposing the reinstatement of Pierre Monatte who was put in charge of the column on social questions. Amédée Dunois took on the job of telling the unlucky conspirators they had been dismissed. He had to face the fury of several of them, and some malicious remarks. But their anger was mainly directed at Cachin, whom they considered a treacherous wretch. They looked for him in vain in the newspaper's offices; he had stayed at home to keep out of the way of the attacks.

As if to prove that the International's decision was correct, they grouped around Frossard, trying to form an embryo party, and published a weekly which directed all its attacks against the International and communism. They demanded compensation for dismissal from **L'Humanité** as they would have done from a bourgeois paper. As for Frossard, he rapidly took the road already followed by Briand and Laval, his true masters. He returned to the Socialist Party, left it, became a minister, and ended his career as one of the many ministers of Pétain. In 1930, he published his memoirs of his short stay in the Communist Party under the title **De Jaurès à Lénine**, in which one can read these surprising admissions: 'Was I ever a communist? As I recreate the atmosphere of the Congress of Tours I feel that I can definitely answer that question in the negative. Twenty times over I looked for an opportunity to free myself, to get myself on the right lines . . . Basically I was much closer to Blum than to Lenin.' (p 177.) That gives a pretty good picture of the strange type of small-time politician he was, and the portrait is complete if one adds the line, on the same page, in which he claims he was 'a dupe of people without honour and without conscience'.[40]

40. On this question, Amédée Dunois, general secretary of **L'Humanité**

★ An account of the Fourth Congress would require considerable space to be devoted here to the question of fascism. Decisive events had just occurred. After a year filled with the deeds of armed fascist bands, operating throughout the country with the complicity and support of the authorities, Mussolini, at the end of that so-called 'March on Rome' which was his first bluff, had been summoned by the King to form a government. The accession of fascism dated from 30 October, a few days before the opening of the Congress. When Bordiga came to the rostrum, on 16 November, to give his report on fascism, it is understandable that he spoke with a degree of emotion not usual for him. 'Special circumstances,' he said, had not allowed him to have all the documentation at his disposal. First of all he gave a brief historical sketch of the fascist movement. Without pinning down those responsible, he recalled what was now clear to everyone, namely, that 'the revolutionary socialist proletarian tendency which had grown stronger in the post-war period, thanks to the enthusiasm which had gripped the masses . . . was not able to take advantage of the favourable situation . . . It may be said that in 1919 and the first part of 1920, the Italian bourgeoisie was to a considerable extent resigned to accepting the triumph of the revolution. The middle classes and the petty-bourgeoisie remained passive, but followed the proletariat.'

His usual schematism led him to formulate a view of the nature of fascism which was only too obviously false: bourgeois democracy and fascism — it was all the same thing. Therefore 'I am not saying that the situation is a favourable one for the proletarian and socialist movement when I foresee that fascism will be liberal and democratic

wrote: 'Frossard had had the fantastic dream that sooner or later he would be able to impose his conditions on the Communist International. This had long been known to the close associates of the cunning secretary of the Party . . . The best planned intrigues do not always succeed . . . For a whole week we were on the verge of a break. But there was no break. There was nothing more to be done except to put into practice the resolutions of the Fourth Congress . . . Those who had been dismissed launched into deafening recriminations. They did more; they used such threats against Frossard — their accomplice, the man who yesterday had been their leader — that he could escape only by resigning from the Party. "The fox was trapped".'

. . . our situation is not tragic.' A Party representative had arrived the day before, bringing information on the most recent events. 'This comrade,' said Bordiga, 'is a worker and the leading member of a local Party organisation. He puts forward the interesting view, shared by many militants, that we may now be able to work better than before.'

Radek, in his report on the capitalist offensive, had judged the situation more correctly and shown more perceptiveness about the meaning of these facts and their development. 'In the victory of fascism,' he said, 'I do not see only the mechanical triumph of fascist weapons. I see also the greatest defeat that socialism and communism have suffered since the beginning of the period of world revolution. It is a defeat greater than that of Soviet Hungary, for the victory of fascism is a consequence of the temporary moral and political bankruptcy of socialism and of all the Italian working-class movements.'

Zinoviev, however, as usual, whether by temperament or as a tactic, felt it necessary to spread his cheap optimism over the delegates. 'The Italian comrades are now arguing among themselves,' he said, 'about the nature of what is happening in Italy at present; is it a *coup d'état* or a comedy? Perhaps both at the same time. From the historical point of view it is a comedy. In a few months the situation will turn to the advantage of the working class.' More than once in the future we were to see him thus transform defeats into successes and announce a communist victory . . . in a few months.[41]

The Italian question, which was on the agenda of the Congress, took on a new importance. The development of fascism had provoked

41. He was not the only one to be mistaken, and one could find a number of erroneous forecasts. I will quote one only, because of its particular significance. For inverse reasons, the socialists, who were frightened of communism, had rejoiced at the failure of the revolutionary upsurge. After the elections in May 1921 Benjamin Crémieux wrote: 'The essential fact about the vote is that it marks . . . the end of Bolshevism in the peninsula . . . The Moscow fashion has had its day. Now Western socialism is coming into fashion again and is preparing to play a fertile rôle.' (**Europe Nouvelle**, 15 May 1921.) And again, on 27 August, in the same magazine: 'To-day Italy is weary of fascism. The socialists have turned away from Bolshevism and have regained the sympathies of the advanced bourgeoisie and the intellectuals.'

a great stir inside the Italian Socialist Party. Serrati and his friends, who had wanted to maintain the unity of the Party at all costs, found, after Leghorn, that it was difficult to coexist with the right wing of Turati and Treves. The split came at the Congress held in Rome in October 1922. The reformists, finding themselves in a minority, left the Party. None the less they got twice the number of votes they had had at Leghorn, 29,000 instead of 14,000, for they were supported by the leaders of the *Confederazione Generale del Lavoro*. Affiliation to the Third International only just got a majority, with 32,000 votes. It should be noted that here Serrati got the support of the so-called *Terzinternationalista* faction which had always supported affiliation. After the Congress D'Aragona broke the agreement between the CGL and the Socialist Party, and withdrew into the comfortable position of the independence and neutrality of the unions. 'We don't want to be involved in politics,' he said, as he humbly submitted to Mussolini. 'We want a trade union movement within the framework of the law. I declared that long ago. Moreover, history proves that the CGL will never participate in illegal activity.'

We had been only too right in Moscow, at the time of the Second Congress, to doubt this character's sincerity and loyalty when he declared his attachment to communism, and signed with us an appeal to revolutionary trade unionists to form a Red International of Labour Unions. It was the clearest possible illustration of the danger of keeping unreliable men at the head of revolutionary organisations. They let themselves be carried along by the stream when it is too strong for them to dam it up, but they are still ready to betray as soon as circumstances become favourable.

Serrati, whom we hadn't seen at the Third Congress, came back to Moscow, this time with a Party that was smaller but more homogeneous. 'The Rome Congress,' he was able to say, 'having expelled the reformists and the open or concealed partisans of collaboration with the bourgeoisie, has voted unanimously for affiliation to the Third International.'

Reporting to the Congress on this question, Zinoviev analysed the new situation in which the Italian Communist Party found itself, and formulated some conclusions. First of all, the united front was more than ever necessary; fusion with the Socialist Party was implied by the very fact of the vote by this Party for affiliation to the International. 'Our Party,' he said, 'has committed errors of doctrine; it has scorned and tried to ignore any movement that developed outside of itself. It was Lenin who taught us that there is a "communist vanity" which claims to know everything and is too infatuated with itself. Mussolini states that the fascist trade unions have already got a million-and-a-half members. That is probably an exaggeration, but that doesn't matter much; it is necessary to join them.'

Bordiga, speaking in the name of the majority of the Italian delegation, expressed his disagreement with Zinoviev's recommendations. He remained opposed to any fusion with the Socialist Party, even after the Rome Congress. Those who wanted to enter the Third International would have to group around the Communist Party. None the less he and his comrades were willing to follow the instructions laid down by the Fourth Congress without discussion or hesitation.

The last sessions of the Congress were devoted to voting on resolutions. These were prepared by special commissions which took into account the discussions which followed the presentations of the reports and submitted the definitive text to the delegates in the plenary sessions. Clara Zetkin came to read the resolution on 'The Russian Revolution and the Perspectives for World Revolution' — it will be remembered that the reports on this had been given by Lenin and Trotsky. One paragraph was drafted as follows:

'The Fourth World Congress reminds workers of all countries that the proletarian revolution can never be victorious within a single country, but only on an international scale, as world proletarian revolution. The struggle of Soviet Russia for its existence and for the gains of the Revolution is the struggle for the liberation of the workers, of all the oppressed and exploited people of the whole world.'

The reading of this resolution was greeted by victorious applause and it was adopted unanimously. For the commission which was to examine the composition of the Executive Committee, the Russian delegation selected Bukharin and Radek as delegates, and Lenin and Trotsky as substitutes.

★ The Second Congress of the Red International of Labour Unions was held at Moscow at the same time, in the great hall of the House of Trade Unions. Its work had been prepared by a meeting of the Central Council — which corresponded to the extended Executive Committees in the case of the Communist International — which had lasted from 17 February to 12 March 1922. The normal evolution of the RILU had come up against two sorts of opponents. The reformists of the Amsterdam International Federation of Trade Unions were pursuing a policy of splits; in France their manoeuvring had led to the split of the national trade union centre. The RILU had issued repeated appeals, wanting to try everything to avoid a split. On 3 December 1921, its Executive Bureau addressed French workers in these terms:

'The leaders of the CGT are peparing a split. After having many times declared their devotion to working-class unity, they are now consciously preparing to destroy it and thus to disarm French workers in the face of reaction. Jouhaux, Dumoulin, Merrheim and their followers are making more and more concessions to the bourgeoisie. In face of the government and the *bloc national* their docility has no limits, and is equalled only by their refusal to compromise with revolutionary workers . . . Through their actions the unity of the railwaymen's union has been broken at this very moment. The federation of clothing-workers is following the same example . . . **L'Information** and **Le Temps** are satisfied. How many times the Amsterdam leaders have invoked working-class unity! But they are willing to destroy it as soon as the majority of trade unionists try to escape from their supervision and that of the bourgeoisie.'

Then, when the danger became imminent, the RILU approached Amsterdam directly with the following telegram, sent on 22 December. 'The French CGT is about to split. We propose a conference bringing together representatives from your federation, from the majority and minority of the CGT, and from the RILU. Our delegates will be: Rosmer, Tom Mann, Lozovsky.' The secretary of the Amsterdam Federation, Oudegeest, waited several days before sending an evasive reply:

'Telegram received. What is happening in France is simply the result of the misdeeds of the Executive of the Third International.

Am glad you now see these misdeeds only serve to support the bourgeoisie. Try to adjourn Congress of the CGT minority. On this condition, I propose to ask the meeting of our bureau, 28 December, to hold conference early January, exclusively with your delegates. Will send details 28 December.'

When common action in defence of the proletariat was proposed to them, the reformists hypocritically concealed their refusal by laying down conditions they knew to be impossible, and, as was the case here, thinking only of winning a pointless victory.[42] They put themselves forward as the champions of trade-union independence, but at the same time linked all their activity to the League of Nations and the International Labour Organisation. In these fragile remnants of Wilsonism they thought they could see the bases of a new democracy and a guarantee against war and fascism. When the League of Nations collapsed, they were among the victims. Even then they refused to understand the terrible lesson.

In Czechoslavakia, the textile workers' federation demanded that every union member should sign a statement promising to give active support to Amsterdam and to give up all propaganda on behalf of the RILU. In Switzerland, where the forces of the reformists amounted to 300,000, and those of the anarcho-syndicalists to 35,000,

---

42. This tactic of the RILU in opposition to any union split was in strict conformity with the principle laid down from the creation of the Communist International. Lenin had defended it, quite harshly even, against excellent revolutionaries, notably, as we have seen, in **Left-Wing Communism, an Infantile Disorder**. And the International had not hesitated to break with those who were persisting in what it considered to be an error. And all the facts showed that the desire to split was on the other side, among the socialists of the Second International and the reformists of the Amsterdam Federation. But these so often accused the communists of seeking a split in the labour movement, they had so many newspapers to say so, with the bourgeois press echoing them, that even more or less objective observers interpreted these moves by the RILU as a total change of direction, a complete repudiation of its earlier attitude. 'An important event,' one of them wrote, 'which has not always been commented on sufficiently accurately, has just oriented the international labour movement along a new path . . . So Moscow is far removed from its policy of 1920.' (**Europe Nouvelle**, 31 December 1921.)

the two competed in a campaign to denigrate the Russian Revolution and repeatedly to attack the RILU.

The other line of attack the RILU had had to put up with from its foundation came from the anarcho-syndicalists and those who claimed to be 'pure syndicalists'. They had tried in vain to impose their views during the First Congress. On their return to their own countries, they took their revenge by launching a violent campaign parallel to — and not very different from — that being carried on by almost all the bourgeois papers of every tendency. All their efforts tended to confuse workers, to destroy in them the enthusiasm which had brought them towards the Russian Revolution at its outset. Their campaigns, coinciding with the ebb of the post-war revolutionary wave, were not wholly ineffective. To some extent they weakened the RILU, but they themselves did not profit from this. None the less, unlike such reformist leaders as D'Aragona, Dugoni, etc. who had travelled to Moscow only to find arguments against the Communist International, they were sincere; or at least the better ones were, for there was no shortage of pretentious windbags among them. What they had seen in Russia was different from what they had imagined. Instead of trying to understand the meaning of the Revolution and its development, and to distinguish which of the roads taken by the Revolution had been deliberately chosen and which had been forced on it by the intervention of the capitalist states and the civil war, they confined themselves to simple assertions; they were against the Red Army, against the dictatorship of the proletariat to which they had rallied in the beginning. Communism had not immediately risen from the ruins, so they turned their backs on it.

The Red International of Labour Unions made every effort to keep sincere syndicalists within its ranks, by giving explanations and dispelling what could only be misunderstandings. At the end of May 1922 it addressed a message to the members of the Spanish CNT. The government had just ended martial law and constitutional guarantees had been re-established. After three years of harsh repression it was an opportunity to draw the lessons from the experiences of the labour movement in all countries during this period packed with important events. The message said that it was hoped a clear direction would be given to the militants of the CNT. Instead there was the Saragossa conference, planned with the dominant concern of manufacturing a majority, where the speeches were stuffed with outdated formulae, unrelated to present reality. Above all, a majority had to be obtained for a break with the RILU. A grave mistake, the message concluded, for there was no room for another International.

The minority, determined to defend affiliation to the RILU, organised in revolutionary syndicalist committees and interpreted the meaning of the vote for the break. They explained: 'The Saragossa Conference has confirmed the existence of an evolutionist current which implies a break with a past full of heroism and sacrifice. The orientation adopted at Saragossa is worse than out-and-out reformism . . . The tendency that triumphed completely disregarded economic factors.' Its leaders were so blind that they refused to believe, even when it was pointed out to them, in the threat of a *coup d'état* which was going to outlaw them again. But Primo de Rivera was to take power on 13 September 1923.

In Portugal, the leaders of the General Confederation of Labour, who also denounced the dictatorship of Moscow, imposed their own. They refused to let supporters of the RILU speak. One member of the organisation, Perfeito de Carvalho, who had returned from Russia, was not able to present his report. The leadership got what it wanted — affiliation to the Berlin Anarchist International, but its manoeuvres demoralised a large number of delegates. 57 of them, almost half, were absent when the vote was taken. In the view of the secretary general, de Souza, 'capitalism was only preserved by a phenomenon of autosuggestion'.

France was now in a peculiar situation. Since the split there had been two national trade-union centres. The CGT had emerged from its manoeuvring considerably weakened; it no longer had even 300,000 members, though it claimed 700,000 in official documents. The new centre, which took the name of the Unitary General Confederation of Labour (CGTU), to stress its desire for unity, had 450,000 members. It held its founding congress at Saint-Etienne from 25 June to 1 July 1922. The provisional leadership, in which, by a chance combination of circumstances, the anarchists and 'pure syndicalists' held a majority, was got rid of. The resolution which was carried by 743 votes to 406, entailed affiliation to the RILU under certain conditions. Article 11 of the statutes, concerning the organic link between the Communist International and the RILU, would have to be deleted and replaced by a clause, drafted as follows: 'The RILU and the Communist International must, if necessary, meet to discuss common action; in the various countries the unions and the communist party must proceed in the same way, without any infringement of the independence of the organisations.'

Thus the Second Congress was able to open under conditions very different from those of the previous year. The debates would not get lost in so-called theoretical dissertations. The situation was clear. On Sunday 19 November the delegates assembled for the first session in the great hall of the House of Trade Unions and immediately began to deal with Lozovsky's secretary's report on the activity of the RILU during the previous year. To make agreement easier, the Executive Bureau of the RILU proposed to adopt the modification of its statutes proposed by the delegates of the CGTU. Article 11 was deleted and replaced by the following clauses: 'In order to co-ordinate the struggle of all revolutionary organisations, the Executive Committee may, if circumstances require it:

1 conclude agreements with the Executive Committee of the Communist International;

2 hold joint meetings with the Executive Committee of the CI to discuss the most important problems of the labour movement and organise joint actions;

3 issue manifestos in conjunction with the CI.'

The discussion in the Congress was brief. Some delegates stated that they could not understand why the rescinding of article 11 was being demanded when it was proposed to replace it by a text which made no basic changes. It had to be admitted, however, that for the French, the difference was significant, since they made it a condition of their affiliation. So they were given satisfaction.[43]

43. Andrés Nin, who at this time was the most active and best informed member of the RILU leadership, next to Lozovsky, wrote on this matter: 'The acceptance of this agreement put an end to our differences with French revolutionary syndicalism. Essentially, the concession was purely formal. Immediately after the Conference there was set up an Action Committee,

★   The question of the relations between the political party and the unions was also on the agenda of the Fourth Congress of the Communist International which was taking place at the same time. Speaking — as he stressed — in the name of the whole Italian delegation, Tasca stated that it might be necessary to make concessions to France or other countries in view of special local circumstances, but that these clauses should not be placed in the general thesis. He explained that we should prevent these concessions 'being something which tends to reinforce the dead-end situation of which several comrades have come here to point out the dangers . . . Even if it were true that in France the unions, because of their historical development, have a leading rôle to play in the proletarian revolution, this would be no reason to give up the creation of communist cells in the unions. On the contrary, it would be an additional reason for setting up cells and ensuring our place in the leadership of the proletarian revolution. The only reason against creating cells in France is the distrust of workers towards the Communist Party. It is a vicious circle in which a clean break must be made. We are convinced that the establishment of conditions for methodical work by communists in the unions is a life-and-death question for the French Communist Party.' (17th session, 20 November 1922.)

★   Once this delicate question was settled, this time easily, the Congress was able to devote all its sessions to the practical tasks facing

including representatives of the two Internationals. The later experience of workers' struggles made it obvious that collaboration between the two bodies was necessary. Moreover, the process of differentiation within the revolutionary syndicalist movement was speeding up. The sectarian elements were returning to their old positions, taking up a hostile attitude towards the Russian Revolution and the RILU. Meanwhile those who had been able to learn the lessons of the war and the Russian Revolution were moving towards communism. Finally — an edifying sight — certain people, like Monmousseau, who feared that the RILU would infringe the independence of the French trade-union movement, were shortly afterwards to convert the revolutionary trade-union centre into a mere dependency of the communist party, thus bringing about a progressive decline in its strength, obviously to the advantage of the reformist CGT.' (**Les organizaciones obreras internacionales**, Madrid 1933.)

the unions: the defence of workers against the capitalist offensive and the manoeuvres of the reformist leaders. The latter, in order to preserve their domination over the unions, resorted to expulsion as soon as an opposition to their policies developed. This posed a new problem, for we had to regroup those expelled, link their activity to that of the unions, attach them to the unions in some way, and stress in the eyes of the workers that the reformists' actions led to splits. Finally considerable attention was given to the urgent task of trade-union organisation and activity in the colonial and semi-colonial countries.[44]

44. In his **Souvenirs**, which a newspaper is publishing as I am completing this book, Victor Serge write: 'The Executive (of the Communist International) had decided, on Russian initiative, of course, to found an international trade union organisation affiliated to the Communist International. It followed logically that in splitting the socialist movement, one should also split the trade union movement.' (**Combat**, 2 December 1949.) In these few lines there are a series of startling errors that one is surprised to find in something written by Victor Serge. What he claims in no way 'logically' followed. On the contrary, logic requires a distinction between a political party which brings together people who are in agreement on a basic programme, and a union which is open to all wage-earners. The split in the socialist parties at the end of the war was inevitable. The differences between the ideas which came into conflict was so deep that they naturally led to a break. Scheidemann and Liebknecht could no longer belong to the same party. As for the trade unions, it is enough for me to refer to the pages where I have dealt with the question, to Lenin's **Left-Wing Communism**, and to the discussions and resolutions of the Second Congress of the Communist International. Far from seeking to split the unions, the communists were told to remain in the reformist unions, and even to entrench themselves there when the leadership tried to exclude them. At the time when Victor Serge was writing these **Souvenirs**, his memory sometimes lapsed. For example, in a passage before the one I have just examined, he stated that 'Trotsky had driven Cachin and Frossard out of Russia in 1920.' Trotsky did nothing of the sort, and neither Cachin nor Frossard was driven out. I have related under what conditions they went to Moscow at this time. They were treated to a 'hot and cold shower'. That is, there was no failure to remind them of their treachery during the war, but at the same time their favourable attitude — even though belated — towards the October Revolution and the Communist International was noted. They left Moscow after having publicly undertaken to support the affiliation of the French Socialist Party to the Communist International; and, of course, they left of their own free will.

1923

1: Poincaré has the Ruhr occupied

1923 was a decisive year — for Germany, for the Entente which finally broke up, and, it is not too much to say, for the world. The occupation of the Ruhr reawakened German nationalism. Hitler had already put in an appearance. It was a decisive year for Soviet Russia and the proletarian revolution. Lenin had been able to resume work partially during the first two months. At the beginning of March he was struck down by a further attack which paralysed him until his death in January 1924.

The crisis was provoked by the eternal question of reparations. It recurred again and again, at conference after conference, and was never settled. The Treaty of Versailles had set up a special reparations commission which was responsible for this problem. The successive sets of conditions which it imposed on Germany turned out to be unworkable, and, as one might expect, Germany for her part made every effort to increase the difficulties of applying them. The Treaty of Versailles had not fixed the total of reparations imposed on Germany. On 5 May 1921, the commission decided to reckon Germany's debt at 132 thousand million gold marks. But how could such a sum be taken from Germany, without finishing off the demolition of the European economy?

The interests of the Allies no longer coincided as they had done during the war; now they were coming more and more plainly into conflict. In Britain unemployment, exceptional unemployment, had established itself permanently. A huge body of two million workers were idle. Industry could not absorb them now, and would not be able to do so in the future either, unless a normal European economy could be re-established. The British government had tried to do this at Genoa, but it was always faced with the obstinacy of France, invoking her devastated regions to support her demand that Germany should pay. Britain retorted that she too had devastated regions — her great industrial centres where the factory-gates were closed, her coal-fields where the workers, reduced to unemployment pay, could only watch the accumulation of stocks of coal for which there were no longer any customers on the Continent.

In Germany, the situation got worse and worse. The controls imposed by the Allies constricted and exasperated the industrialists. The enormous war-time expenses weighed heavily on the budget. The Social Democrats had several ministers in the Government; sometimes there was a Social Democrat Prime Minister. After having broken the first revolutionary wave, they were reduced to asking platonically for an 'equitable distribution of the burden of reparations'. But Stinnes, who was then speaking for the magnates of heavy industry, replied in the negative, and the government remained powerless while poverty spread. The value of money fell. Each crisis saw a new fall in the mark. At the beginning of 1922 the first serious collapse made the mark fall so low that there were 650 to a pound sterling. After Genoa the rate was 1,650 and ten days later 2,500. An occupation would mean an endless fall. Nationalists of every variety agitated and became aggressive. Men who were looking for an agreement with the Allies on the basis of reasonable and practicable conditions were picked out by them for destruction. Walter Rathenau, former head of the powerful General Electricity Company, who had become Foreign Minister, had declared at Cannes that Germany was willing to pay 'everything that was possible'. He was assassinated in June. (Erzberger, leader of the Catholic Centre, who had agreed to sign the peace treaty, had been killed on 26 August 1921.)

In France the internal situation was difficult for other reasons. During the war the various governments had financed the exceptional expenditure almost exclusively by means of loans. The bourgeoisie wanted the war to be continued 'until victory', but it did not want to pay; it left the financial burden for later generations. Successive governments had only struck token blows against the enormous profits made by entrepreneurs of every kind and by middlemen who had got rich out of war work. The state budget collapsed under increasing expenditure — former debts, war debts, pensions to war victims, etc. The enormous deficit got bigger, for although a serious degree of disarmament had been imposed on Germany, the French military budget had not been cut. Indeed it was taking on such proportions that the government were concealing an important part of it by tricks of bookkeeping. They replied to the growing discontent by denouncing 'Germany's defaulting'. Thus the ground remained favourable for the chauvinistic current which had sent a nationalist majority to parliament, and above all for the anti-German feeling that the war had raised to its highest level.

During 1922 tension between France and Britain went on increasing. Germany, not being able to meet the dates fixed for payment by the decision of 5 May, asked that she should be granted loans; only after this would she be able to pay. In August, at a new conference meeting in London, Poincaré agreed to give her the moratorium she was asking for, but in return he demanded new measures of control stricter than the previous ones. Early in 1923, another conference had become necessary; Britain, France and Germany again took up the same positions. But this one was to be the last of its type. Poincaré had been nursing the idea of occupying the Ruhr for too long not to end by putting it into practice. He had asked military and civilian technicians to study the idea closely and to draw up a detailed plan. According to him and the men around him, this move, in effect equivalent to a resumption of the war, would finally compel Germany to pay up. There were risks. A break with Britain would become inevitable. But he felt sure that he would not come up against more than an insignificant degree of opposition within France. Briand himself had sometimes used a threatening style — 'send the bailiff to Germany', 'take her by the scruff of the neck' — and he had given the order for coercive measures, in the form of an occupation. But this occupation had been confined to the three key towns of the Ruhr basin, Duisburg, Düsseldorf and Ruhrort, and it had not lasted long. It was, in fact, a symbolic show of force.

The conference had lasted from 2 to 4 January. Poincaré had been obstinate, intimating that his decision to occupy the Ruhr was irrevocable. From this point on all discussion was pointless. The British, no less determined, declared that the French would have to go through with the adventure on their own. They expressed regret at not being able to help them, wished them good luck, as was fitting between Allies, but they found it hard to conceal their anger at having to deal with such an uncomprehending partner. But Poincaré was not left completely on his own. When the French soldiers entered the Ruhr on 11 January, they were accompanied by a Belgian contingent.

The President of the German Reich issued a solemn appeal to resistance which was almost unanimously confirmed by the Reichstag. It was to be passive resistance by the whole population; workers were to refuse to work for the occupiers. There was a series of incidents. The French government arrested and sentenced Fritz Thyssen and other big industrialists.

In France, the Communist Party, which had only just carried out the reorganisation deriving from the decisions of the Fourth Congress of the Communist International, was immediately put to the test. The struggle against the occupation of the Ruhr fell entirely on its shoulders. The Socialist Party offered only token opposition. It did not approve Poincaré's policy, but remained a spectator of the operation. It refused to call on its forces for active opposition because it did not dare to make a frontal attack on the dangerous anti-German feeling maintained and encouraged by the nationalists. It didn't even dream of co-ordinating its activity with that of the German Social Democracy.

The new leadership of the French Communist Party immediately took steps to establish a link with the German Communist Party. They helped to prepare, and participated in, a Franco-German Conference held at Essen, in the heart of the Ruhr. Poincaré responded by having the French delegates to the Conference arrested and imprisoned — Cachin, Treint, the new secretary general of the Party, and Monmousseau, the secretary general of the CGTU. The Ruhr commission of factory councils, replacing the union leaderships which had failed to act, issued an appeal to the various Internationals, to the national trade-union centres, to the social democrats and labourites. It asked them to send delegates to the Conference it was proposing to organise at Cologne. The Conference took place, not at Cologne, because of difficulties caused by the occupying forces, but at Frankfurt on 17 March.

But it didn't achieve the results the workers had hoped from it. The leaders of the social democratic and reformist organisations decided to boycott it and to forbid their members to take part in it. In France, a 'week of protest', during which meetings took place in every town, had only limited success. The workers were fundamentally opposed to Poincaré's domestic policy, but the hatred for Germany, maintained by almost all the press, dominated. They allowed Poincaré to carry out his operation; perhaps he would manage to squeeze something out of Germany, who was refusing to repair the ruins caused by her aggression.

The Communist Youth intervened courageously, defying all risks. They ensured the publication and distribution of **L'Humanité**, which was banned by the military authorities. The paper was edited and set up in Paris and printed in Germany. It carried out vigorous propaganda among the troops, calling for fraternisation with the German working masses. This propaganda produced such results that the French government took fright and launched huge police operations. Many young soldiers were arrested and the court-martial imposed heavy penalties. But propaganda and activity continued.

In Germany agitation and confusion produced by the occupation increased. The collapse of the currency made the provision of food an agonising problem for working-class families. Nothing could be done to make wages keep up with prices. There was poverty, unemployment and food riots. Anger and revolt were expressed in two distinct forms. The arrests of industrialists and mayors and the heavy fines imposed on towns assisted recruitment and activity on the part of the nationalists. Their leaders tried to mobilise all the sections of the population against an occupier who was trying to detach a piece of German territory, by encouraging separatist movements, in particular the creation of an independent Rhineland Republic.

For the workers the situation appeared more complex. Of course they were opposed to the occupying forces. But they were also opposed to Thyssen and Krupp, to the Ruhr magnates, harsh masters who were pillars of the régime that had led Germany into war. Spontaneous movements, many and frequent, broke out here and there, sometimes in the form of occupations of factories and mines, and sometimes the seizing of power in the towns. One tendency among the Communist Party militants urged that these movements should be helped and encouraged, and that direct action by workers should be advocated. But the Party leadership considered they were small risings doomed to failure, which ran the risk of turning the masses away from the Party. They thought that working-class action should first of all be directed against the occupying forces.

The nationalists had organised sabotage teams. They prepared acts of violence, blew up bridges, tore up railway lines, trying every means to prevent the French from exploiting the wealth of the coal-field. One of their men, Schlageter, was captured, sent before a court-martial and condemned to death. His execution on 26 May sent a wave of emotion through the whole country. The situation was becoming grave. The occupation was continuing and getting worse. How far would it go and what would it lead to? The leadership of the Communist International decided to convene an extended Executive Committee.

Once again the journey to Moscow was long and complicated. It was necessary to avoid regions under the control of French militarism. One communist deputy returning from Moscow at this time was unaccustomed to 'irregular' journeys, and, following his instructions badly, he wound up in the police station at Kehl after various mishaps. But he was in such a state that the police authorities refused to believe he was a deputy and telephoned Paris to check.

The first session took place on 12 June 1923. After the usual general report, Clara Zetkin gave a long statement to open the debate on 'the struggle against fascism'. On the afternoon of the 21st, Šmeral and then Gyptner had spoken, when Radek came to the rostrum. His appearance was unusual and the speech he was going to make was not less so. He began as follows:

'Throughout comrade Clara Zetkin's speech, I was obsessed with the name of Schlageter and his tragic fate. The fate of this martyr of German nationalism must not be passed over in silence or honoured only by a passing word. He has much to teach us as well as the German people. We are not sentimental romantics who forget hatred in front of a corpse, or diplomats who say that at a grave one must praise or be silent. Schlageter, the valiant soldier of the counter-revolution deserves a sincere homage from us soldiers of the revolution. His co-thinker Freks published a novel in 1920 in which he described the life of an officer who died in the struggle against the Spartacists. It was called **The Wanderer into Nothingness**. If those German fascists who want to serve their people faithfully do not understand the meaning of Schlageter's fate, then indeed he died in vain and they can inscribe on his tomb: "The Wanderer into Nothingness".'

The delegates were disconcerted. What did this strange preamble mean? What followed did not explain it, but, on the contrary, strengthened the first impression. Continuing his speech, Radek evoked a Germany beaten down and crushed by the victor. 'Only fools,' he said, 'could imagine the Entente would treat Germany differently from the way Germany treated Russia. Schlageter is dead. On his grave, his companions in arms swore to carry on: against whom? with whom?'

Now Radek recalled the battle of Jena, Gneisenau and Scharnhorst. Why this literary mediocrity about a nationalist 'hero'? He was not the first victim of the occupation. Before Schlageter workers had been imprisoned and executed. Others had been assaulted and brutally treated by Schlageter's friends. Listening to Radek, one had the impression that he was reading an article he had just hastily improvised, and which was a purely personal thing. Only the conclusion was plausible: 'We believe that the great majority of those masses now stirred by nationalist feelings belong, not to the camp of the capitalists, but to the camp of labour.'

For that indeed was the question posed by the nationalist agitation which, assisted by Poincaré's policy, was developing in a disturbing fashion.[45] It was already a problem before the occupation.

45. During a conference for the foreign press on 30 June 1924, Stresemann declared: 'To the French Ambassador who communicated to me M Poincaré's worries about the nationalist movement in Germany, I said, last November,

An article published in **Correspondance Internationale** on 30 December 1922 under the signature of H Tittel, pointed to the threat presented by its military form of organisation and its demagogic programme. In substance this article said that the fascist danger was real in South Germany. In Bavaria, and recently in Württemburg, the schemes of the National Socialist Workers' Party were taking on a very clear significance — brutality against workers, bloody clashes at Stuttgart and Geislingen, and a serious outbreak of rifle-fire at Goeppingen. It was a systematic campaign carried on with the help of posters, leaflets and meetings. The National Socialist movement was anti-semitic and pan-German. Its demagogy — 'against Jewish high finance, usurers and speculators' — sometimes won it too much of a welcome among the disappointed masses. Organised on a military basis it denied being a party. In the first instance it recruited among the middle classes and the petty-bourgeoisie. But we should not deny that there were also workers. Its most important support came from the big industrialists and the landowners. The 'active' members were bound by oath and pleged to risk their life if their leaders demanded it. Everywhere they benefited from a kindly attitude, even support, on the part of the police. The article ended as follows: 'The boldness of the National Socialists has earned them, especially in South Germany, a certain prestige. We cannot doubt that their energy may rapidly increase their forces and make them, tomorrow, a real danger for the working class.'

If, as we have seen, the National Socialist danger was clearly perceived and precisely defined in its distinctive features, the situation none the less remained peculiarly difficult. It was not purely and simply the struggle of the workers against their exploiters. The occupation was pushing sections of the petty-bourgeoisie towards the National Socialists, and even workers who had to be held back. Radek's unbelievable declamation was not designed to ease the task of worker militants who had given their activity a carefully judged

that it was entirely up to the Allies to check this movement. I think I recall telling him that every time M Poincaré spoke on a Sunday the nationalists gained a hundred thousand votes. I was wrong, but only because I was far below the true figure.' (**The Stresemann Papers**, I, p 255 in the French translation.)

orientation. On the other hand, it was of great value to the Social Democratic leaders who were remaining passive in face of the advances of the National Socialists and were glad to have a pretext — which seemed excellent — to denounce the 'collusion of the communist and fascist leaders'. Their papers hastened to reproduce Radek's speech and comment on it, just as had also been done by the papers of the German People's Party and the **Vossische Zeitung**, a venerable liberal democratic daily.

Radek then had to reply. He did so in an article free from the lyrical flights that had marked his speech, but with his usual caustic and ironic touch. After devoting a few lines to the editors of **Die Zeit** and the **Vossische Zeitung** he attacked **Vorwärts**, which had headlined its article 'Radek celebrates Schlageter'. 'Fascism,' he wrote, 'constitutes a grave danger, perhaps greater than the gentlemen of **Vorwärts** suspect, for they have frequently proved that they are scarcely capable of calculating correctly . . . The Communist Party is the only force which is at the moment organising the struggle of the proletariat against the armed fascist bands. But it is ridiculous to believe that fascism can be beaten simply by force of arms. One can smash small minority movements with government terror; but that is impossible against the fascists in Germany for the simple reason that the whole government apparatus is in the hands of fascists and fascist sympathisers.' What had to be done was to win for socialism the sections of the petty-bourgeoisie whose material and moral wretchedness was driving them towards National Socialism. 'Socialism was never merely a struggle to win a morsel of bread for the workers. It always strove to be a burning torch for all the wretched.' **Vorwärts** would concede that Germans ought to struggle against the enslaving clauses of the Treaty of Versailles 'but it will not be able to say how to struggle because it doesn't know itself.' The workers' government that the communists want to establish would start by putting the charges laid down in the Treaty on the shoulders of those who can carry them, and it would struggle against the Treaty of Versailles as the Russians struggle against every attempt to enslave them. Radek ended by saying: 'One of the greatest crimes of the German Social Democracy is to destroy all faith in socialism, all confidence in the strength of the popular masses.' (**Correspondance Internationale**, 10 July 1923.)

This article had been written in Moscow on 2 July 1923, ten days after the extraordinary homily on Schlageter. It had a quite different tone, and posed the problems clearly. One could still wonder what reasons Radek had had for delivering his speech, but that had only a very limited interest now.

2: Hamburg: Fusion of the Second International and the Vienna International

In accordance with its tactics, the Communist International addressed an appeal to the Second International and the International Union of Socialist Parties with the object of mobilising working-class forces to the maximum degree against the invasion of the Ruhr, the Treaty of Versailles and the dangerous activity of the nationalists. Neither replied. It is important and extremely significant to note that during this period the Second International and its sections were growing stronger. Left-wing elements who had left them, affirming that they would never again accept collaboration with men who had betrayed socialism during the war, were now returning to them. Their hesitancy in the face of decisive actions, of actions that lived up to promises, finally led them to turn to the side of the Second International. Already the German Independents had reunited with the Social Democracy of Scheidemann and Noske. There had been conferences to prepare the fusion of the two Internationals which was to be sealed by a Congress arranged in Hamburg.

As a final attempt, the Communist International had decided to send a delegation to Hamburg which would ask to be heard by the Congress. The Polish Communist Walecki was made leader: Lozovsky was representing the Red International of Labour Unions; A Andreev the All-Russian Central Council of Trade Unions; Heckert the German Communist Party; Tom Bell the British; and I was selected to represent the French Communist Party.

We had taken different routes to Hamburg. The delegation held a preliminary meeting to organise its work. This involved looking over the text of the appeal, and that of the letter to be communicated to the Secretariat of the Congress, and co-ordinating the interventions by the representatives of the various organisations if they should be permitted to address the Congress. This work had scarcely begun when I was summoned by representatives of the Young Communists. A meeting called by the Young Communists was taking place at this moment. In this period of tension between the French and German governments the participation of a French Communist would be of exceptional value.

The meeting was being held in a theatre quite a long way from where our delegation was assembled. The urban railway we travelled by spanned docks, ran along noisy quaysides and passed through busy quarters; night was falling and there was an element of fantasy in the trip. The meeting was less receptive than we might have expected. The hall was only part filled and there were gaps in the galleries. The organisers agreed it was only a partial success, but said that this should not lead one to conclude that the population was passive. The nationalist tendency was already strong and growing as the occupation continued. And the workers had launched several important protest actions against both the chauvinists and the government of Cuno, the man of the Hamburg-America Line. Later events proved that indeed they could not be accused of passivity.

Our delegation soon realised that all its efforts would be in vain. The Second International had a fully settled position. Its 'successes' made it more intransigent than ever, and the Vienna Union was no longer in any position to put the slightest pressure on it. It was coming in the rôle of a repentant sinner and had to accept everything — which it did. In the course of the debates a single discordant voice was heard — that of Steinberg, the Left Social-Revolutionary. He was now hostile to communism, but far from anxious to join up again with the discredited leaders of the Second International. He refuted the arguments put forward to justify the fusion one by one, and declared: 'It is said we must unite with the Second International because the great mass of the working class is with it. Did we not see during the war the great mass go over from social democracy to social patriotism? Were there more than a handful of militants at Zimmerwald and Kienthal? All of you here are only parties of legal reformism.

Those who lack the courage to start the revolution in their own country ought to be a bit more careful in their criticisms. As far as the reactionary danger is concerned, I will answer: yes, this danger does exist, but it must be sought first of all in our own parties. The social democratic parties are the essential factor of reaction at the present time. In Germany it is **Vorwärts** which is making the most energetic defence of the interests of the bourgeoisie. Do you know what the Second International is? It was and it remains the International of nationalists.' These words were greeted with shouts and produced uproar, but they had no effect; the final decisions had already been taken.

Waiting for the reply which the Congress secretariat was in no hurry to give us left plenty of spare time. One afternoon Lozovsky suggested we should visit the port. Andreev was with us; he was a friendly and modest companion, who didn't mind us joking about his name — Andrei Andreevich Andreev. A member of the leadership of the Central Council of Trade Unions, he had been in a bloc with Trotsky at the time of the great debate on the trade union question. On our return to town we entered a café; the friends who were ahead of me winked to point out a notice fixed on the door: 'Entry strictly prohibited to French and Belgian dogs'. Dogs was written in capitals. It was no empty warning; the day before Vandervelde and his friends had been asked to leave in a pretty rough fashion. It was not the only place; similar notices could be seen on a number of establishments. The invasion of the Ruhr and the sufferings it had led to had brought hatred of the French and Belgians to a climax.

Around August there was a rapid sequence of events. A big strike, in which the Reichsbank printers took part, forced the Cuno cabinet to resign. Streseman took power, forming a 'big coalition' government, in which were representatives of four parties. His programme was: at home, merciless struggle against communism; abroad, an orientation towards Britain in order to unite with her against France and obtain an advantageous arrangement of the payment of reparations, although, from this point of view, the result was disappointing. Britain condemned the occupation, but was unable to do anything at all to put a stop to it.

3: Confusion in the leadership of the Communist International. Revolutionary situation in Germany

These long months of deep crisis had seriously shaken the very structure of the Reich. The authority of the central government was frequently repudiated. Bavaria, which was nationalist, and where this took the form, not of a separatist tendency, but of a desire to dominate over Berlin and the whole of Germany, openly flouted it. In Thuringia and Saxony, on the other hand, socialism was dominant, a left-wing socialism in revolt against the leadership of the Social Democratic Party. The situation was becoming very serious. Berlin was proving to be powerless. The revolutionary forces in Thuringia and Saxony appeared to be the real centre of resistance to the reactionary threat coming from Bavaria. The leadership of the International decided to convene, not an extended Executive Committee, but a secret conference with the participation of delegates from the Communist Parties of states bordering on Germany in order to co-ordinate their activity and organise the support they would have to give to the workers' government that was to be set up in Saxony by left socialists and communists, and which would become the centre from which revolutionary action would be directed.

I cannot give personal evidence on this important meeting. I had had to stay in Paris, for I was then responsible for the Party's daily paper, **L'Humanité**. Cachin was still the editor, but there was never an editor who edited less. He confined himself to producing a short and superficial daily article of general propaganda, avoiding tricky subjects and constantly evading responsibility. When our delegates returned, it became difficult to produce the paper. They brought back contradictory information, such divergent accounts that it was impossible to know exactly what had happened at Moscow and what had been decided there. If, on the basis of a piece of precise information, we maintained a guarded tone about the preparation of the movement, we were assailed with angry protests. Germany was on the eve of revolution! The French Communists must be kept in a state of alert! Articles in the **Bulletin Communiste** were headed 'On the Threshold of the German Revolution' and 'The Proletarian Revolution is in Sight'. Bu we could not write that every day when we had no other *facts*, no other sign of revolution except the entry of three communists into the cabinet of the left socialist Zeigner. Finally, after having announced the Revolution, we had to record the dispatch, laconic to a terrible degree, saying that the 'workers' government' had collapsed and that the Reichswehr had entered Dresden with a military band at its head.

What then was happening in Moscow, in the leadership of the Communist International? This hesitancy, this inconsistency in face of a situation considered to be revolutionary, were alarming symptoms. They suddenly revealed a change which could not be ignored, although its nature and causes could not be discovered. The importance of the German events had thrust into the background what was happening elsewhere. For this reason appropriate attention had not been given to the attitude of the Bulgarian Communist Party in two situations of indisputable gravity.

Bulgaria, a nation with a population that was 85 or 90 per cent peasant, was favourable territory for peasant parties. The head of the government, Stambulisky, was the leader of one of these peasant parties and his policy was a first attempt at an anti-bourgeois peasant policy. He had sent the former ministers responsible for the war to trial, driven out the bourgeois officers and created a peasant militia. On 9 June 1923, a *coup d'état* led by Professor Alexander Tsankov succeeded in Sofia, but fierce struggles continued and spread through the countryside. The whole country was involved in the action. But the Communist Party took up a neutral position. 'Two hostile cliques are fighting; it's nothing to do with us,' stated its central committee, urging the working class to stand on the sidelines. The *tesnyaki* (narrow socialists) thus well deserved their name. They had let the peasants be crushed, and the Tsankov government consolidated in position.

To make up for this unfortunate passivity, the Bulgarian Communist Party leaders prepared, at Zinoviev's instigation, a rising against Tsankov. They organised a 'committee of revolutionary war', distributed arms, issued a call for insurrection to set up a 'workers' and peasants' government'. It was a total and humiliating failure. Kolarov and Dimitrov fled to Moscow. Brainless passivity had been followed by a disastrous putsch; but for the latter the Communist International, in particular Zinoviev, bore the responsibility.

When one went over this list of defeats, and more than the defeats, their causes, then it was impossible to avoid the question: what was going on in Moscow? The explanation emerged suddenly when Zinoviev decided to bring before the sections of the International the conflicts which had developed inside the central committee of the Russian Communist Party.

In 1922 Lenin had been able to resume work only during the last months of the year, and even then he could take up only some of the jobs he had done previously. As we have seen, he had to shorten the report he was to give to the Fourth Congress. He spoke to the Congress on 13 November at the expense of a huge effort which probably helped to bring about a relapse which was more a warning than a simple repetition of the first attack. Convinced that he had only a short breathing-space at his disposal, he set about the tasks he considered essential and urgent. His first concern was the leadership of the Party. On 25 December he dictated a note addressed to the central committee. It contained his final recommendations. There now seemed to be a risk of a split which must at all costs be averted. He tried to give a precise characterisation of the men of the Party, speaking of each of them with great consideration, in terms that were as far as possible from being offensive. He thought that if the old disagreements were toned down or explained, reconciliation would thus become easier, and the collective task would be continued without him as it had been carried on with him. With regard to one only of the members of the central committee, Stalin, did he express the fear that he might abuse the power he assumed as general secretary of the Party. Because his fear was so strong, and because it was doubtless confirmed by new and alarming manifestations of this abuse of power, ten days later, on 4 January 1923, Lenin dictated a postscript to his note of 25 December, entirely devoted to Stalin. This time it was brutal and peremptory. Stalin was to be removed from the post of general secretary.

The tenor of this postscript, followed by Lenin's actions in early 1923, allow us to describe the path taken by Lenin's thought. For he did not stop with this particular measure. Two months later, and, significantly, just because of Georgian affairs, he broke off all relations with Stalin, personal relations and relations as a Party comrade. A conflict set Stalin against the Georgian communist militants. Lenin clearly sided with the latter.

On 6 March, he sent them the following telegram:

To comrades Mdivani, Makharadze and others (copy to comrades Trotsky and Kamenev).

'Dear comrades, I am with you with all my heart in this matter. I am scandalised at the arrogance of Ordjonikidze and the connivance of Stalin and Dzerzhinsky. I am preparing notes and a speech in support of you. LENIN.'

Besides the drafting of his notes to the central committee and his intervention in Georgian affairs, Lenin had written five articles in this period in early 1923. When he had returned to work after his first stroke, he had been alarmed by the development of the bureaucracy. Renewed contact after four months of complete absence allowed him to appreciate the situation very well. An expensive and incompetent bureaucracy was weighing heavily on the Soviet apparatus. The Party leaders had always been concerned about this threat of bureaucratic excrescence. They had therefore created a special commissariat, the Workers' and Peasants' Inspection, the name of which indicated precisely its function. The workers' and peasants' organisations were to watch and supervise the bureaucracy in order to forestall its mistakes. But this commissariat itself had become a model of incompetence and inefficiency. Lenin wrote on 2 March: 'Let us say frankly that the People's Commissariat of the Workers' and Peasants' Inspection does not at present enjoy the slightest authority . . . Everybody knows that no other institutions are worse organised than those of our Workers' and Peasants' Inspection.'

Here again he came up against Stalin, for the commissar of this Inspection which was failing so badly in its task was Stalin. So Stalin had serious reasons to be worried about what might happen if Lenin was once more able to overcome his illness, while reasons of a different sort obliged him to manoeuvre to keep his position in the clandestine leading circle in case Lenin should die. This important article was to be the last. On 9 March Lenin was struck down by a third stroke from which he was not able to recover.

During these months when Lenin was partially or totally paralysed, the thoughts of certain Party leaders were obsessed by what they saw as the problem of the succession. A triumvirate (*troika*) was formed, consisting of Zinoviev, Kamenev and Stalin. Evidence that it already existed as far back as March 1923 can be found, but it was only from this date that it became a real institution, though outside the regular channels of the Party. The first task it gave itself was the elimination of Trotsky, whom a huge majority of communists and sympathisers inside and outside Russia saw as the only man worthy to take over the leading position from Lenin. Long and subtle manoeuvres were therefore necessary.[46]

However, serious problems were coming up. Abroad there was the new situation created in Germany by the occupation of the Ruhr, and the internal situation in Soviet Russia offered much cause for concern. The peasants had been freed from the requisition. They were able to dispose of their surplus production, but the gap between agricultural prices and industrial prices was such that they scarcely profited from this freedom. Trotsky had characterised the situation with a striking image: it was the problem of the 'scissors'. The two arms representing industrial prices and agricultural prices went on moving further and further apart. They had to be brought closer together, until eventually they could be made to meet. The peasants were discontented, and the Party militants likewise. Forty-six eminent Bolsheviks, including Pyatakov, Sapronov, Serebriakov, Preobrazhensky, Ossinsky, Drobnis, Alsky and V M Smirnov, published a statement, which included the following noteworthy passage:

'The régime established within the party is completely intolerable; it destroys the independence of the party, replacing the party by an . . . apparatus which acts without objection in normal times, but which inevitably fails in moments of crisis, and which threatens

46. 'On 26th May 1922, Lenin was struck down by the first paralytic attack; for some time the Party leadership kept the news secret. Lenin, who had always been concerned about the health of his comrades, had himself been an inexhaustible source of energy. Now his illness was so serious that it was not known whether he would ever be able to resume work. The manoeuvres for the succession began immediately. Precisely because Trotsky appeared as the obvious heir, the Party leaders united against him. Thus developed the historical circumstances which were going to permit Stalin to become leader.' (Ruth Fischer, **Stalin and German Communism**, p 235.)

to become completely ineffective in the face of the serious events now impending. The position which has been created is explained by the fact that the régime of the dictatorship of a fraction within the party, which was in fact created after the Tenth Congress, has outlived itself.'

Various opposition groups were formed. But all protest was in vain. This 'intolerable régime' was precisely what the triumvirs wanted to impose on the Party. According to them, it was the only possible régime, as they had explicitly stated when Trotsky, during a meeting of the Political Bureau had denounced it — already before the 'forty-six' — as intolerable, protesting vigorously against this denial of the teaching and practice of Lenin. They were wholly in agreement on this key point — discussion was no longer allowed, the apparatus decided and acted on behalf of the Party, but, of course, this must not be said. On the contrary, to appear to satisfy those who were protesting, Trotsky and all those demanding a return to democracy in the Party, they got the central committee on 5 December to pass a resolution solemnly affirming this democracy. But it was all a façade; at the very time they were voting for it, they were preparing the tactics by means of which all opposition would be made impossible. It was to be first gentleness, then violence. For those who had taken the text of 5 December seriously were not willing to be duped. The conflicts got sharper.

During this discussion, which for some time was public, Trotsky had alluded to the possible degeneration of the Bolshevik 'old guard'. Stalin replied with his usual vulgarity. The 'old guard' was sacred; it was sacrilege even to mention the hypothesis that it could degenerate; all criticism was forbidden. Now at this time the members of the Political Bureau were: Bukharin, Rykov, Kamenev, Stalin, Tomsky, Trotsky and Zinoviev. Stalin had four of them executed: Bukharin, Kamenev, Rykov and Zinoviev. He drove Tomsky to suicide, and after having exiled Trotsky he had him assassinated by one of his professional killers.

However, if the triumvirs were in agreement about setting up a régime which already had the essential features of a totalitarian régime, there was a veiled struggle between Stalin and Zinoviev. The latter was convinced that only he could replace Lenin. He had a reliable supporter in Kamenev, and Bukharin was at this time on his side. At bottom, no one — except the man himself — believed that Stalin could even aspire to the first place.

All these protests, resolutions, manoeuvres, and rivalries were completely unknown in the International. We learnt of them only later on, and fragmentarily. We then remembered certain facts which took on a meaning that had not been fully understood at the time. I can only give a brief summary of them here, and say just enough to explain the hesitations, inconsistencies and disasters that marked this year.

The campaign against Trotsky had begun at the start of 1923. Hitherto the great argument always aimed against him was that he wasn't an 'old Bolshevik'. Yet a number of 'old Bolsheviks' had pasts that were none too spotless, for they had failed to face up to events during the war or in October. Trotsky, on the other hand, could counterpose his past, his rôle in 1905 and in October, his attitude during the war. But this was discounted, for he wasn't an 'old Bolshevik'.[47] But now a rumour was spreading everywhere pointing to a well-prepared and less harmless manoeuvre: 'Trotsky thinks he is Bonaparte, Trotsky wants to play at being Bonaparte.' The rumour circulated to the ends of the country. Communists returning to Moscow sometimes came to tell me about it. They realised something was being plotted against Trotsky. 'You ought to tell him about it,' they said to me.

At the regular sessions of the Political Bureau, Trotsky tried to keep the attention of the members on the problems of the moment, which were certainly grave enough. He was listened to, but nothing

47. Lenin had already come up against this sort of 'old Bolshevik' as soon as he arrived in Petrograd, in April 1917, and he spoke of them in these terms: 'The Bolshevik slogan and ideas have been completely confirmed *as a whole*, but, concretely, things have happened in a manner *different* from what could have been predicted, in an original manner, remarkable and more varied. To ignore or forget this fact would mean being assimilated to those "old Bolsheviks" who have more than once played a sad rôle in the history of our party by repeating a formula that has been foolishly *learnt* instead of having *studied* the original nature of the new and living reality.' (Quoted by Trotsky, **History of the Russian Revolution**, Volume I.)

was decided.[48] For the real Political Bureau was not the one known to the Party; Trotsky was eliminated from it and replaced by Kuibyshev. By chance I happened to attend one of these meetings. It was in May 1923, at the time of the extended Executive Committee convened to study the situation created by the occupation of the Ruhr. On the day I arrived in Moscow, Zinoviev had asked me to go and see him during the evening. I went straight to his home, where I found him together with Bukharin. As they both seemed surprised and amused to see me come in, I asked 'What's the matter then?' 'You don't come to Zinoviev's house like that any more,' laughed Bukharin. 'You have to go through the secretariat.'

Great changes had occurred within the French Communist Party since the Fourth Congress. Zinoviev was impatient to ask about them, which explained his quite unusual hurry to see me. The conversation had been going on for quite some time when Kamenev arrived, then Rykov, Tomsky . . . I had just had time to glimpse Stalin's sly face — I had never seen him before despite my frequent stays in Moscow — and then Olga Ravich came up to me and gently turned me out, saying: 'It won't be very entertaining for you now; they're all going to start talking Russian.'

All the decisions were taken without Trotsky; sometimes even by Zinoviev alone, as in the case of the 'insurrection' launched in Bulgaria in September. Trotsky had known nothing of this disastrous operation. When he asked Zinoviev for explanations, the latter merely replied in an aloof manner: 'In war it sometimes happens that one loses a division.'

It is now clear why the French delegates to the secret meeting in Moscow brought back confused and contradictory accounts. For inconsistency and hesitation reigned among the leaders of the Russian Communist Party and the Communist International. They were too worried about grabbing Lenin's succession by carrying on a policy that was the opposite of his. That forced them to scheme, to constantly

48. 'During 1923, Trotsky's participation in the Political Bureau was reduced to the status of a pure formality. All the questions were studied and the decisions taken in secret sessions of all the members other than Trotsky.' Ruth Fischer, **Stalin and German Communism**, Harvard University Press, p 236.

deceive the Party, to replace thorough discussions with secret meetings from which the most competent militants were excluded.

These deliberations were so secret that Trotsky himself was mistaken about the position taken by Stalin on the German question. It was the first time the latter had participated in the life of the Communist International. His attitude at this time was revealed only much later, in 1929, when Brandler, expelled from the International, published, to justify himself, the letter that Stalin had sent to Zinoviev and Bukharin. It is an important letter for the history of the events in Germany and for the biography of the character. Stalin had finally declared against the insurrection. 'It is in our interest,' he wrote, 'that the fascists should attack first. That will rally the whole of the working class round the communists (Germany is not Bulgaria). Moreover, according to all information, the fascists are weak in Germany.' This beginning was obviously not marked by percipience. Zinoviev tended to be favourable to the insurrection, but he hesitated. Doubtless he was thinking of precedents that were not encouraging. When finally, after all these waverings, it was decided to prepare for insurrection, the right time was already past, and Brandler was forced to assume the leadership of an action he had been opposed to. The Communist Parties in the countries bordering on Germany, which had been put in a state of alert, were disconcerted by this capitulation without struggle. Stalin and Zinoviev agreed to try and clear the International of the responsibility by claiming it was all Brandler's fault. It was the first use of the scapegoat tactic which later became standard practice.

1924

1: Lenin's Death

THE DECAY of communism was already obvious when Lenin died on 21 January 1924. After his death, it proceeded at increased speed. In his last speech, at the Fourth Congress of the Communist International, Lenin had warned the communists of all countries against mechanical and slavish imitation of Russian methods. Zinoviev made such imitation into a compulsory rule. Moreover, under the pretext of 'Bolshevising' the parties, he introduced totalitarianism into the whole life of the Communist International. By means of the emissaries he sent into the sections, he suppressed all opposition just before the Congress. Wherever resistance appeared, the most varied means were used to crush it. It was a war of attrition where the workers were doomed to lose to the functionaries, who, having all the time they needed, imposed endless discussions. Tired of the struggle, all those who had indulged in criticism and were overwhelmed by the weight and authority of the International gave way provisionally, or left.

At the Fifth Congress of the Communist International, in July 1924, Zinoviev, beaming, proclaimed: 'We have achieved one hundred per cent "Bolshevisation".' He thought his rule was assured. At the peak of his personal triumph, he could not imagine that the most obscure of the triumvirs would rise above him within two years, and ten years later would have him felled with a bullet in the cellars of the Lubyanka prison. From now on it was Moscow without Lenin.

Appendix

1: Lenin's Final Recommendations to the Central Committee of the Russian Communist Party, considered as his political testament

BY THE stability of the central committee I mean the measures to prevent a split, inasmuch as such measures can be taken. For, of course, the White Guard of *Russkaia Mysl* (I think it was S E Oldenburg) was right when, in the first place, in his play against Soviet Russia, he banked on the hope of a split in our Party, and when, in the second place he banked for that split on serious disagreements in our Party.

Our Party rests upon two classes, and for that reason its instability is possible, and if there cannot exist agreement between those classes its fall is inevitable. In such an event it would be useless to take any measures or in general to discuss the stability of our central committee. In such an event no measures would prove capable of preventing a split. But I trust that this is too remote a future, and too improbable an event, to talk about.

I have in mind stability as a guarantee against a split in the near future, and I intend to examine here a series of considerations of a purely personal character.

I think that the fundamental factor in the matter of stability — from this point of view — is such members of the central committee as Stalin and Trotsky. The relation between them constitutes, in my opinion, a big half of the danger of that split, which might be avoided, and the avoidance of which might be promoted, in my opinion, by raising the number of members of the central committee to fifty or one hundred.

Comrade Stalin, having become general secretary, has concentrated enormous power in his hands; and I am not sure that he always knows how to use that power with sufficient caution. On the other hand comrade Trotsky, as was proved by his struggle against the central committee in connection with the question of the People's Commissariat of Communications, is distinguished not only by his exceptional abilities — personally he is, to be sure, the most able man in the present central committee — but also by his too far-reaching self-confidence and a disposition to be too much attracted by the purely administrative side of affairs.

These two qualities of the two most able leaders of the present central committee might, quite innocently, lead to a split; if our Party does not take measures to prevent it, a split might arise unexpectedly.

I will not further characterise the other members of the Central Committee as to their personal qualities. I will only remind you that the October episode of Zinoviev and Kamenev was not, of course, accidental, but that it ought as little to be used against them personally as the non-Bolshevism of Trotsky.

Of the younger members of the central committee, I want to say a few words about Bukharin and Pyatakov. They are, in my opinion, the most able forces (among the youngest), and in regard to them it is necessary to bear in mind the following: Bukharin is not only the most valuable and most important theoretician of the Party, but he may legitimately be considered the favourite of the whole Party; but his theoretical views can only with very considerable doubt be regarded as fully Marxist, for there is something scholastic in them (he has never learned, and I think has never fully understood, the dialectic).

And then Pyatakov — a man undoubtedly distinguished in will and ability, but too much given over to administration and the administrative side of things to be relied on in a serious political situation.

Of course, both these remarks are made by me merely with a view to the present time, or assuming that these two able and loyal workers do not find an occasion to increase their knowledge and correct their one-sidedness.

25 December

Postscript: Stalin is too rude, and this fault, entirely supportable in relations among us communists, becomes insupportable in the office of general secretary. Therefore, I propose to the comrades to find a way to remove Stalin from that position and appoint to it another man who in all respects differs from Stalin in one superiority — namely, that he be more patient, more loyal, more polite and more considerate to comrades, less capricious, etc. This circumstance may seem an insignificant trifle, but I think that, from the point of view of preventing a split and from the point of view of the relation between Stalin and Trotsky which I discussed above, it is not a trifle, or it is such a trifle as may acquire a decisive significance.

4 January

2: Fortunes of Lenin's Testament

To begin with and for more than a year these 'notes' were known to only two people — the secretary Lenin had dictated them to, M Volodicheva, and Lenin's companion, N Krupskaya, who kept them carefully locked up for as long as it was possible to hope, if not for a cure, at least for an improvement in his condition . . . Lenin died on 21 January 1924. Krupskaya then handed the testament over to the secretariat of the central committee of the Russian Communist Party so that it should be, as Lenin had wished, communicated to the next Congress of the Party, the Thirteenth.

The *troika* (Zinoviev, Kamenev, Stalin) who had installed themselves in power during Lenin's illness first of all planned to suppress the document just as they had planned to suppress the article denouncing the misdeeds of the bureaucratic apparatus. On Krupskaya's insistence, they made the following arrangements. The leaders of the provincial delegations to the Congress would be gathered together. Kamenev would read the testament — which he did before the session on 22 May 1924. Then it would be read to each delegation separately afterwards. It would be strictly forbidden to take notes during the readings and it would likewise be forbidden to make any reference to the testament in the plenary sessions. Krupskaya had remarked that such a procedure was against Lenin's wishes, for the question was supposed to be brought to the attention of the Party by means of the Congress. But the *troika* had refused any concessions and insisted on the procedure it wished to enforce.

But from now on the testament was known. It was impossible to prevent it being spoken of, in Russia and abroad, or even to prevent the text being published. The triumvirs' instruction was now a pure and simple denial: the so-called testament was only a forgery fabricated by the Opposition. But a time came when this tactic was no longer possible — or essential. It was necessary to admit to it. The authenticity of the document was confirmed by Stalin. In a speech to the October plenary session of the central committee and central control commission of the Communist Party of the Soviet Union, he stated:

'It is claimed that Lenin, in this testament, proposed to the Party Congress that it should examine the question of replacing Stalin in the post of general secretary by another comrade. This is true.' (**Correspondance Internationale**, 12 November 1927.)

He had waited to speak until the time came when, in sole command after having ousted his two partners, Zinoviev and Kamenev, and put men he trusted in all the important Party posts, he had nothing more to fear. There was no longer any voice to speak out against him.

3: Lenin's last speech to the Communist International (Fourth Congress; 13 November 1922)

I have said that we have done a host of foolish things, but I must also say a word or two in this respect about our enemies. If our enemies blame us and say that Lenin himself admits that the Bolsheviks have done a host of foolish things, I want to reply to this: yes, but you know, the foolish things we have done are none the less very different from yours. We have only just begun to learn, but are learning so methodically that we are certain to achieve good results . . . That is easily proved. Take, for example, the agreement concluded by the USA, Great Britain, France and Japan with Kolchak. I ask you, are there any more enlightened and more powerful countries in the world? But what has happened? They promised to help Kolchak without calculation, without reflection, and without circumspection.

It ended in a fiasco, which, it seems to me, is difficult for the human intellect to grasp.

Or take another example, a closer and more important one: the Treaty of Versailles. I ask you, what have the 'great' powers who have 'covered themselves with glory' done? How will they find a way out of this chaos and confusion? I don't think it will be an exaggeration to repeat that the foolish things we have done are nothing compared with those done by the capitalist countries, the capitalist world and the Second International. That is why I think that the outlook for the world revolution — a subject which I must touch on briefly — is favourable. And given a certain definite condition, I think it will be even better. I should like to say a few words about this.

At the Third Congress, in 1921, we adopted a resolution on the organisational structure of the Communist Parties and on the methods and content of their activities. The resolution is an excellent one, but it is almost entirely Russian, that is to say, everything in it is based on Russian conditions. This is its good point, but also its failing. It is its failing because I am sure that no foreigner can read it. I have read it again before saying this. In the first place, it is too long, containing fifty or more points. Foreigners are not usually able to read such things. Secondly, even if they read it, they will not understand it because it is too Russian. Not because it is written in Russian — it has been excellently translated into all languages — but because it is thoroughly imbued with the Russian spirit. And thirdly, if by way of exception some foreigner does understand it, he cannot carry it out. This is its third defect. I have talked with a few of the foreign delegates from different countries during the Congress, although I shall not take part in its proceedings, for unfortunately it is impossible for me to do that. I have the impression that we made a big mistake with this resolution, namely, that we blocked our own road to further success. As I have said already, the resolution is excellently drafted; I am prepared to subscribe to every one of its fifty or more points. But we have not learnt how to present our Russian experience to foreigners. All that was said in the resolution has remained a dead letter. If we do not realise this, we shall be unable to move ahead. I think that after five years of the Russian revolution the most important thing for all of us, Russian and foreign comrades alike, is to sit down and study. We have only now obtained the opportunity to do so. I do not know how long this opportunity will last. I do not know for how long the capitalist powers will give us the opportunity to study in peace. But we must take advantage of every moment of respite from fighting, from war, to study, and to study from scratch.

The whole Party and all strata of the population of Russia prove this by their thirst for knowledge. This striving to learn shows that our most important task today is to study and to study hard. Our foreign comrades, too, must study. I do not mean that they have to learn to read and write and to understand what they read, as we still have to do. There is a dispute as to whether this concerns proletarian or bourgeois culture. I shall leave that question open. But one thing is certain: we have to begin by learning to read and write and to understand what we read. Foreigners do not need that. They need something more advanced: first of all, among other things they must learn to understand what we have written about the organisational structure of the communist parties, and what the foreign comrades have signed without reading and understanding. This must be their first task. That resolution must be carried out. It cannot be carried out overnight; that is absolutely impossible. The resolution is too Russian, it reflects Russian experience. That is why it is quite unintelligible to foreigners, and they cannot be content with hanging it in a corner like an icon and praying to it. Nothing will be achieved that way. They must assimilate part of the Russian experience. Just how that will be done I do not know. The fascists in Italy may, for example, render us a great service by showing the Italians that they are not yet sufficiently enlightened and that their country is not yet ensured against the Black Hundreds. Perhaps this will be very useful. We Russians must also find ways and means of explaining the principles of this resolution to the foreigners. Unless we do that, it will be absolutely impossible for them to carry it out. I am sure that in this connection we must tell not only the Russians, but the foreign comrades as well. We are studying in the general sense. They, however, must study in the special sense, in order that they may really understand the organisation, structure, method and content of revolutionary work. If they do that, I am sure the prospects of the world revolution will be not only good, but excellent.

Conclusion

'Are you happy about the Russians? Of course, they will not
be able to maintain themselves in this witches' Sabbath, not
because statistics show economic development in Russia to
be too backward as your clever husband has figured out, but
because social democracy in the highly developed West
consists of miserable and wretched cowards who will look
quietly on and let the Russians bleed to death. But such an
end is better than "living on for the fatherland"; it is an act of
historical significance whose traces will not have disappeared
even after many ages have passed. I expect great things to
come in the next few years, but how I wish that I did not have
to admire world history only through the bars of my cage.'
— ROSA LUXEMBURG, Letter to Luise Kautsky. Breslau
Penitentiary prison, 24 November 1917.

'Immediately after the war the victory of the proletariat was a
historical possibility. But the possibility was not fulfilled,
and the bourgeoisie has shown that it knows how to take
advantage of the weaknesses of the working class.' — LEON
TROTSKY, Speech to the Third Congress of the Communist
International, July 1921.

I HAD intended to write 'The End' under the last line of my account.
I had produced enough facts, texts and discussions to recreate the
period I had planned to summon up, in order to disentangle it from
legends and false interpretations, or simply to rescue it from oblivion.

As far as a conclusion was concerned, I could leave the reader the job of formulating it, for it seemed to me so obvious that from now on it would be impossible to confuse the first phase of the Russian Revolution with what it became after Lenin's death, as Stalin made his way towards absolute personal power. But perhaps it will not be without value to stress certain points, to take up again problems that the Revolution had to solve, and which can be better understood at thirty years' distance.

The way in which the history of that period is too often written today is such that readers may perhaps think, observing in my work the absence of certain names and the amount of space devoted to others, that I too, for the purposes of my argument, have suppressed, falsified and distorted. I can say that this is not the case. I had no 'argument' to put forward, only facts and texts to present and to bring out the importance of them. If Stalin's name does not appear in my story, it is because he is never mentioned in the debates which took place during those four years, although they were varied and bore on all aspects of the labour movement. Likewise he does not figure in John Reed's book, **Ten Days that Shook the World**, because the author, an eye-witness, did not see Stalin among the heroes of those memorable days. From 1920 to 1924 I caught only two glimpses of Stalin; once in the circumstances I have related, furtively plotting with Zinoviev and Kamenev against Trotsky; and again, in the Kremlin corridors, during the Fifth Congress of the Communist International. He had never been seen there before, and he was noticed all the more because he was wearing military uniform, although the civil war had finished four years earlier, and he had boots on, even though it was July. Besides, he took no part in the debates. He simply wanted to make first contacts with the delegates from the sections of the International, doubtless hoping to establish a clientèle among them.

★   The succession of important events which have occurred in the world since the first world war at an ever increasing speed tend to dissipate the attention which should be given to each of them in order to understand their interconnections and their meaning, and thus to be able to draw the lessons. There have never been more abundant and meaningful experiences; but never has the working class so failed to learn from them. Starting from a socialist revolution, the social transformation which was to lead to the liberation of man, to a classless society, progressively declined in Russia into a totalitarian régime, while, outside Russia, there was the parallel development of fascism and Hitlerism. This is the question which dominates the life of our period, and it concerns each one of us. How was it possible?

The history of the four decisive years already provides the answer. And the two short texts I have quoted as epigraphs illuminate and explain the developments of the period which followed the first world war. The warning that I have quoted from the anarchist Malatesta gives a more precise confirmation: 'If we let the favourable moment (for making the revolution) go by, we shall have to pay with tears of blood for the fear we are now causing the bourgeoisie.' The bourgeoisie was frightened until 1920; but the European proletariat left the Russians on their own. The bourgeoisie regained confidence and the results were fascism, Hitlerism, Stalinist totalitarianism and the second world war. Lenin and Trotsky were wrong — but what Western worker would dare reproach them for it? They could not imagine that the Western workers, especially the Germans, emerging from a slaughter of which they could now see the tragic futility, would lack the necessary revolutionary audacity to overthrow a régime which the war-years had shaken to its foundations. They saw the Russian Revolution merely as the advanced guard of the German and European Revolutions. And this view was so concrete for them that they were already preparing for the new tasks they would have to take on. 'The Russian proletariat,' wrote Lenin, 'must stretch all its forces to come to the aid of the German workers; we must create a reserve of wheat for the German Revolution.' But at the same time they gave the peoples an ultimate warning — and here they were not wrong: 'Communism or barbarism: if the working class proves unable to respond to the appeal of the revolution, the world will slip back into barbarism.' If they overestimated the revolutionary will of the Western workers, they were right in their prediction of what would be the results of their passivity.

★ Rosa Luxemburg's pessimistic judgment, harshly expressed, has been confirmed by the facts. Western Socialists did not remain silent during the bitter struggles the Russian Revolution had to undergo. They gave solemn proof of their solidarity with the Russian proletariat and the October Revolution and hailed the soviets. They stopped work in the munitions factories, and prevented the transport of weapons intended for the mercenaries of the Entente. This was not enough, and in the last resort they remained spectators, refusing to risk the decisive revolutionary act. Why? Doubtless a large part of the responsibility falls on the syndicalist and socialist leaders who, during the war, had tied themselves to their governments, and who, when peace came, had offered their assistance to the bourgeoisie. Even in Italy, where the situation was particularly favourable, since the Socialist Party and the unions had opposed the government's policy of intervention in the war, the factory occupations in 1920, which logically could be only a prelude to the revolutionary seizure of power by the workers, ended up with the anti-climax of a demoralising compromise for the working class. The road was open for Mussolini and his fascist bands. In Germany, there was the Weimar Republic. The Socialist leaders were ministers and sometimes even Prime Minister. With Noske they went so far as to massacre revolutionary workers. They were blinded and infatuated to the point that they believed that fascism could only be a purely Italian invention, and they were incapable of seeing that one day they could know worse under Hitler.

Yet whatever the leaders' responsibility may have been, we must go deeper in seeking the causes of the relative passivity of the workers. If the impetus from below had been eager and resolute, it would have pushed aside and rejected all those who tried to break it or divert it. Should we conclude that henceforth Western workers are incapable of going to the point of revolutionary insurrection? Another idea which Lenin and Trotsky frequently returned to was that it would be more difficult to start the revolution in the West than in Russia, but easier to continue it. This was so obvious that it was generally agreed. But this brings us back to the same question: why? What are these greater difficulties to be overcome at the start?

Perhaps the main cause of this lies in the long years of parliamentary practice, in the habits of a more or less real democracy? In the European labour movement before 1914, the word 'revolution' was frequently in use, but as the socialist parties increased in strength, and their parliamentary representation became greater, it was no longer anything more than a ritual term, with no precise meaning, stripped of any commitment it implied. And in the long term the idea crept in and became dominant that henceforth an insurrection would no longer be necessary to take power, that it would be possible to save the expense of a revolution like those of the past with their sufferings and sacrifice of human lives. Only the revolutionary syndicalists, the anarchists and a few socialist groupings escaped the influence of the 'cajolers'. These were the first to respond to the call of the October Revolution.

★ The Soviet Republic had to fall back on its own strength. But it could not even use this as it wished. Passionately wanting peace, concentrating its thoughts on the construction of a new society, it found itself forced to put almost all its energies into the war. This leads us to another lesson that is often neglected. A revolution does not develop as it wishes. The dispossessed privileged class attack it by every means, open and underhand. They call the privileged classes of other countries to their assistance. The revolution has to defend itself, a task that is all the more exhausting since it begins amid the ruins. It has to create an armed force and a body for the repression of counter-revolutionary schemes — plots, outrages and sabotage. These are, once again, not measures it takes because it wants to but because it is forced to. At the beginning, in the enthusiasm of the first days, it is all generosity and mercy. It releases on parole generals from the former régime who will soon be found at the head of counter-revolutionary forces. The French bourgeois Revolution followed exactly the same course, and when the socialist Renaudel criticised the Bolsheviks for their dictatorship, it was precisely the historian of that Revolution, Albert Mathiez, who reminded him that the Revolution of 1789 had taken the same safety measures and had resorted to the same dictatorship.

But not only does the revolution have to arm itself and fight at home and abroad; war and repression make it run other risks. The harsh régime of this period, known under the name of 'war communism', involved a requisition of cereal crops, for the towns and the army had to be fed. But requisition is always an unpopular and demoralising measure. Continuing after the end of the civil war, this régime became dangerous for the Republic itself. In this respect the Kronstadt rising was the most tragic of awakenings . . . But the October Revolution had not yet exhausted its vigour, as subsequent events were to prove. Far from taking pleasure in and exalting — as was to be done later after the Kirov assassination — a repression undertaken unwillingly, the Bolshevik militants studied the causes of the rising with the desire to put right the mistakes that had produced it, by applying measures which could prevent a recurrence. All these measures were to constitute the New Economic Policy (NEP). The requisition was done away with; the re-establishment of a private sector gave greater flexibility to food supplies and made an industrial recovery possible.

In the same year, the leaders of the Communist International vigorously opposed those sections, and there were a good number of them, who were calling for a general offensive by the working class in all countries, without worrying about particular circumstances, but with the support of the Communist International and Soviet Russia. To oppose this, they developed the tactic of the workers' united front, intended to enable workers to come together on a programme of common demands. In November 1922, at the Fourth Congress of the Communist International, speaking for the last time, Lenin took stock. The NEP was eighteen months old, and its application had produced the results he expected. Not that all the aspects of the situation were favourable. Lenin was not one of those demagogues who always declare that everything is for the best and who assert that an obvious failure is a certain victory. In analysing a situation, he would systematically paint the picture a little blacker than it was in reality. Just as the last article he was able to write was a merciless criticism of the bureaucratic practices which had made their way into the Soviet apparatus, so too the conclusion of his last speech to the Congress was a vigorous warning against a slavish imitation of the Russian Communists.

There was nothing of this sort once Lenin had gone. The Russian workers and foreign delegates would not hear such words again. Indeed, the Congresses were called only at infrequent intervals, and there was no longer any discussion, for they were merely gatherings of unanimous approval, of glorification of the 'leader', a new figure in the Communist world.

★ The period of transition, the passing from the feeble régime, which the revolutionaries needed only to finish off, to the new society which had to be built, was the most difficult test. The civil war made it longer and harder, and foreign interventions encouraged practices and habits which were dangerous for the revolution. The leaders now risked losing contact with the masses; the party in power lost the sense of responsibility incumbent on the sole party in a one-party system. If it no longer expressed the aspirations, if it was ignorant of the needs, of the men who had accepted it as a guide, then it was no longer possible to speak of the dictatorship of the proletariat. From now on it was the dictatorship of a party, of a small group of men, a dictatorship which became intolerable to those very men who were supposed to be the builders of the socialist society. The exercise of power was then revealed with all its weaknesses; why discuss with an opponent when it is easy to imprison him?

★ Even before Lenin died a split had occurred inside the leadership of the Communist Party. On one side were the men who wanted to continue his work, to maintain his policy of free discussion inside the party, of revolutionary audacity with the possibility of mistakes which could be corrected. On the other side were those who claimed that such a policy was no longer possible, that it involved too many risks, in short that it was too difficult. In their view, it was now possible to govern only by relying on a repressive police apparatus. Their dictatorship was established even inside the party and its central committee. An opposition was formed which refused to follow them in what it considered to be a betrayal of the October Revolution. It was hounded and driven out. Stalin used Zinoviev and Kamenev — with whom he had formed the triumvirate — to get rid of Trotsky; then he used Bukharin to get rid of his two partners. Then he remained alone. Triumphant Stalinism hoisted itself up over the bodies of Lenin's faithful companions.

★   Lenin had foreseen his fate when he wrote, about Marx's destiny, that there is an attempt to convert revolutionary leaders, after their death, into inoffensive icons. Stalin presented him to the admiration of the crowds, claiming to be his humble disciple when he was betraying both the man and the revolutionary. Yet there is no shortage of writers, historians and socialists who claim that Stalin is continuing Lenin's work, or that at least there is a direct continuity between them. Stalinism is said to be 'a logical and almost inevitable development of Leninism'. It is, they say, still the same one-party régime, based on dictatorship and the absence of democratic liberties, and if today the repressive apparatus is called the MVD, under Lenin it was called the Cheka.

Starting with a witty observation, with isolated facts, with second- or third-hand information, they see reality only through distorting spectacles which they cannot get rid of when dealing with the October Revolution, being glad to show in this way that Stalinism is of the same nature as Bolshevism. The odious Stalinist régime becomes a sort of belated justification of their policies. The way they write or interpret history is that already used by Taine. When he set out to write the history of the French Revolution, he read and studied the texts only through the spectacles of a French bourgeois who had been frightened during the Commune and was still trembling even though it had been defeated. One can write the history of a revolution only if one sympathises with it; otherwise one can collect a lot of facts and fail to see their meaning. If one treated the history of the Commune in this way, there would not be much left for socialists. Nothing but empty chatter when action was necessary, dictators playing at being Jacobins, the taking and shooting of hostages. Yet the workers do not make such a mistake. They know that, despite its mistakes and weaknesses, the Commune remains a great date in the history of the labour movement. And the revolutionaries from all countries who responded to the call of the October Revolution would have had to have been very stupid or very blind if they could have mistaken for a socialist revolution what in fact was only the embryo of a totalitarian régime and a personal dictatorship.

★ A measure which is wholesome if it is shortlived becomes fatal if it lasts too long. The centralisation of all the forces of the revolution which is necessary for a victorious defensive struggle stifles those same forces if it becomes no more than a convenient way of governing. The sun may ripen or scorch the crops, and it is the same water which makes the land fertile or destroys it. It is very easy to declare against all dictatorship, to demand the full exercise of freedom, but for a revolutionary this is to indulge in empty words and to dodge the real problem which it is easier to wish away than to solve. This problem was given an excellent formulation by the Italian anarchist Berneri, who was in Spain at the beginning of the Civil War. He was alarmed by certain consequences of the 'sacred union' of all anti-fascist forces against Franco, and he was distressed to see 'a certain bending by the CNT' — the powerful anarcho-syndicalist Confederation of Labour. He wrote then: 'We must reconcile the "necessities" of the war, the "will" of the revolution and the "aspirations" of anarchism. That is the true problem. This problem must be solved.'

★ The conception of the role of the state is of capital importance. Lenin wrote a book to show this: socialism and the state develop in parallel but in opposite directions. The rise of one coincides with the decline of the other. And the death of the state marks the advent of socialism. Stalin, here, repudiated his 'master' so totally and so openly that he had to admit it. His state was an all-powerful monster, and it was through this that socialism was supposed to be achieved.

The trial of the Social-Revolutionaries took place in 1921 when the civil war had scarcely finished. The accused were self-confessed opponents of the régime. They had been in a state of open war against it since the dissolution of the Constituent Assembly, and they had planned outrages. They were tried in public; they had to defend them socialist leaders from Belgium, France and Germany; they admitted their acts with pride. It was a trial such as is seen in all revolutions, but it had nothing in common with the 'Moscow Trials' of 1936 to 1937, when Stalin got old revolutionaries to accuse themselves of crimes they had not committed. These were disgusting scenes, a degradation of reason, which have had no parallel in any revolution.

Lenin himself was anxious that he himself should write an introduction to the Russian translation of John Reed's book **Ten Days that Shook the World**. Having read it with 'the greatest interest' and 'never-slackening attention' he recommended unreservedly to the workers of the world that they should read it; he wanted it to be published in millions of copies and translated into all languages. It gave a truthful and most vivid exposition of the events which were significant to the comprehension of what the proletarian revolution and the dictatorship of the proletariat really were. Stalin did not share this opinion; he put John Reed's book on the index and it became a crime to read it. An internationalism which was ceaselessly affirmed gave way to a narrow nationalism, to an abject chauvinism, on occasion to a revival of pan-Slavism. And between Chicherin and Vyshinsky there is neither resemblance nor continuity.

The division of the Revolution into two phases, the second moving constantly further from the first until it becomes its absolute negation; this is neither arbitrary nor tendentious, but corresponds to reality. But should one conclude from this, or deduce that I believe, that until 1923 Soviet policy was free of errors and mistakes and that everything must be approved and admired? Lenin would have been the first to burst out laughing if such a claim had been made in his presence.

★   Many other questions could be raised here, for example the place and rôle of individual men in a revolution, indeed, all the questions connected with revolution. From a more general point of view, we could raise all the questions which must be solved by men today, if they want to break the infernal sequence of world wars, if they want to preserve themselves from a reversion to the barbarism of which only too many signs are already visible. The October Revolution was an attempt in this direction. Its ambition was to put an end to the division of society into classes, the source of conflict and harsh battles. It will take its place along with the succession of working-class risings and revolutions of the last century, a new Commune covering a whole country, with effects radiating out into the whole world, Europe and America, leading on the populations of the economically backward countries as well as the workers of the great capitalist factories. The Russian revolutionaries knew well the history of these movements. They had searched among them eagerly to take advantage of their lessons, their victories and their defeats. In their turn they wrote a chapter of this history which we must study both for itself and in the light of other working-class movements, in particular the Spanish Civil War, where, quite the opposite of what happened in Russia, the 'antifascists' fought in extended order, but under a government in which anarchists were to be found side by side with Stalinist agents.

★   It is not always easy to distinguish the moment at which a revolution becomes a counter-revolution. Its opponents usually proceed by means of a series of amputations, suppressions of men and institutions which fully accomplish their work of destruction only at the end of a period of time. In Napoleonic France, the word 'Republic' still appeared, and Napoleon was only able to finally get rid of it in 1808, by a decree which stipulated that 'coins minted after 1st January 1809 will carry on the back the inscription "French Empire" instead of "French Republic".' The royalist attempts on his life in the rue Saint-Nicaise had served as a pretext to deport the Republicans who were hindering his march to empire. Stalin, who pulled himself to power by different means, has not yet been able to get rid of the vocabulary of the Revolution; it has been enough for him to deform it.

Stalinism, to preserve itself, to keep its influence over the working class, needs to appear as the continuer, the preserver of the socialist revolution, as the incarnation of the Russian Revolution. This is a lie; it is neither one nor the other. Why should it be allowed to lay claim to a revolution it has betrayed? To identify its totalitarian state with the October Revolution is to do it a service; it is grist to its propaganda mill. For its empire will only disintegrate when the socialist mask it wears has been snatched from it, and the workers, seeing it as it is, in its totalitarian nakedness, will cease to give it their support.

I shall have fulfilled my intention if I have succeeded in drawing attention to a forgotten period, and if my contribution to the study of it helps it to be better understood.

Alfred Rosmer
December 1952

Biographical Notes

The following notes do not claim to be either complete or free of errors. This is partly because the vicissitudes of revolution pluck individuals from obscurity and fling them back there; partly because of the contradictory and inaccurate material to be found in even the most reputable sources. I would like to acknowledge the assistance of Norah Carlin, Charlie Hore and Anne Showstack in compiling these notes; the responsibility for errors is wholly my own.   **I.B.**

Abramovich, Rafail (1879-1963): Russian Bundist; during war Menshevik Internationalist; arrested 1921; after leaving Russia became leading figure in Second International.

Adler, Frederich (1879-1960): Son of Victor Adler, one of founders of Austrian socialism. Before 1914, secretary of Austrian Socialist Party. Leader of left faction; in opposition to war assassinated Austrian Prime Minister in 1916. In 1923 elected secretary of Socialist International.

Andreev, Andrei A (1895-1971): Member of Politburo 1930-52, deputy premier 1946-53; one of the few members of Stalin's Politburo not to fall into disfavour under Khrushchev.

Antoine, André-Léonard (1858-1943): Paris theatre-director; founded *Théâtre Libre* (1887) out of own savings, specialising in naturalist drama.

Antonov-Ovseënko, V A: Tsarist officer, rebelled in 1905; Menshevik; organiser of anti-war paper **Nashe Slovo**, of which Trotsky was joint editor (1915). Led storming of Winter Palace in October 1917, and became Commissar for War. Close friend of Trotsky and oppositionist in 1923; broke with Trotsky to support Stalin's 'left turn' of 1927; became Russian consul-general in Spain 1936, recalled to Moscow and disappeared 1937.

Arlandis, Hilario: CNT delegate to RILU founding congress; joined Spanish CP; director of school for commissars during civil war.

Avksentyev, Nikolai D (1878-1943): Russian right-wing Social-Revolutionary leader; after February 1917 member of executive committee of Petrograd Soviet; Minister of Interior in Kerensky government; active counter-revolutionary during civil war; later émigré.

Bakunin, Michael (1814-1876): Russian anarchist; joined First International 1869 but broke with it 1872.

Balabanova, Angelica (1878-1965): Joined Italian Socialist Party 1900; well known throughout European socialist movement; active supporter of Zimmerwald; 1919 secretary of Communist International and acting Commissar of Foreign Affairs in Ukrainian government; resigned 1920, left Russia 1922; later secretary of International Bureau of Socialist Parties; after second world war helped found Saragat's right-wing breakaway from Italian Socialist Party.

Barmin, Alexander: Soviet chargé d'affaires in Athens, came over to Trotsky in 1937.

Barrès, Maurice (1862-1923): French novelist; originally an aesthete, gravitated to right under influence of Boulangism and Dreyfus case. Exalted mystical sense of region and nation against idea of abstract humanity. Wrote daily patriotic articles in **Echo de Paris** during and after first world war.

Barthou, Jean-Louis (1862-1934): French right-wing politician, Prime Minister 1913, minister in many governments. President of Reparations Commission 1922; assassinated with King of Yugoslavia.

Bauer, Otto (1881-1938): Austro-Marxist, collaborator with Friedrich Adler. Wrote study of nationalities in Austria-Hungary. Prisoner-of-war in Russia; on return leader of left in Social Democratic Party; Austrian Foreign Minister 1918-1919; exiled 1934.

Bell, Thomas (1882-1944): Member of Associated Ironmoulders of Scotland, of which president in 1918; member of ILP, SDF and SLP; founder-member of British CP and later its National Organiser; in CP till death.

Beneš, Edward (1884-1948): Czech professor; worked with Masaryk in national liberation movement during first world war; president of Czech Republic, resigned after Munich; supported government of coalition with communists in 1945.

Berneri, Camillo: Italian anarchist intellectual; led Ancona revolt of 1914; escaped from Mussolini; murdered by communists in Spain in 1937.

Bernstein, Eduard (1850-1932): German Social Democrat; theoretician of 'revisionism', wishing to subtract from Marxism ideas of revolution and essential rôle of working class; ambiguous position on war; deputy, and after 1918, minister.

Blum, Léon (1872-1950): Main leader of French Socialist Party after split with communists in 1920; Prime Minister 1936-37 and 1938 of Popular Front government; deported during war; Prime Minister again 1946-47.

Blumkin, Jacob (1898-1929): Left Social-Revolutionary, member of Cheka, assassinated Count Mirbach, German Ambassador, during Brest-Litovsk crisis; later joined Bolsheviks, won distinction in civil war, rejoined

Cheka. Trotskyist sympathiser, remaining in GPU; visited Trotsky on Prinkipo, arrested and shot while returning with message.

Body, Marcel: French communist in Russia; in 1921 in disillusion got himself sent to Soviet Embassy in Oslo; worked with Rosmer and Monatte in 1930s and remained lifelong revolutionary syndicalist.

Bombacci, Nicola (1879-1945): Italian maximalist socialist; founder-member of CP, member of central committee; censured by Communist International for sympathy with Mussolini, expelled 1928; thereafter loyal follower of Mussolini, giving him a 'proletarian' front, even after overthrow; shot 1945.

Bordiga, Amadeo (1889-1970): Italian communist; on left of Socialist Party before war; opposed war, supported Third International, but differentiated himself from Gramsci and Togliatti by total opposition to parliamentary participation; criticised for 'Trotskyism' in 1925, expelled 1930; active until death with small, dogmatic 'Bordigist' groups that exist in Italy and France.

Borghi, Armando: Prominent Italian anarchist; secretary of *Unione Sindacale*.

Brandler, Heinrich (1881-1967): German building-worker, veteran Spartacist, founder-member of German CP, leader with Thalheimer until 1923. Made scapegoat for failure of 1923 actions; led right-wing in Party till 1929, when expelled. Then led with Thalheimer KPO, critical of German CP, but failing to analyse rôle of Stalinism in Russia.

Briand, Aristide (1862-1932): French politician; began as socialist, associate of Jaurès, but expelled from Socialist Party in 1906 for accepting government office; eleven times Prime Minister, including during first world war; smashed 1910 railway strike; advocate of concessions to defeated Germany and Franco-German reconciliation.

Brion, Hélène: Secretary of French teachers' union (CGT) in 1914; originally pro-war, became anti-war activist.

de Brouckère, Louis (1870-1951): Belgian professor; member of Belgian Socialist Party; early opponent of ministerialism; social patriot during first world war; member of Executive of Second International; several times member of Belgian cabinet and Belgian delegate to League of Nations.

Browder, Earl (1891-1973): American socialist and syndicalist before 1914; became general secretary of Communist Party of USA 1930, replacing Foster; launched slogan 'communism is twentieth-century Americanism'; in 1944 dissolved CPUSA; this 'right deviationism' was repudiated by the international Communist movement, and Browder was purged; the CPUSA was reconstituted under Foster.

Bryant, Louise: American journalist, author of **Six Red Months in Russia** (1982); her life up to 1920 depicted in the film *Reds*.

Budienny, S: Civil war cavalry leader; survived purges to become Marshal in second world war.

Bukharin, Nikolai (1888-1938): Bolshevik from 1906; in exile 1910-1917; a 'left communist', opposed to Brest-Litovsk treaty; member of Political Bureau 1919-1929, and editor of **Pravda**; supported Stalin against left from 1923 to 1928; then Stalin broke with him, and he was removed from all posts of importance; after capitulation to Stalin in 1933 editor of **Isvestia**; executed in 1938 in last of Moscow trials; author of **Imperialism and World Economy** (1972). (see S Cohen, **Bukharin and the Bolshevik Revolution** (1980) and M Haynes, **Nikolai Bukharin and the Transition from Capitalism to Socialism** (1985).)

Cachin, Marcel (1869-1958): French socialist councillor and deputy, Guesdist before 1914; fervent nationalist during war, visited Italy and Russia to encourage support for Allies; elected editor of **L'Humanité** in 1918; founding member of Communist Party, of which he remained a leader until his death.

Chambelland, Maurice: Revolutionary syndicalist, CP member; resigned from **L'Humanité** with Monatte, expelled from Party October 1924, helped found **La Révolution Prolétarienne**, to which he still contributed after second world war.

Chernov, Victor M (1876-1952): Russian Social-Revolutionary leader and theoretician; Minister of Agriculture in Provisional Government; opponent of Soviet régime, abroad after 1920.

Chicherin, G V (1872-1936): Tsarist diplomat; became socialist after 1905 revolution and emigrated; joined Bolsheviks 1918; Commissar of Foreign Affairs 1918-1930; died in disgrace under Stalin.

Clemenceau, Georges (1841-1929): French politician, Prime Minister at end of first world war; smashed army mutinies, and instigated blockade and intervention against Soviet Union.

Colombino, Emilio: Right-wing socialist and CGL leader before first world war.

Crémieux, Benjamin (1888-1944): French essayist and literaray critic; introduced Pirandello into France; deported, died in Buchenwald.

Crispien, Arthur (1875-1946): German Social Democrat, became member of Independent Socialist Party; opposed 'twenty-one conditions', broke with International after Second Congress.

Cuno, Willhelm (1876-1933); German politician and businessman; president of Hamburg-America steamship line; leading member of Centre Party; chancellor of Weimar Republic 1922-23, resigned over reparations issue; chancellor again 1926-29.

D'Aragona, Ludovico (1876-1961): Italian right-wing socialist and one of leaders of reformist wing in CGL. Took capitulationist attitude to fascism. Supported Saragat's right-wing pro-American split from Socialist Party 1947.

Däumig, Ernst (1866-1922): German Social Democrat journalist; chairman of Independent Socialist Party 1919; joined German CP 1920; rejoined Social Democrats 1922.

Delaisi, Francis: French economist and journalist, moved between anarchism and radicalism.

Denikin, Anton Ivanovich (1872-1947): Tsarist general; leader of counter-revolutionary forces in South during civil war; defeated 1920, fled abroad.

Dimitrov, Georgi (1882-1949): Joined Bulgarian Social Democratic Party 1902, leading member of left wing (narrow socialists). Exiled after failure of 1923 uprising; active in Communist International; 1933 defendant in Reichstag trial, acquitted; secretary-general of Executive Committee of Comintern 1935-43; leading protagonist of 'Popular Front' line; Premier of Bulgaria from 1946.

Dittman, Wilhelm (1874-1954): German Social Democrat; followed Kautsky's centrist position during war; joined Independent Socialist Party in 1917, but returned to Social Democrats 1922; emigrated to Switzerland when Nazis took power.

Doriot, Jacques (1898-1945): French communist; broke with CP in 1934 in opposition to 'Third Period' line, advocating a form of popular front before this became Comintern line. Founded the Parti Populaire Français, which rapidly evolved to fascism. During the second world war a violent pro-Nazi, fought on the Russian front.

Dreyfus, Alfred (1859-1935): French Jewish army officer, convicted for spying for Germany, sent to Devil's Island. After various attempts to reverse sentence he was eventually cleared and reinstated 1906. Public controversy over the affair led to polarisation in France between left and anti-semitic, militaristic right. In the socialist movement, Jaurès argued for support for bourgeois republicanism, while Guesde claimed this meant abandoning the class struggle.

Drobnis, Y I: Shoemaker, active revolutionary at fifteen, served six years in Tsarist prison, survived three death sentences. Later secretary of Ukrainian central committee. 'Democratic centralist'; sentenced to death in 1937 Moscow trial.

Dugoni: Reformist CGL leader; representative of national league of co-operatives; socialist deputy, wanted to join government after July 1922.

Dumoulin, Georges (1877-1963): French miner; centrist during first world war; later joined Jouhaux and right wing; in second world war collaborated with Vichy.

Dunois, Amédée (1879-1944): French socialist, opposed war, supporter of Zimmerwald, founder-member of French CP, which he left in 1927. Rejoined Socialist Party, but never happy there. Died in German concentration-camp after arrest for clandestine publication.

Dzerzhinsky, Felix (1877-1926): Polish Social Democrat, became prominent Bolshevik leader and permanent chairman of Cheka (Extraordinary Commission for Struggle against the Counter-Revolution).

Eastman, Max (1883-1969): American writer; 1913-18 editor of **The Masses**, radical monthly which sent John Reed to Russia; associated with left opposition from inception; published Lenin's **Testament** in English 1925; translated Trotsky's **History of the Russian Revolution**; always philosophically opposed to Marxism, he broke with socialism around 1940, and ended up a roving editor for **Reader's Digest**.

Enver Pasha (1882-1922): Turkish general, member of nationalist Young Turk movement which made revolution of 1908; leader of Turkish army in Caucasus and Dardanelles during first world war. Advocate of a greater Turkey including Turkestan, hoped for alliance with Bolsheviks to this end, but became anti-Bolshevik.

Erzberger, Matthias (1875-1921): German politician of Catholic Centre; encouraged arms drive before first world war; 1918 accepted Armistice while pressing for concessions because of Bolshevik threat; as Minister of Finance in 1919 pressed for acceptance of Treaty of Versailles, which won undying hostility of nationalists; forced to resign 1919 by corruption charges; assassinated 1921.

Fischer, Ruth (1895-1961): Founder of Austrian Communist Party, later leader with Maslow of left faction in German CP; led Party 1924-26, but replaced and expelled when Stalin broke with Zinoviev.

Foster, William Z (1881-1961): American IWW militant, then advocate of work in AFL ('boring within'). Leader of Workers' Party (front of underground CP), its presidential candidate in 1924. Loyal follower of Moscow, but replaced by Browder as secretary in 1930. Reassumed leadership in place of Browder 1945.

Fraina, Louis C (1892-1953): American communist and publicist; 1919 editor **The Revolutionary Age**, first paper to popularise ideas of Lenin and Trotsky in USA; broke with communist movement 1922; later became anti-communist economist under name of Lewis Corey; died amid deportation proceedings begun in the McCarthy period.

Frossard, Ludovic-Oscar (1889-1946): French socialist, follower of Longuet tendency during war. Became secretary of Socialist Party in 1918, secretary of French CP 1921-23; resigned from Party 1923; rejoined Socialist Party which he left in 1936; held ministerial posts in several Third Republic governments and in Pétain's first government.

Gneisenau (1760-1831): Prussian field-marshal; played leading rôle in campaigns against Napoleon in 1813 and 1815.

Godonnèche, Victor: French syndicalist of pro-RILU tendency; resigned from **L'Humanité** together with Monatte.

Gompers, Samuel (1850-1924): President of American Federation of Labour; ultra-conservative bureaucrat, aimed at organisation based on skilled workers; considered Amsterdam International Federation of Trade Unions too red.

Gorky, Maxim (1868-1936): Russian novelist; arrested for seditious poem 1901; worked with Bolsheviks 1905-17; went to USA to collect funds for them; critical of repressive measures in early years of Soviet régime; in 1932 became chairman of Union of Soviet Writers and advocate of 'socialist realism'.

Görter, Hermann (1864-1933): Dutch poet and founder of Dutch CP; defended line of KAPD against Lenin.

Gotz, Abraham R (1882-1937): Social-Revolutionary, then supporter of Kerensky; imprisoned 1922-27; then worked for state bank; probably shot 1937.

Gramsci, Antonio (1891-1937): Italian revolutionary; joined Socialist Party 1914; founded weekly **Ordine Nuovo** 1919; a leader of Italian Communist Party 1921-26, opposing Bordiga's sectarianism; imprisoned 1926; wrote copiously while in prison; works available include two volumes of **Political Writings** (1977 and 1979) and **Prison Notebooks** (1973). (C Harman, **Gramsci versus Reformism** (Bookmarks 1986) provides a refutation of the view that Gramsci was some sort of premature 'Eurocommunist'.)

Graziadei, Antonio (1873-1953): Italian Socialist; right-wing till 1914; founder-member of Italian CP; later criticised for rightist deviation, expelled 1929. Later made self-criticism, readmitted to CP.

Guesde, Jules (1845-1922): From 1880s a leading advocate of Marxism in France; in united Socialist Party formed in 1905, represented revolutionary wing against Jaurès, but tended to dogmatism and sectarianism; nationalist in 1914; minister in war cabinet 1914-1916; hostile to Bolshevism; remained in Socialist Party after split.

Guilbeaux (1885-1938): French socialist; took part in Kienthal conference 1916; later became anti-Semite and supporter of Mussolini.

Heckert, Fritz: Member of Saxon government with Brandler in October 1923; German CP leader in thirties, supported Ulbricht in faction-fight, stayed loyal to Stalin; reported executed by GPU after Moscow trials.

Henderson, Arthur (1863-1935): British Labour politician; member of war-time government till resignation in 1917; Foreign Minister in first Labour government.

Hilferding, Rudolf (1877-1944): Leading German Social Democrat theorist and economist; Finance Minister in Müller government of 1928-30; author of important books on imperialism and finance-capital; arrested by Vichy régime, handed over to Nazis in 1940.

Höglund, Zeth (1884-1956): Swedish Social Democrat; attended Zimmerwald; in 1917 became chairman of breakaway left-wing Social Democratic

Party, later Communist Party of Sweden; disputed authority of Communist International in 1924 and returned to Social Democrats.

Humbert-Droz, Jules (1891-1971): Swiss protestant pastor; refused military service 1916, supported Zimmerwald; campaigned for affiliation of Swiss Socialist Party to Third International; elected secretary of Communist International 1921; main responsibility Latin countries; supported Bukharinite opposition; leader of Swiss CP 1936-41; expelled 1943; secretary general of Swiss Socialist Party 1946-59; later active in peace movement.

Huysmans, Camille (1871-1968): Belgian Socialist; secretary of International Socialist Bureau of Second International 1904-19; centrist during first world war; Prime Minister of Belgium 1946-47.

Ibáñez, Jesús: Member of CNT, later joined Spanish CP; escaped to Russia after Primo de Rivera took power; participated in reorganisation of Party.

Jaurès, Jean (1859-1914): Leader of reformist wing of French Socialist Party; founding editor of L'Humanité 1904; anti-militarist; assassinated on eve of first world war.

Jean, Renaud (1887-1961): French farm-worker; member of Socialist Party from 1908; founder-member of CP; elected deputy in 1920, 1924, 1932, 1936; nearly broke with Party over Hitler-Stalin pact; thereafter distrusted by Party leadership, and excluded from parliamentary or party office. (For Jean at the end of his life, see Gordon Wright, Rural Revolution in France, pp 192-197.)

Jouhaux, Léon (1879-1954): Pre-first world war French revolutionary syndicalist; secretary general of CGT 1909-40 and 1945-47; supported first world war; led pro-American breakaway from CGT in 1947 to form 'Force Ouvrière'; rewarded by Nobel Peace Prize 1951.

de Jouvenel, Robert (1881-1924): French journalist and political satirist; editor of L'Oeuvre, a radical and anti-clerical daily.

Kamenev, Leon (1883-1936): Bolshevik leader; editorial board of Pravda; deported to Siberia during war; resigned from central committee 1917; entered Political Bureau 1919; 1923 sided with Zinoviev against Trotsky; 1926 with Trotsky against Stalin; imprisoned 1934, executed 1936.

Kautsky, Karl (1854-1938): Chief theoretician of Second International and German Social Democratic Party before 1914, giving a dogmatic and mechanical interpretation of Marxism; failed to oppose first world war; after war a firm opponent of Bolshevism — replied to in Trotsky's Terrorism and Communism — while retaining Marxist terminology.

Ker, Louis-Antoine (1886-1923): Student before war; combatant, received croix de guerre; joined Socialist Party 1919; became international secretary of CP 1921; resigned posts 1922 because of freemasonry.

Keynes, John Maynard (1883-1946): Major economic theorist; British representative at Versailles peace talks 1919; resigned because felt reparations imposed on Germany threatened world economy. Published **The Economic Consequences of the Peace** (1919), attacking Lloyd George and President Wilson.

Kobietsky, Mikhail: Born 1881. Joined Russian Social Democratic Party 1903; Bolshevik; emigrated to Denmark 1908; after 1917 held important posts in Bolshevik Party and Communist International.

Koenen, Wilhelm (1868-1963): Member of German Social Democratic Party, and after 1917, Independent Socialist Party; member of central committee of German CP, in anti-Levi majority; 1927 communist deputy; in exile in London helped launch appeal for German Popular Front 1937; returned to East Germany 1945; held government and party posts.

Kolarov, Vasil (1877-1950): Leading Bulgarian 'narrow socialist'; attended Zimmerwald; early leader of Bulgarian CP; in USSR during second world war; returned to Bulgaria after war, held various government posts; succeeded Dimitrov as Premier in 1949.

Kolchak, Alexander V (1873-1920): Tsarist admiral; led Czech counter-revolutionary forces in civil war; handed over to Bolsheviks by discontented Czechs and shot.

Kollontai, Alexandra (1872-1952): Menshevik, then Bolshevik, 'left communist' and leader of 'Workers' Opposition'; after Trotskyist sympathies became orthodox Stalinist; Russian diplomat in Mexico, Norway and Sweden. (See **Selected Writings** (ed. Alix Holt 1977) and pamphlets **Communism and the Family** and **Sexual Relations and Class Struggle** (both Bookmarks 1985).)

Krasin, L B (1870-1926): Russian engineer; active in clandestine work during youth. Led delegation which signed Anglo-Soviet trade agreeement; ambassador to Paris and London.

Krasnoshchekov, Alexandr: Russian radical with anarchist connections; in US before Revolution; Prime Minister of Far Eastern Republic, recalled to Moscow 1921; first director of Bank for Industry 1922; charged with embezzlement 1924; later shot.

Kropotkin, Pyotr (1842-1921): Russian price; support for Polish rising of 1861 brought him to revolutionary ideas; involved in zoological and anthropological research; briefly associated with First International from 1872, but rejected Marxism; exiled in Western Europe from 1874; developed theory of anarchism on what he claimed to be a scientific foundation.

Krupp, Gustav (1870-1950): German diplomat, married into famous German steel family; arms producer and supporter of Nazism; after war Allies proposed to indict him as war criminal, but for health reasons never brought to trial.

Krupskaya, Nadezhda (1869-1939): Helped form Petersburg League of

Struggle for the Liberation of the Working Class; 1896, arrested and exiled to Minusinsk; there married Lenin; abroad 1901-5, 1908-17; secretary of **Iskra**; after Revolution held government positions, especially in relation to labour education.

Kuibyshev, V V (1888-1935): Leading Bolshevik; army commissar in Turkestan during civil war; secretary of central committee when Stalin took over Party secretariat April 1922; member of Politburo from 1927.

Kun, Bela (1886-1939): Born in Transylvania, became socialist in youth; first contacted Bolsheviks as prisoner-of-war in 1917; leader of Hungarian CP and of short-lived Hungarian Soviet Republic in 1919; leading figure in Third International; supported Zinoviev then Stalin; tried by Party tribunal 1937, killed 1939.

Labourbe, Jeanne (1879-1919): French communist; from February 1919 conducted underground work among French sailors and soldiers in Odessa.

Labriola, Antonio (1843-1904): Theoretician who introduced Marxism into Italy.

Lafargue, Paul (1842-1911): Son-in-law of Marx; founded *Parti Ouvrier Français* with Guesde in 1880; deputy 1885-1893, later an opponent of participation in government. Author of several works popularising Marxist theory; he and his wife committed suicide on approach of old age.

Laval, Pierre (1883-1945): French politician; socialist 1903-20, then moved to the right; Prime Minister 1931 and 1935; head of collaborationist Vichy government 1942; sentenced and shot 1945.

Lazzari, Costantino (1857-1927): One of the founders and leaders of Italian Socialist Party; its secretary 1912-1919; sympathetic to Soviet Union but opposed to Communist International discipline.

Lefebvre, Raymond (1890-1920): French writer; wounded in first winter of war; developed as internationalist and republican, moved sharply to Bolshevism in 1919.

Legien, Karl (1861-1920): Turner; became president of German trade unions, then from 1913 president of International Federation of Trade Unions; right-wing Social Democrat.

Lepetit: French syndicalist; labourer; worked on **Le Libertaire**; broke with Committee for the Resumption of International Relations in 1917 to form Committee of Syndicalist Defence.

Leval, Gaston: Anarchist writer of French extraction; later wrote study of Spanish civil war, **Collectives in the Spanish Revolution** (1975).

Levi, Paul (1883-1930): Rosa Luxemburg's lawyer; a leader of German Independent Socialists, co-founder of *Spartakusbund* and early leader of German CP; in 1921 issued pamphlet denouncing 'March Action', for which expelled from CP (though Lenin was sympathetic to the substance of his argument); later joined left of Social Democratic Party; probably committed suicide.

Litvinov, Maxim (1876-1951): Member of Russian Social Democratic Party from inception; worked abroad, including Britain during war; Soviet plenipotentiary representative to Britain 1917-18; Commissar for Foreign Affairs 1930-39; negotiated US government recognition of Soviet Union.

Lockhart, Sir Robert Bruce (1887-1970): British vice-consul in Moscow 1911, acting consul-general 1915-17; head of special mission to Soviet government January 1918; imprisoned in Kremlin, exchanged for Litvinov September 1918; director-general of Political Warfare Executive 1941-45; published his account of the 'Lockhart plot' in **Memoirs of a British Agent** (1932).

Longuet, Jean (1876-1938): Son of Charles Longuet (member of Paris Commune) and of Jenny Marx; French Socialist Party journalist and international expert before 1914; did not oppose war, but supported left tendency of Socialist Party, where he remained after foundation of Communist Party.

Loriot, Fernand (1870-1932): French school-teacher and member of Socialist Party. Pro-war in 1914, opposed it from 1915, co-operating with Trotsky. One of signatories of protocol arranging Lenin's journey though Germany. Founder-member of French CP; left party in disillusion in 1926. Published article in Monatte's **Révolution Prolétarienne** rejecting idea of Leninist party.

Lozovsky (or Dridzo-Lozovsky), Salomon A (1878-1952): Russian Social Democrat from 1901; in exile 1909-17; mainly in Paris; supported Zimmerwald; expelled from Bolshevik Party 1918 for views on party and unions; rejoined 1919; general secretary of RILU 1921-37; sent to a concentration-camp 1949; shot 1952; later rehabilitated.

Lunacharsky, Anatoly V (1875-1933): Soviet politician and intellectual; dramatist and critic; wrote on art and literature; associated with Lenin from 1904; People's Commissar for Education 1917-29.

Lutovinov, Yuri: One of leaders of 'Workers' Opposition'; opposed economic policy again in 1923; committed suicide 1924.

MacDonald, Ramsay (1866-1937): One of founders of British Labour Party; centrist during war; Prime Minister 1924 and 1929; in 1931 broke with Labour to become Prime Minister of National Government.

MacLaine, William (1891-1960): British engineer; leading member of Shop Stewards' Movement in first world war; member of British Socialist Party, and one of its delegates to Second Congress of the Communist International; 1920, member of central committee of CP; later left CP, became assistant general secretary of AEU.

Makharadze, F I (1886-1925): Important Bolshevik leader in Georgia; president of Georgian central executive committee, member of Caucasian Party bureau.

Malatesta, Errico (1853-1932): Italian anarchist, disciple of Bakunin and Cafiero; took part in rural revolts in Bologna (1874) and Sicily (1894); frequently imprisoned; lived in England, France, Switzerland and USA; opposed vigorously anarchists who went over to nationalism in first world war.

Mandel, Georges (1885-1944): French conservative politician, associate of Clemenceau, opponent of appeasement, murdered by Vichy militia.

Mann, Tom (1856-1941): Led London dock-strike 1889; secretary of ILP, 1894; travelled in USA, Australia, New Zealand, South Africa — did trade-union organising. Attracted by ideas of IWW and French syndicalism. Founder-member of British CP; leader of Minority Movement; signed **Unity Manifesto** 1937.

Manuilsky, Dimitri (1883-1952): Russian Social Democrat from 1903; deported 1906, worked with Trotsky in exile, supported Zimmerwald; joined Bolshevik Party 1917; secretary of Executive Committee of Communist International 1929-34; Foreign Minister of Ukraine 1945-52.

Marchand, René: Petrograd correspondent of **Figaro**; member of French communist group in Russia; later went to Turkey, renounced Bolshevism; became supporter of Kemal Ataturk.

Martinet, Marcel (1887-1944): French revolutionary socialist, poet, novelist and dramatist; author of **La Nuit**, described by Trotsky as 'the drama of the French working class'; literary editor of **L'Humanité** from 1921; in bad health from 1923 but close to **La Révolution Prolétarienne** in 1930s.

Martov, L (Tsederbaum) (1873-1923): Russian Social Democrat, Menshevik leader, centrist during first world war; opposed Bolshevik revolution; emigrated 1920.

Masaryk, Thomas (1850-1937): Czech professor and sociologist; led Czech national liberation movement; president of Czech Republic 1918-35; father of Jan Masaryk, Czech Minister who committed suicide in 1948.

Mathiez, Albert (1874-1932): Historian of the French Revolution, notably author of study of popular living standards; admirer of Robespierre.

Maurin, Joaquín (1897-1937): Spanish syndicalist; after attempt to form syndicalist organisation joined CP; expelled 1931 for supporting Trotsky, though criticised sharply by Trotsky; leader of Workers' and Peasants' Bloc, fused with Nin's Communist Left to form POUM. Imprisoned in Galicia before civil war started.

Mdivani, P G (1887-1937): Georgian revolutionary, old Bolshevik, civil war commissar; member of Caucasian Bureau of the central committee and of the central committee of the Georgian CP until the collective resignation of this committee in October 1922 because of opposition to Stalin's policies on national question. Soviet commercial representative in France from 1924, deputy chairman of the Georgian government from 1931-36. Later purged.

Merrheim, Alphonse (1871-1925): French copper-worker; Guesdist socialist, then syndicalist; strike-leader; opposed first world war, attended Zimmerwald; went over to right in 1918; supported Jouhaux; violently anti-communist.

Mesnil, Jacques (1872-1940): French socialist writer; supported Rolland's opposition to war; 1916 joined Society for Documentary and Critical Studies on the War, under Charles Gide, a tendency to the right of the Committee for the Resumption of International Relations; associate of Serge in Comintern in Russia.

Millerand, Alexandre (1859-1943): French socialist, deputy; in 1899 entered Waldeck-Rousseau's government of 'republican defence', provoking profound debate about participation in bourgeois governments in French socialist movement; War Minister 1914-15; Prime Minister 1920; President 1920-24.

Mirabeau, Honoré-Gabriel (1749-1791): One of most notable orators of French Revolution; advocate of constitutional monarchy.

Monatte, Pierre (1881-1960): Printing worker, revolutionary syndicalist; founded **La Vie Ouvrière** in 1909; founder-member of CGTU after CGT split in 1921; joined CP in 1923; expelled in 1924; founded **La Révolution Prolétarienne** in 1925, continued to work with it till death. returned to factory-floor until retirement.

Monmousseau, Gaston (1883-1960): French railwayman; as anarchist refused to join trade union till 1910. Joined Monatte in opposition to Bolshevik views on trade unions; later became loyal CP member; member of Political Bureau 1926-45.

Moutet, Marius (1876-1968): French lawyer; member of League for the Rights of Man and Socialist Party (from 1895); deputy at various times from 1914, later senator; intimate of Léon Blum. Minister for colonies 1936-38 and 1946-47; one of architects of French war in Vietnam.

Mühsam, Erich (1878-1934): German poet and dramatist; editor of a number of anarchist periodicals; took a prominent part in Bavarian left-wing movements, for which he was imprisoned for six years in 1919; further revolutionary activities led to his death in a Nazi concentration camp.

Murphy, J T (1888-1966): British militant engineer in pre-war period; leading member of shop stewards' movement during war; leading member of British CP until resignation in 1932.

Nettlau, Max (1865-1944): Austrian-born historian; joined Socialist League in London (1885), then turned to anarchism under influence of Kropotkin. Collected documentation on libertarian politics; wrote biography of Bakunin.

Neumann, Margaret Buber: Wife of Heinz Neumann, German Communist, Comintern emissary to China, recalled to Moscow 1937, arrested and disappeared; she was imprisoned in a concentration-camp and handed by the GPU to the Gestapo after the Stalin-Hitler Pact but survived to write her memoirs.

Nin, Andrés (1892-1937): Delegate from CNT to First Congress of RILU, stayed on in Russia and supported Trotsky against Stalin; returned to Spain and founded Oposición Comunista, fused with Maurin's Workers' and Peasants' Bloc to become POUM (1936); Councillor for Justice in Catalonian government 1936; resigned December 1936; arrested by Russian agent Orlov and murdered while under arrest, June 1937.

Noske, Gustav (1868-1946): German Social Democrat; Minister of National Defence in Scheidemann government; smashed Spartacist rising; pensioned by Hitler.

Ordjonikidze, Grigory (1886-1937): Old Bolshevik; Georgian; Party's military and administrative leader in Caucasus during civil war, and Party plenipotentiary there until 1926. Rose to central committee in 1921, and Politburo in 1930. Head of Soviet heavy industry from 1930 till suicide in 1937.

Ossinsky, Valerian V (Prince Obolensky) (1887-1938): Russian economist and writer; chairman of Supreme Economic Council 1917-18; 'left communist' over Brest-Litovsk; member of 'democratic centralist' group; went over to Stalin 1926; tried 1937; probably executed 1938.

Oudegeest, Jan (1870-1950): Founding secretary of Dutch trade union federation; joint secretary of IFTU; resigned 1927 following dispute between British and Continental trade unions over relations with Russia.

Overstraeten, War Van: Belgian CP leader; later became Trotskyist.

Pankhurst, Sylvia (1882-1960): Active with mother and sister in militant wing of suffragette movement; excluded for agitation in East End; her East London Federation of Suffragettes changed name to Workers Socialist Federation in 1919; her weekly **Workers Dreadnought** was strongly anti-war.

Pannekoek, Antonie (1873-1960): Dutch astronomer; left socialist before 1914; founded **De Tribune** 1907; Zimmerwaldist during war; founded CP of Holland 1918, which affiliated to Third International 1919; withdrew 1920. He left CP 1921, soon retired from politics.

Parijanine, Maurice: Poet, worked with Victor Serge on translations for Communist International. (See Serge's 'Twice Met', **International Socialism** 1:20.)

Pascal, Pierre: Collaborated with **La Révolution Prolétarienne** 1925; in thirties a Sorbonne professor, noted historian of Russian Church and more or less conservative.

Pataud, Emile: French anarchist; led strikes and direct action such as disruption of Opera and Elysée receptions; expelled from CGT in 1913; had anti-semitic tendencies, involved in Action Française; dropped out of politics after first world war.

Pelloutier, Fernand (1867-1901): French journalist; broke with Guesdists to become anarcho-syndicalist; prolific writer before early death of tuberculosis.

Péricat, Raymond: French anarcho-syndicalist, born 1873; plasterer and leader in building unions; opposed first world war, calling for insurrection; formed Committee of Syndicalist Defence 1917; advocated foundation of Communist Party from 1918; one of first leaders of CGTU; did not join CP.

Pestaña, Angel (1881-1937): Leader of moderate wing of Spanish CNT; his Syndicalist Party signed pact creating Spanish Popular Front 1936; later became deputy and vice-commissar of Republican Army.

Petrichenko: One of leaders of 1921 Kronstadt rising; escaped to Finland; worked there with pro-Soviet émigré groups; repatriated to Russia 1945, died in prison 1946.

Pichon, Stephen (1857-1933): French Radical politician and diplomat; Foreign Minister 1917-20, signatory of Treaty of Versailles.

Pilsudski, Joseph (1867-1935): Polish leader, born in Russian Poland; deported to Siberia for five years for socialist agitation; joined Polish Socialist Party; 1914 agreed with Austrian government to lead Polish Legion against Russia; dictatorial head of state of Poland 1918-21 and 1926-35; led Polish Army against Bolsheviks 1919-20; concluded non-aggression pact with Germany 1934.

Poincaré, Raymond (1860-1934): French president 1913-20; Prime Minister 1922-24 and 1926-29; ordered occupation of Ruhr 1923.

Pokrovsky, Mikhail N (1868-1932): Russian Marxist historian; old Bolshevik, active in 1905; emigrated to Western Europe 1907-17; internationalist during war; chairman of Moscow Soviet 1917; 'left communist' over Brest-Litovsk; 1918-32 assistant Commissar of education, edited various historical publications.

Pouget, Emile (1860-1931): French anarchist; one of founders of French trade unionism; advocate of sabotage of production (go-slow, etc); withdrew from politics through ill-health before 1914.

Pozzani: Reformist CGL leader.

Preobrazhensky, E A (1886-1937): Old Party member, economist, secretary of Party central committee 1920-21; expelled from Party for Trotskyism 1927; later readmitted, but finally perished during the purges.

Price, Morgan Philips (1885-1973): Russian correspondent of **Manchester Guardian** during October Revolution; later Labour MP 1929-31, 1935-39.

Primo de Rivera, Miguel de (1870-1930): Spanish general; dictator of Spain 1923-30.

Pyatakov, G L (1890-1937): Bolshevik militant from 1910; deported to Siberia and exiled; president of first Soviet government of the Ukraine; member of central committee of the Bolshevik Party from 1921; devoted himself to economic questions; tried with Radek and executed.

Quelch, Thomas (1886-1954): British socialist, member of BSP; later communist; resigned from CP towards end of life.

Radek, Karl (Sobelsohn) (1875-1939): Active revolutionary in Germany and Poland before Russian Revolution; then became Bolshevik leader; one of leaders of left opposition until 1929 when he capitulated to Stalin; sentenced to ten years' imprisonment in Moscow trials.

Rakovsky, K G (1873-1941): Bulgarian socialist; joined Bolsheviks in 1917; headed the Ukrainian Council of People's Commissars 1918-23; ambassador in Paris and London; expelled from Party in 1927 for Trotskyism; readmitted 1935; arrested and sent to camp 1938. (See his **Selected Writings on Opposition in the USSR 1923-1930** (1980).)

Ramsay, David (1883-1948): Scottish pattern-maker; active in SDF, SLP; national treasurer of Engineering Amalgamation Committee and of Shop Stewards and Workers Committee Movement. Active in 'Hands off Russia' Committee; founder member of British RILU and of CP; elected to Executive of CP in 1926.

Ransome, Arthur (1884-1968): English writer; visited Russia several times before and after Revolution; opposed British intervention; author of children's books.

Raskolnikov, Fedor (1892-1939): Naval officer and Bolshevik, Kronstadt leader in October 1917; Soviet envoy in Kabul 1923; directed Eastern work of Comintern in accordance with Stalin's policy for Chinese revolution; author of **Kronstadt and Petrograd in 1917** (1982).

Rathenau, Walter (1867-1922): German Jewish businessman and liberal bourgeois politician; from 1916 organised 'war socialism' for German government, with strict control over labour; as Minister of Foreign Affairs, advocated close alliance of Germany and Russia; murdered summer 1922.

Ravich, Olga (Karpinskaia): Bolshevik, active in Switzerland during war; after 1917 active in Russian public education; oppositionist from 1925; said to have been deported 1938.

Reed, John (1887-1920): American journalist; studied at Harvard where set up socialist circle; came to Russia summer 1917; on return to New York 1918 wrote **Ten Days that Shook the World** (1970); returned to Russia 1919.

Reinhardt, Max (1873-1943): Theatre-director in Germany and Austria; emigrated to USA when Hitler came to power, became film-director; reputation as an innovator, especially with spectacular stage-effects.

Renaudel, Pierre (1871-1935): Journalist; Jaurès's assistant; became leader of right in French Socialist Party.

Rolland, Romain (1868-1944): French writer, novelist; idealist follower of Tolstoy; humanitarianism became more explicitly pacifist from 1915; interested in Buddhism, fellow-traveller with communism; participated in CP peace and cultural fronts; intervened in defence of Victor Serge, but refused to condemn Moscow Trials.

Roy, Manabendra Nath (1890-1954): Indian politician; participated in struggle against British 1910-15; became communist; member of Executive Committee of Communist International from 1924; Comintern representative in China 1927; expelled as Brandlerite 1929; from 1940 headed People's Radical Democratic Party of India.

Ryazanov, David B (1870-1933): Entered labour movement in Odessa in 1895; imprisoned and deported; worked with Lenin on Iskra; organised railway workers' union during 1905 revolution; joined Bolshevik Party during July Days in 1917; organised the Marx-Engels Institute; arrested and deported.

Rykov, A I (1881-1938): Russian revolutionary; imprisoned and exiled; met Lenin in Geneva; member of Party central committee in 1905; after October 1917 president of Supreme Economic Council; succeeded Lenin as president of Council of People's Commissars; sentenced at third Moscow trial and shot.

Sadoul, Jacques (1881-1956): French socialist and army officer; supported war; sent to Russia as member of French military mission; became communist, joined Red Army; later hanger-on of French CCP.

Sandomirsky, German B: Russian Kropotkinite; imprisoned after 1905; after Revolution worked in Commissariat of Foreign Affairs; 1936, exiled to Siberia, probably shot.

Sapronov, T: One of leaders of 'democratic centralist' group; oppositionist from 1923 on; regarded by Trotsky as ultra-left; deported to Crimea.

Scharnhorst (1755-1813): Prussian general; reorganised Prussian army for struggle against Napoleon.

Scheidemann, Philipp (1865-1939): Leader of right-wing of German Social Democratic Party; chauvinist during war; head of government in 1919; carried out repressive policy against working-class movement.

Schlageter, Albert Leo (1894-1923): German nationalist, executed by French during Ruhr occupation for attacks on the means of comunication of the French troops; a monument to him erected near Düsseldorf in 1931 was removed after the second world war.

Serebriakov, Leonid: Russian metal-worker; political commissar in civil war; secretariat of central committee of Party 1920; expelled from Party for Trotskyism 1927; exiled to Central Asia; went over to Radek and Preobrazhensky 1928; tried and executed 1937.

Serge, Victor (1890-1947): Writer and revolutionary; born in Belgium of Russian parents; active as anarchist in France; came to Russia 1919, worked for Communist International; imprisoned 1933-36; then in France and Mexico; anti-Stalinist but had differences with Trotsky; author of **Memoirs of a Revolutionary 1901-1941** (1968) and of novels **The Case of Comrade Tulayev** (1970), **Birth of Our Power** (1970) etc.

Serrati, Giacinto M (1872-1926): Leader of maximalist left of Italian Socialist Party; attended Zimmerwald; when Italian Socialist Party split in 1921 did not join CP but worked for reconciliation; joined CP 1924.

Shablin: Bulgarian communist; said to have been burnt alive in furnace after CP blew up Sofia Cathedral 1925.

Shapiro, Alexander M (1882-1946): Russian anarchist; abroad for 25 years; member of Jewish Anarchist Federation of London, Anarchist Red Cross; secretary of International Anarchist Bureau 1907; returned to Russia 1917; held position in Commissariat of Foreign Affairs; left Russia 1922, continued campaigning for imprisoned anarchists; died in New York.

Shatov, Bill (Vladimir): Russian anarchist; emigrated to US, worked as machinist, longshoreman, and printer, active in IWW; in 1914 reprinted secretly Margaret Sanger's **Family Limitation**. Returned to Russia 1917; August 1917 on military-revolutionary committee of Petrograd Soviet; 1919 officer in Tenth Red Army; 1920 Minister of Transport in Far Eastern Republic; later supervised construction of Turk-Sib Railroad; 1936, sent to Siberia, probably shot.

Shlyapnikov, A G (1885-1943): Bolshevik metal-worker; agitator in large Petersburg steel-works; 1908-14 in Western Europe; organised international contacts during war; 1917 member of executive committee of Petrograd Soviet; Commissar for Labour; 1920-22 leader of Workers' Opposition; described build-up to Revolution in his book **On the Eve of 1917** (1982).

Sklyansky, E M (1892-1925): Bolshevik, graduate of Kiev medical faculty; Trotsky's deputy on Revolutionary War Council of the Republic; compared by Trotsky to Carnot (the organiser of the armies of the French Revolution); dismissed from Commissariat of War 1924.

Šmeral, Bohumir (1880-1941): Member of Czech Social Democratic Party from 1895; founder-member of Czech CP in 1921 and member of its central committee; on Executive of Communist International 1921-25 and from 1935; lived in USSR from 1938.

Smirnov, V M (1887-1937): Bolshevik from 1907; after 1917 member of Presidium of Supreme Economic Council. 'Left communist' over Brest-Litovsk; 1920-21 member of 'democratic centralist' group; expelled from Party 1926; exiled; did not join Trotsky who considered him ultra-left; deported.

Souvarine, Boris (Lifschitz) (1893-1971): Born in Kiev; naturalised French 1906; member of Longuet tendency in Socialist Party during war;

founder member of CP in 1920; expelled 1924; after struggle for readmission became anti-communist; wrote biography of Stalin and much other anti-communist material.

Stambulisky, Alexander (1879-1923): Bulgarian statesman and peasant leader; head of Agrarian Party; opposed Bulgarian entry to world war; Prime Minister from 1919 till overthrown by military coup 1923.

Stauning, Thorvald (1873-1942): Right-wing leader of Danish Social Democratic Party and Second International; supported first world war; member of several governments and Prime Minister.

Steinberg, I: Left Social-Revolutionary; People's Commissar for Justice after Revolution.

Stinnes, Hugo (1870-1924): Wealthy German industrialist, who subsidised nationalist press and movements.

Stresemann, Gustav (1878-1929): German Foreign Minister 1923-29; negotiated Dawes Plan and Locarno Treaty which established Germany's post-war relations with rest of Europe.

Taine, Hippolyte (1828-93): French philosopher and literary critic; produced interesting if crude work on influence of social factors on literature; after Paris Commune devoted himself to history of French Revolution, which he saw as source of all ills in modern society — essentially a catalogue of alleged atrocities.

Tanner, Jack (1890-1965): British fitter and turner; on executive of Industrial Syndicalist Education League; delegate of shop stewards' movement to Second Congress of Communist International. On close terms with CP, but in later years an active anti-communist; president of AEU 1939-54.

Tardieu, André (1876-1945): French conservative politician, associate of Clemenceau, several times Prime Minister.

Tasca, Angelo (1892-1960): Italian socialist; co-founder of **Ordine Nuovo** and founder-member and early leader of Italian CP; worked clandestinely under Mussolini; expelled for 'rightism' 1929; spent rest of life in France, publishing prolifically, under name A Rossi, works on communist movement from a critical point of view.

Terracini, Umberto (1895-1983): One of founders of Italian CP; 1926-43 imprisoned in Italy; after war president of National Assembly, later chairman of communist group in Senate.

Thalheimer, August (1883-1948): Leader of German CP with Brandler 1921-24; later followed same line as Brandler.

Thomas, Albert (1878-1932): Member of French Socialist Party, followed Bernstein's attempt to 'modernise' Marxism, developed ideas of technocratic socialism. Under-secretary of state for armaments during first world war; after war became first director of International Labour Office.

Thomas, Norman (1884-1969): American Presbyterian minister, became socialist before first world war; opposed US intervention in war; member of Socialist Party, its presidential candidate in 1928 and several times subsequently.

Thyssen, Fritz (1873-1951): Son of German industrialist and Ruhr steel baron August Thyssen. After first world war he and father used money for political manipulation detrimental to Weimar Republic and beneficial to Hitler.

Togliatti, Palmiro (1893-1964): Co-founder of **Ordine Nuovo** and founder-member of Italian CP; 1926-44 in exile; participated in Spanish Civil War; minister in several post-war Italian governments; after Stalin's death a leading advocate of 'liberalisation' of Stalinism; died in Soviet Union.

Tomsky, M P (1880-1936): In Party from 1904; head of Soviet trade unions till ousted in 1928 as one of leaders of 'rightist deviation'; member of Politburo from 1922; committed suicide to escape trial.

Treint, Albert: French school-teacher, born 1889; joined Socialist Party 1910; reached rank of captain in war, won *légion d'honneur*; founder-member of CP, member of its first central committee, joint secretary 1923-24; regained leadership later 1924; removed from Political Bureau 1926, expelled 1927; brief links with Trotskyist opposition, joined Socialist Party 1934.

Treves, Claudio (1868-1933): One of reformist leaders of Italian Socialist Party; centrist during world war.

Tsankov, Alexander (1879-1959): Bulgarian politician; led military-intellectual opposition which overthrew Stambulinsky 1923; Prime Minister 1923-26; in 1944 tried to set up pro-German National Bulgarian government after Soviet invasion.

Tukhachevsky, Mikhail (1893-1937): Former officer of Russian Imperial Guard, went over to Revolution 1917; made head of Fourth Red Army by Trotsky; urged Tsarist officers to come over to Bolshevik régime; played leading rôle in building Red Army, civil war, and suppression of Kronstadt rising; purged and killed by Stalin; rehabilitated by Khrushchev 1961.

Turati, Felippo (1857-1932): One of pioneers of reformist socialism in Italy; opposed Italian participation in first world war; strongly anti-communist; exiled 1926.

Uritsky, Mikhail S (1873-1918): Bolshevik from 1917; 'left communist' and chairman of Petrograd Cheka in 1918; assassinated by Social-Revolutionary.

Vaillant, Edouard (1840-1915): Leading figure of Paris Commune, knew Marx in exile in London; leading figure in French Socialist Party and Second International; together with Keir Hardie called for general strike against war in amendment for Vienna Congress of Second International (never held).

Vandervelde, Émile (1866-1938): President of POB (Belgian Workers' Party) and of Second International; joined government of national defence in 1914; several times minister in Socialist-Catholic coalitions.

Varga, Eugene (1879-1964): Hungarian economist, chairman of Supreme Economic Council in Hungarian Soviet Republic; leading Comintern economist during 'Third Period' and 'Popular Front'.

Vergeat, Marcel: French anarchist; became secretary of Committee for the Third International August 1919.

Volodarsky, V (1891-1918): Bolshevik; Petrograd Commissar of Press, Propaganda and Agitation; assassinated by Social-Revolutionary.

Vuyovich, Voya: Yugoslav revolutionary, active in French CP and secretary-general of Young Communist International. Only member of Executive of Communist International to support Trotsky in 1927; expelled as Zinovievite; capitulated 1928; withdrew from political activity; later deported to Siberia and died.

Vyshinsky, Andrei (1883-1954): Lawyer, Menshevik; joined Bolsheviks only after civil war; prosecutor in Moscow Trials; later Russian Foreign Minister.

Walcher, J: German communist from early years; member of Brandlerite right wing, expelled 1929; later led centrist SAP (Socialist Workers Party).

Walecki, Henryk (1877-1937): Polish socialist; repeatedly arrested and exiled before 1914; Zimmerwaldist during war; one of founders and leaders of Polish CP; removed from Party leadership 1925; 1935 became editor of **Communist International**; 1937 arrested by NKVD and executed; rehabilitated after 1956.

Wauters, Joseph (1875-1929): Belgian socialist, minister in post-war coalition government.

Wels, Otto (1879-1939): Right-wing German Social Democrat; military commander of Berlin who crushed Spartacist uprising of December 1918; in Reichstag 1933 called for 'lawful non-violent opposition' to Hitler.

Wijnkoop, David (1877-1941): One of founders of Dutch Social Democratic Party; on left of Party; internationalist during war; became communist.

Wilson, Thomas Woodrow (1856-1924): US president from 1912; decided US entry to first world war; exercised great influence on post-war settlement in Europe — creation of League of Nations, right of national independence and self-determination.

Wolf, Felix: Pseudonym of N Krebs, Moscow secret emissary to Western Europe (also known as Rakov, Inkov).

Wrangel, Petr (1878-1928): Descendant of German baronial family; served in Russian Imperial guards; supported Kornilov's attempt to overthrow Petrograd Soviet; served under Denikin in civil war; led own forces in Crimea; defeated 1920.

Yudenich, N N (1862-1933): Tsarist general; commander-in-chief of counter-revolutionary North-Western army in civil war; after defeat emigrated to Britain.

Yvetot, Georges (1868-1942): Typographer, French anarchist; specialised in anti-military activity, but withdrew from trade-union activity in 1914; thereafter pacifist; signed manifesto for 'immediate peace' in 1939 and shortly before death associated with collaborationist trade unionists.

Zetkin, Clara (1857-1933): German socialist; friend of Engels; participated in founding of Second International; member of left of Second International; 1915 organised international women's socialist conference against war; militant in Spartacus League and Independent Socialist Party; joined German CP in 1919; communist deputy from 1920; member of Presidium of Communist International and head of international women's secretariat of Communist International.

Zhdanov, Andrei A (1896-1948): Secretary of central committee of Soviet Communist Party from 1935; leading enforcer of ideological orthodoxy, notably 'socialist realism' in literature; prominent in founding of Cominform.

Zinoviev, Grigory (1883-1936): Bolshevik from 1903; opposed Lenin over taking power in 1917; president of Petrograd Soviet and President of Third International 1919-26. Allied with Stalin and Kamenev against Trotsky 1923, with Trotsky against Stalin 1925; expelled from Party 1927, capitulated 1928; again expelled and readmitted 1932; executed 1936 after first Moscow Trial.

Bloc National: Grouping of right-wing French political parties which won overwhelming majority in French parliament in 1919 (the skyblue Chamber), but was defeated by the alliance of Socialists and Radicals in 1924.

Bulletin Communiste: Weekly theoretical journal, founded by Souvarine in 1920 as pro-communist organ in Socialist Party; continued as theoretical journal of French CP, mainly under Souvarine's editorship, until 1924, when replaced during 'Bolshevisation' by **Cahiers du Bolchévisme**.

Central Committee (of French CP): Originally the central body of 24 members was known as the Comité Directeur (literally 'leading committee', but rendered in this translation as 'central committee'). Its name was changed to central committee in 1924.

CGT (*Confédération Générale du Travail* — General Confederation of Labour): French trade-union body, founded 1895; in 1922 revolutionary wing formed CGTU (*Confédération Générale du Travail Unitaire* — Unitary General Confederation of Labour). The two bodies were reunited in 1936.

CGL (*Confederazione Generale del Lavoro* — General Confederation of Labour): Italian national trade-union body, founded 1906, uniting most non-Catholic tendencies till syndicalists split to form *Unione Sindacale*

Italiana in 1912. Grew to 300,000 by 1910, two million by 1920. Fascist régime reduced it to purely formal existence; executive committee voted to disband 1927; a clandestine CGL was reconstituted in Paris.

CNT (*Confederación Nacional del Trabajo* — National Confederation of Labour): National confederation of Spanish anarchist federations, founded 1911; reached 700,000 members by 1918; entered Republican government in civil war.

The Entente (or Triple Entente): Collaboration of Britain, France and Russia 1907-1917; in 1914, the three powers agreed not to make a separate peace; this was disavowed by the Bolsheviks in 1917.

L'Humanité: French daily paper, founded by Jaurès 1904; from 1921 to present CP organ.

IWW (Industrial Workers of the World): American trade-union centre founded 1905, in opposition to American Federation of Labour, on principles of industrial unionism and class struggle. led many struggles in pre-war period, and reached 100,000 members in 1917, but declined thereafter.

Internationale Communiste: French edition of **Communist International**; also appeared in English, German and Russia; Russian edition was fullest and most regular, but other editions sometimes contained items not in the Russian edition; hence references in this translation are always to the French edition.

International Federation of Trade Unions (Amsterdam or Yellow International): Founded 1919 in Amsterdam, organising workers in 14 countries, notably Britain, Germany and US; disappeared at end of second world war with creation of World Federation of Trade Unions which brought in Russians and American CIO.

KAPD (*Kommunistiche Arbeiterpartei Deutschlands* — Communist Workers Party of Germany): Left split from German CP in 1920; reduced to a sect after a few years.

League for the Rights of Man (*Ligue pour la Défense des Droits de l'Homme et du Citoyen*): French organisation, founded at time of Dreyfus case, under Radical influence; Fourth Congress of International declared membership of league was 'absolutely incompatible with the calling of a communist and contrary to the elementary conceptions of the communist world outlook'. Co-operated in various appeals and meetings leading to establishment of the French Popular Front.

Narrow Socialists: Left-wing minority tendency of Bulgarian socialist movement, founded by Blagoev, who had participated in Russian populist and Marxist circles. Opposed war; later constituted Bulgarian CP.

Ordine Nuovo: Italian revolutionary paper, launched as weekly by Gramsci, Togliatti, Terracini and Tasca in 1919; merged with **Avanti!** and became daily in 1921; **Ordine Nuovo** fraction dissolved itself into CP in 1921, though paper was not official Party organ; forced to cease publication October 1922; reappeared as bi-weekly 1924.

RILU (Red International of Labour Unions): Also known as Red Trade Union International or Profintern.

Small Bureau: From 1921 this was renamed the Presidium.

Social-Revolutionaries: Russian Peasant socialist party, formed at beginning of century from fusion of several Narodnik tendencies; in Revolution split between Left S-RS, anarchistic but supporting Bolshevik rule for a time, and Right S-RS supporting Kerensky.

Le Temps: French daily paper, founded 1861; right-wing in orientation; from 1929 organ of industrialists' group Comité des Forges. Ceased publication 1942; not allowed to reappear after the war and replaced by **Le Monde**.

Unione Sindacale Italiana (Italian Syndicalist Union): Founded 1912 as a syndicalist split from CGL; in 1914 advocated insurrection in event of war; had 300,000 members in 1920.

Treaty of Versailles: Peace Treaty concluding first world war (28 June 1919). It removed from Germany its colonies and parts of its territory; limited German level of armement and imposed reparations, settled in 1921 at £6,600 million. Germany signed under protest while the US Congress refused to ratify the treaty.

Vie Ouvrière: Journal founded 1909 by Monatte, as voice of syndicalists in CGT; ceased publication 1914, reappeared 1919; in 1922 Monatte abandoned editorship, and after considering Rosmer as editor gave editorship to Monmousseau (who then seemed closer to him on trade-union question). Now exists as mouthpiece of official line in CGT.

Vorwärts: Berlin daily, organ of German Social Democratic Party from 1891 to Hitler period.

Zimmerwald: Conference held 5 to 8 September 1915, in a village near Berne; the first meeting during the first world war of delegates from socialist parties and trade unions who had opposed the war; followed by a second conference at Kienthal.

Index

This index covers the Introduction, text and appendix. Items marked * also have entries in the notes on pages 255-77 (individuals) and 277-9 (organisations).